Patrick Boudreault.

D0072768

Significant Gestures

Significant Gestures

A History of American Sign Language

JOHN TABAK

Westport, Connecticut
London

Library of Congress Cataloging-in-Publication Data

Tabak, John.
   Significant gestures : a history of American Sign Language / John Tabak.
p. cm.
   Includes bibliographical references and index.
   ISBN 0–275–98974–7 (alk. paper)
1. American Sign Language—History. 2. Deaf—Means of communication—United
States. 3. Deaf—Education—United States. 4. Deafness—United States. I. Title.
HV2474.T3 2006
419'.7—dc22   2006021001
British Library Cataloguing in Publication Data is available.

Library of Congress Catalog Card Number: 2006021001
ISBN: 0–275–98974–7

First published in 2006

Praeger Publishers, 88 Post Road West, Westport, CT 06881
An imprint of Greenwood Publishing Group, Inc.
www.praeger.com

Printed in the United States of America

∞

The paper used in this book complies with the
Permanent Paper Standard issued by the National
Information Standards Organization (Z39.48–1984).

10 9 8 7 6 5 4 3 2 1

Copyright Acknowledgments

The author and publisher gratefully acknowledge permission for use of the following
material:
Excerpts are reprinted by permission of the publisher from *The Deaf Experience: Classics
in Language and Education,* edited by Harlan Lane, translated by Frank Philip, pp. 35,
40, 52, 130, 140, 148, Cambridge, Mass.: Harvard University Press, Copyright © 1984
by the President and Fellows of Harvard College.

Für Herrn und Frau Wehner und ihre Kinder Paul, Irmgard und Harald, mit denen ich so viel über die Sprache und das Leben im Allgemeinen entdeckt habe.

For Mr. and Mrs. Wehner and their children Paul, Irmgard, and Harald, with whom I discovered so much about language and life in general.

Contents

Acknowledgments

I could not have completed this book without the generous and knowledgeable assistance of many individuals from around the country. Gary Wait, the archivist at the American School for the Deaf, cheerfully shared his considerable expertise time and again. I was extremely fortunate to interview Bernard Bragg, who, as a witness to, and participant in, many historically important events, shared his considerable insights with me and also rescued a substantial portion of the book by providing important historical documents that were otherwise unavailable. As a longtime fan of Audree Norton, it was very meaningful for me to correspond with her about her views on the *Experiment in Television* controversy, and I took her words of encouragement to heart. I was fortunate to also correspond briefly with George Fellendorf, formerly Executive Director of the Alexander Graham Bell Association. I appreciate his patience and candor.

Betty Henderson, activist and historian of the now-defunct Texas Blind, Deaf, and Orphan School (BDO), provided many crucial insights and is, in my opinion, a national treasure. Franna Camenisch, of the Texas School for the Deaf Alumni Association, expended considerable time and creativity in obtaining for my use what I believe is the best historical record in existence of the first few decades of the Texas Institute for the Deaf, Dumb, and Blind Colored Youth. My friend and long-time interpreter Rob Granbury was an invaluable source of information as was Clark Grundle of the Granbury Care Center.

Brenda Wells of St. Mary's School for the Deaf contributed her artistry; Leo Christian-Tabak (my son) contributed his expert camera work, and Anke Tremback, an excellent translator, provided invaluable assistance.

Mary C. Zatta of the Perkins School for the Blind taught me about the history and implementation of the Tadoma method, and Nancy O'Donnell of the Helen Keller National Center for Deaf-Blind Youths and Adults could not have been more helpful and generous with her expertise.

Librarians can never be thanked enough. Susan Pierce, research librarian for the Brownell Library in Essex Junction, Vermont, Donna Meehan of the CLARKE School for the Deaf, Center for Oral Education, and Jan Seymour-Ford of the Perkins School for the Blind were of particular importance in the preparation of this work.

I conducted many interviews while preparing this book for publication, most of which, for reasons of space, did not make it into print. I wish to explicitly thank Harry Anderson, the late Oliver Blaylock, Harvey Corson, Elizabeth L. Broecker, and Sharon Gold-Johnson for their patience with me as I tried to tap their numerous and valuable insights. I also need to thank Sue Ellen Schaudt for her remarkable insights into language and communication.

I am grateful to Edward Peltier and the faculty and the staff of the Austine School for the Deaf, Brattleboro, Vermont, for allowing me into their classes as an observer.

Finally, I want to express my appreciation to Diana Marsan, Project Manager at BeaconPMG, for her keen eye and expert help in the preparation of this book. It is a better book for her efforts.

Introduction

Winters are long in Brattleboro, Vermont, the state's seventh largest city (pop. 12,100), and this one is particularly cold and snowy. The Connecticut River, the largest and the longest of New England's rivers, winds past Brattleboro. It has been frozen over for weeks, and long sinuous snowdrifts lie upon the ice. A solitary set of animal tracks linking the Vermont side of the river to the New Hampshire side is visible in the snow that clings to the river's surface.

To drive to the Austine School for the Deaf and Hard of Hearing, I turn off Route 9 in Brattleboro and cross a wooden covered bridge. The one-lane bridge is painted barn red. Because the bridge is not aligned with the road, driving across is not a simple matter. Cars on both sides must stop to (1) peer through the latticework that makes up the sides of the bridge to see whether the bridge is currently in use, (2) check the road on the opposite side to see if a driver is waiting to use the bridge, and (3) when the coast is clear, turn onto the bridge and drive across. I wait my turn. No one is in a hurry.

The neighborhood on the far side of the bridge is composed of old, well-maintained houses and the Living Memorial Park. The citizens of Brattleboro take their winter recreation seriously. The Living Memorial is built on the side of a hill and is equipped with a T-bar, a sort of low-budget chairlift that carries skiers and snowboarders to the top of the park's trail. The T-bar is funded and managed by a group of local volunteers—decisions are made democratically—and the city pays the insurance. An all-day pass costs $5.00; children under six ride free. At 8:15 A.M., with the temperature only a few degrees above zero (Fahrenheit) and hours before the T-bar opens, there are already a few locals hiking up the hill and skiing down.

Two minutes after I pass Living Memorial Park I turn up the steep drive that leads to the Austine School for the Deaf and Hard of Hearing. Established in 1912, Austine is a K–12 residential school. The campus consists of a few well-maintained buildings of various ages and levels of occupancy. Before going inside the main academic building I take a few minutes to enjoy the view: Below me is Interstate 91 and beyond the highway lie Brattleboro's old neighborhoods, snow-covered evergreens, and a few of the tall, narrow, wooden steeples that characterize so much church architecture in old New England. On my right I notice icy tracks on the snow on the hill above the school's soccer field, tracks worn smooth by students' sleds, toboggans, and flying saucers. This morning the trails are abandoned; the students are in class.

I have received permission to observe classes and talk with teachers. The school's secretary meets me at the entrance to the academic building and hands me a schedule—designed to accommodate my preferences—and escorts me to my first class. This sets the pattern for the entire day. At the end of each class a teacher or administrator appears promptly at the door and ushers me to my next appointment. I pause only for lunch, which I share with the soccer coach and several proud members of the soccer team. Everyone is focused.

My favorite class turns out to be the first: Sharon Gold-Johnson's third and fourth grade English class. Hers is a small classroom with big windows and a stunning view of Austine's snow-covered environs. In addition to the usual desks, chairs, computer, and white board, the classroom is crowded with books, crafts, games, hats, coats, boots, globes (2), abacuses (2), a microscope, an upholstered love seat, and from the ceiling, suspended by short strings, are numerous, carefully crafted, white, paper snowflakes. In the corner, out of the way, I notice a small poster about American Sign Language; it is the only indication that this is a classroom for Deaf students.

The topic during my visit is grammar. The students are seated around a single table by the white board while their teacher stands before them and reviews the parts of speech. All communication is in signed language. The class is silent. Lip reading plays no role. (Sometimes signers pronounce certain easy-to-lip-read words while signing, but that is not the case here.) This is American Sign Language—the signs, the signed grammar, and the *tempo* of the signs all have much in common with what, 150 years earlier, was called the "natural language of signs," and on this day the natural language of signs is being used to convey information about the grammar of that other language that is so important to these children, English. But it is English as Latin. Reading and writing skills are essential; scant attention is given to the spoken word. "If you don't know English, you're doomed" is how Ms. Gold-Johnson later describes her work, but she means written, as opposed to spoken, English. When these students talk with their teacher or with each other, they sign. It is no accident; it is a matter of policy. After class Gold-Johnson informs me that at Austine, faculty and staff may use one language or the other to communicate, but the two languages are kept separate in the sense that one does not impose English word order or English vocabulary on American Sign Language nor does one impose American Sign Language vocabulary or grammar on written English.

The children are attentive, and initially I am very impressed. Their teacher writes a sentence on the board, and the students compete to correctly identify nouns, verbs, adjectives, prepositions, and definite and indefinite articles by drawing specific ideograms above each word in the sentence. Each ideogram represents a part of speech. Their analysis is quite detailed for such young students—more detailed, in fact, than what I would have expected from hearing third and fourth graders. Later I learn that there is some controversy about this type of grammar lesson. During a subsequent conversation at the school, another teacher expresses dissatisfaction with Gold-Johnson's approach. "They [the children] are good at it." She agrees. "But it's a pattern that they memorize. As they get older, they can correctly diagram sentences even when they have no idea what the words mean." Perhaps. I could not tell whether her criticism was valid, but in the months since visiting the class I have remained impressed with how expert the children seemed, and I remain curious with what that expertise might represent.

When the students' attention begins to wander, Gold-Johnson changes tact: She writes flawed sentences on the board—each sentence has an incorrectly conjugated verb or a missing article—and students supply the missing article or correct form of the verb. Each student gets a turn. When someone makes a mistake, there is a quick flurry of small hands. I notice that as left hands shoot upward to request recognition from the teacher, right hands offer opinions about the correct solution, a simple case of the right hand not caring what the left hand is doing. It is cute, but Gold-Johnson does not smile. Like my class-to-class escorts, she remains firmly focused on the task at hand.

Later, during our conversation, I realize that she is under some pressure. There are test scores for which she and her school are held accountable. (Test scores can always be higher.) Furthermore, not all parents are satisfied. Some parents have voiced dissatisfaction with their children's progress. It is easy to understand why: Most hearing parents with Deaf children never become fluent in American Sign Language. The signed language that their children absorb so effortlessly at school—the language that many will later proudly claim as their own—will always remain more or less incomprehensible to the majority of parents, the very people who want most to communicate with these children. The kinds of conversations that so many parents imagine themselves having with their children—conversations where ideas, feelings, and family histories are shared—must happen via pad and pencil if they are to happen at all, and it is by no means certain that these students will acquire the written language skills necessary to have these conversations. Many Deaf students do not. This is true regardless of the school a child may attend and regardless of the methodology employed to teach him or her. In this case the dissatisfied parents are concerned about what Luzerne Rae, one of the first teachers of the Deaf in the United States, called "deafisms," expressions that make perfect sense when signed but are meaningless when put to paper. When I glance at samples of the written work of some of these students I notice that a few samples are rife with American Sign Language expressions.

I ask Gold-Johnson why she uses American Sign Language as the language of instruction in an English class. She is, as all teachers of the Deaf are, ready with an answer: The policy was arrived at by the faculty in conjunction with the administration and incorporating the best available research. When I suggest to Ms. Gold-Johnson that virtually everyone admits that a majority of Deaf students will *regardless of the methodology by which they are instructed* still graduate without developing sufficient proficiency in reading and writing English, she does not disagree. So, I ask, what difference does signed language really make? The second part of her answer is more revealing: Austine School provides a signed language environment. "A school for the Deaf," she asserts, "is a place where students can feel *free*." Austine, her school for the Deaf, provides a place where students can communicate freely and easily with everyone they meet. As she continues, her answer becomes more animated, "In a Deaf school, children have autonomy. They don't depend on interpreters. This [Austine] isn't a stepping stone to get into the public school. This is where they are taught in a way that best meets their needs."

She expresses her ideas directly and eloquently and at some length. As I listen, I almost forget that this approach to communication is only the most recent of many that Austine has adopted. As many schools for the Deaf have done, Austine had previously discouraged the use of American Sign Language. There was a time when Austine used oral methods of education; that is, students were taught without signed language. Information was conveyed verbally from teacher to student and student to teacher. Students were expected to communicate as if they could hear, and if oral methods sometimes proved to be awkward and prone to misunderstanding, this simply indicated the need for additional practice on the part of the student. To the faculty of the time, it did not indicate a shortcoming in the method itself.

Austine's move away from oral education was slow. The school did not embrace American Sign Language for decades, preferring instead to gradually introduce various "sign systems," pseudolanguages devised to represent the grammatical structure of the English language on one's hands. Such sign systems are not new. In the eighteenth and nineteenth centuries conceptually similar systems were called "methodological signs," and they were adopted and abandoned at various times in both the United States and Europe. In the United States during the latter part of the twentieth century methodological signs again came into vogue under a variety of names, but the educational results obtained by using these systems for manually coded English were (again) not very impressive—hence the recent swing toward American Sign Language, the only fully developed American signed language available. Unfortunately for English teachers, American Sign Language has little in common with English—the grammar, vocabulary, and rhythm are all at odds with the spoken word—and that turns out to be part of the problem: proficiency in one language (English or American Sign Language) is a poor predictor of proficiency in the other.

Whatever the merits of using American Sign Language in the classroom—and all teachers I questioned during my visit to Austine supported its use—I know that other generations of teachers here and elsewhere have faced essentially the same problems and essentially the same alternatives and made radically different choices. These earlier generations of teachers are mostly gone now, but their writings reveal that they were just as articulate and just as sure of themselves as the teachers I met at Austine. And later, in a discussion with a long-retired member of Austine's faculty, a teacher who used a sign system in the classroom, I realize that although he has followed the change in language policy at Austine with interest, and although he will not openly criticize the new policy, he believes his generation got it right.

Gold-Johnson's emphasis on the freedom and autonomy that mastery of one's own language provides does, however, explain the surprisingly few references to deafness or to American Sign Language in the classrooms, the hallways, or the gym. On this campus, during the spring of 2004, deafness is not a barrier to communication, but the *inability* to sign is. Here the students are communications experts: When they walk to and from classes, they communicate effortlessly with each other and with their teachers in sign; when cheerleaders perform before spectators at a sporting event, they do so in sign; when aspiring scholars seek help from the librarian, they ask in sign, and it is in signed language that their questions are answered. Students flirt in sign; they learn in sign; they argue in sign. Signed language does not make all of this possible, of course, but signed language does make all of this *easy and graceful*. A skilled signer is a joy to watch. American

Sign Language—a language developed largely by the Deaf for their own use—enables these Deaf students to effortlessly express those casual, stream-of-consciousness observations, witticisms, and insights that most hearing people take for granted.

For the students, the decision to use American Sign Language is empowering. When American Sign Language is used as the medium of communication between teacher and student, the language in which their thoughts are conveyed becomes practically transparent. Students and teachers concentrate on the content of their discussions rather than their form. These students, unlike Deaf students educated without signed language, do not depend on continual feedback from their teacher about the volume of their voices relative to the background noise, nor do they depend on their teacher for help in the pronunciation of various words. American Sign Language evens the relationship between student and teacher; the students are as capable of excelling in American Sign Language as anyone else on campus, and that, of course, is part of the language's attraction. The decision to use American Sign Language as a sort of *lingua franca* contributes to the sense of freedom so apparent around campus. While one remains on campus the condition of deafness no longer hinders ordinary conversation. Here one finds ordinary American life expressed in an extraordinary language.

Methodological Signs and the Roots of American Sign Language

We shall show in the clearest manner how to proceed in order to convey by the window what cannot be introduced at the door,...[1]

—Charles-Michel de l'Epée

The signed language used by a majority of Deaf Americans today has its roots in eighteenth century France in the work of Charles-Michel de l'Epée (1712–1789), a Catholic cleric and religious dissident. De l'Epée was a proponent of Jansenism, a belief system out of favor with the Catholic Church at the time, and so the Church forbade the young de l'Epée from practicing the profession for which he had trained. In response, de l'Epée turned to the practice of law, but he did not enjoy it. He continued to look for an outlet through which he could express his talents and insights. His epiphany occurred in his late 40s during a visit to a mother with twin daughters both of whom were Deaf. When he arrived at their house, the mother was not yet present. The girls' attention was directed downward toward their needlework. When he spoke to them, neither looked up; neither responded.[2] When the girls' mother entered the room, de l'Epée complained to her about her daughters' rudeness. The mother explained that the girls did not acknowledge his remarks because they had not heard him speak. She went on to express her anguish at the difficulty of educating her daughters. The experience left a profound impression on de l'Epée. He began to tutor the girls himself. Gradually he added more students. In 1771 at the age of 59, de l'Epée opened his first school for the Deaf with a population of 30 students. By 1789, the year of his death at age 77, de l'Epée had opened three schools with a total enrollment

ABBE
CHARLES MICHEL DE L'EPEE
1712 — 1789

HER OF THE DEAF—ADVOCATE OF   MANUAL ALPHABET & LANGU

ERECTED BY THE
NATIONAL
ASSOCIATION OF THE DEAF
1930

This statue of the abbé de l'Epée by the Deaf sculptor Eugene A. Hannon was presented to St. Mary's School for the Deaf by the National Association of the Deaf during the Third World Congress of Educators of the Deaf in 1930. Courtesy Brenda Wells/St. Mary's School for the Deaf.

of over 100 students. He had also written extensively about the education of the Deaf.

From the outset, de l'Epée taught his students via signs. To him, visual language seemed the logical choice, and it was logic that motivated de l'Epée. "My only goal," he wrote when describing his initial efforts, "was to get them [the students] to think systematically and to combine their ideas. I supposed this might be brought about with representative signs reduced to a method from which I constructed a kind of grammar."[3]

However logical his decision to use signs, his choice of language was hardly an informed one. In fact, he made all of his most important choices about educational methodology with no awareness of the work of any of the teachers and researchers who had preceded him. In particular, he never considered the possibility of teaching speech or speech reading because at the outset of his work he believed such things were impossible.[4] But during the century or so preceding de l'Epée's involvement in the education of the Deaf, others had attempted to teach the Deaf speech and/or speech reading (also known as lip reading) with some success. In 1620 Juan Pablo Bonet published a widely circulated book describing in detail his methods of teaching speech. (Bonet considered instruction in speech reading an unproductive use of one's time.) In addition to Bonet, the English mathematician John Wallace had developed a highly acclaimed method of educating the Deaf of which de l'Epée was also unaware. Initially, de l'Epée was even unaware of the ideas and methods of Jacob Rodriquez Pereire, a contemporary of his who had presented a highly acclaimed paper describing his experiences in the education of the Deaf to the French Academy of Sciences. Instead, de l'Epée drew his inspiration from the indigenous signed language then in use among the Deaf of Paris.

Today little is known about the signed language of eighteenth century Parisians, but it is certain that the language existed and that it was an important and expressive mode of communication. Pierre Desloges, a Deaf contemporary and admirer of de l'Epée and author of *A Deaf Person's Observations about an Elementary Course of Education for the Deaf,* wrote that de l'Epée studied the signed language of the Deaf because he had "... observed that they possessed a natural language for communicating to each other ... de l'Epée was not the inventor or creator of this language; quite the contrary, he learned it from the Deaf; he merely repaired what he found defective in it."[5] De l'Epée's initial impulse to seek insight and inspiration in the language of the Deaf rather than in his own (spoken) language distinguished him from his contemporaries as well as from those who preceded him. He sought to create a method of instruction that would appeal to his students' intellects in a manner that was as simple and as direct as possible. He was the first to use signed language in the classroom in this way. Unlike his predecessors, de l'Epée did not begin the education of his students by attempting to correct for their weaknesses in speech and hearing. Instead, he began by appealing to their intellects via their sense of vision. These were their strengths. Or that, at least, was his initial impulse.

Upon further study, however, de l'Epée identified many "defects" in the signed language of Deaf Parisians, and his program of repairs was extensive. In his book, *The True Method of Educating the Deaf Confirmed by Long Experience,* de l'Epée describes how he created a complex secondary set of gestures to augment those he had learned from the Deaf in order to convey active, passive, and intransitive verbs, the declension of nouns, the difference between adjectives ending in *-able* and those ending in *-ible,* and other aspects of grammar that are characteristic of written or spoken French. It is doubtful that these gestures added much to the expressiveness of the signed language already in use, but that mattered little to de l'Epée. He had something else in mind entirely.

De l'Epée wanted his students to produce accurate *written* transcriptions of *signed* translations of works originally *written* in French, Latin, and other languages. Despite his expressed emphasis on the importance of teaching systematic thinking and his habit of always referring to his students as scholars, de l'Epée measured his success by his students' ability to take dictation. The procedure worked like this: De l'Epée or one of his more accomplished Deaf scholars would sign an excerpt from a book or letter and his scholars would write down what had been signed. French, of course, was emphasized, but de l'Epée also experimented with dictation from Latin, Spanish, English, and Italian sources. Finally, the transcriptions were compared with the original. Accurate transcriptions were presented as proof of the validity of de l'Epée's method. Errors consisted of deviations from the original written text. De l'Epée wrote that by using his system of methodological signs, a term that he coined himself, his scholars could distinguish between the words *intellect, intellectual, intelligent, intelligence, intelligibility, intelligible, unintelligible, intelligibly, unintelligibly,* and *unintelligibility.* (Today, if it were important to distinguish between these closely related words when translating from English to signed language, the relevant words would be fingerspelled. No one would try to *sign* the difference between *unintelligibility* and *unintelligible.* American Sign Language has its own vocabulary and its own grammar; it is ill suited for translating this kind of wordplay.) What is unique about de l'Epée's methodological signs is that he claimed to have created a system of signs—independent of fingerspelling—that enabled the user to represent the French language manually.

In his writings de l'Epée repeatedly and proudly describes the accomplishments of his scholars in the not especially scholarly work of transcription. His manual version of French must have been quite difficult for his scholars to learn, and his efforts may not have improved their skills at signed language; it may not have opened their minds to the larger world of ideas that had always been so important to de l'Epée, but it must, at least, have required a great deal of effort and practice. Theirs was a strange but impressive accomplishment: The set of grammatical gestures that they were required to master was of value only in the classroom. De l'Epée's version of manual French was unintelligible to most hearing and, quite probably, most Deaf Parisians. In any case, de l'Epée clearly considers the transcriptions that they produce to be the best proof of the validity of his method.

De l'Epée also makes a number of references in his writings to a sort of grammar table that his students used to demonstrate their understanding of that subject. With the help of the table and a pointer de l'Epée writes that a scholar could describe how "...the verb *bring* is the present tense of the imperative mode, and *would bring,* the imperfect of the conjunctive of *to bring,* a verb active, irregularly conjugated."[6] Through these exercises the teacher measured his students' progress in "scholarship."

Even religious instruction, a very important part of the curriculum, was an exercise in memorization and grammar. De l'Epée drilled his scholars in the elements of the Catholic faith one day and the following day required them to write what they had learned. Even prayers were reduced to exercises in the use of methodological signs. De l'Epée wrote, "The signs which are executed [in the course of reciting one's prayers] exhibit not only the simple signification of the words, but their grammatical position as to tenses, modes, genders or cases...."[7] De l'Epée's approach to education seems to consist of little more than exercises in grammar followed by numerous sessions of dictation.

De l'Epée's scholars left few clues about what they thought about their education, and this is surprising because Deaf writers had already begun to make their mark in France. There were two Deaf contemporaries of de l'Epée who wrote important and interesting books and whose works have been preserved: Saboureux de Fontenay, one of the very few students of Jacob Rodriguez Pereire, wrote a brief autobiography and a work on meteorology, and the self-educated Pierre Desloges, bookbinder and paperhanger, wrote the previously mentioned *A Deaf Person's Observations about an Elementary Course of Education for the Deaf.* They were the first major Deaf authors, and neither was associated with de l'Epée. Even Desloges, whose book is, in part, a defense of de l'Epée's method, claims not to have known the French cleric. Despite the large number of students that de l'Epée taught and the controversy and acclaim that surrounded their teacher and his methods, the students themselves wrote little on their own, a consequence, perhaps, of de l'Epée's emphasis on accurate transcriptions rather than self-expression.

Public demonstrations of his students' ability to accurately transcribe signed renditions of the written word brought great fame to de l'Epée. His classes were visited by some of the most prominent philosophers and most powerful monarchs of his time. Especially important was a brief visit by the philosopher Étienne Bonnot de Condillac, whose ideas about the existence of a highly expressive primeval language of gestures out of which all spoken languages arose—he called it the "language of action"—played an important role in the history of American Sign Language. De l'Epée welcomed Condillac into his classroom as he welcomed all of his many visitors. The two of them apparently had little conversation during the visit, and they never formed a friendship, but Condillac later wrote admiringly about how de l'Epée's system of methodological signs made possible the expression of "ideas more exact and precise than those one usually acquires with the aid of hearing,"[8] an opinion, of course, that was little more than guesswork on his part; the great philosopher knew no sign. In any case, Condillac's conception of signed language went beyond its role in the history of the evolution of language. He also wrote that signed language, by which he seems to have meant the methodological signs of de l'Epée, could form the basis for a universal language, a language that would enable European scholars to communicate across the many linguistic divides that separated them. He summarized his observations of de l'Epée's methods and innovations in a single long footnote in an essay on language. Condillac's essay and that footnote—especially the footnote—would resonate for many decades among those interested in signed language, because Condillac's ideas about the origin of language provided a framework in which succeeding generations of signed language scholars posed and answered questions about the nature of signed language and its relation to the naturally occurring gestures with which everyone is familiar.

Those who disapproved of de l'Epée's methods focused their criticism on his use of signs as the *principal* medium of instruction. His critics believed that articulation, the teaching of speech, as well as speech reading, should be given more emphasis. The arguments on both sides were often exaggerated for effect. Some of de l'Epée's harshest critics used some signs in the instruction of their students, and at least some of de l'Epée's students learned speech and participated in public "orations" to demonstrate their capabilities in this area. What separated de l'Epée from his critics was not that he used signs, but rather that he used *only* signs in his students' early education. He believed that instruction via signs was the most efficient path to scholarly achievement for the Deaf, which, as previously noted, he defined as the ability to "think systematically," and which, in practice, meant grammatical analysis. Whatever contributed to this goal was worthwhile. Whatever did not was not.

De l'Epée's insights into his own innovations and his contemporaries' objections to his method are clearly stated in a series of letters that he exchanged with Samuel Heinicke, an innovative German educator and critic of de l'Epée. As a young soldier with little formal education, Heinicke nurtured an unusual talent for languages. He became interested in Deaf education while still in the army when he read *The Talking Deaf* by the Swiss doctor Johann Conrad Amman. *The Talking Deaf* changed Heinicke's life. After a period of imprisonment—he was captured by the Prussians during the Seven Years War—Heinicke worked for a Danish ambassador and eventually, with the ambassador's help, opened the first German school for the Deaf. Heinicke's influence in the field of education, both inside and outside the subdiscipline of Deaf education, was felt by many generations of German educators, and his belief in the importance of teaching the Deaf speech has been shared by most German educators who succeeded him.

In retrospect, Heinicke may not have been the best representative of de l'Epée's critics. His letters show him to be idiosyncratic and disagreeable. In them, he lays claim to great secrets in the field of Deaf education—secrets that he refuses to share without payment. He claims, for example, to have found a way to substitute his students' sense of taste for their sense of hearing, an assertion that sounded almost as ridiculous in his time as it does today. Nevertheless, de l'Epée took Heinicke's criticisms seriously and responded to them in detail. The resulting set of letters offers clear statements by the elderly French cleric and one of his most prominent critics about what they perceived was most important about their respective innovations.

In his letters de l'Epée emphasizes the importance of visual communication for the Deaf. He repeatedly uses the metaphor of the eye as a window through which ideas and images can easily pass. He also recognizes that for his Deaf scholars, signs are simply more appealing than speech. Visual language is the right choice, according to de l'Epée, because for the Deaf it is more efficient than speech. Students learn signs quickly, he writes Heinicke, and so are able to quickly proceed to "higher matters." He also recognizes that for the Deaf communicating via signs is more fun than communicating via speech and speech reading. His scholars *enjoy* signing, and it is through the use of signs that his students are "lifted to the participation of social life and business."[9]

De l'Epée's emphasis on the joy that his students experienced and the quickness with which they were able to learn also explains his aversion to the introduction of speech and speech reading early in their education. De l'Epée considered the teaching of speech to be tedious work for both student and teacher. Worse than tedious, it was also extremely time-consuming. He contrasts his approach with that of a teacher who claimed that it took only 12 to 15 months to teach students speech and speech reading. De l'Epée states that such a course of instruction is ill suited for aspiring scholars because it consisted of 12 to 15 months of work that failed to challenge the intellect: ". . . we are far from fettering [the students] for twelve or fifteen months in the dismal exercise of pronunciation. . . ."[10] Training of this type, in de l'Epée's view, shut the students off from more intellectual pursuits. The goals of daily training in speech and speech reading were too narrow, too dehumanizing, to justify the ends.

Not only did de l'Epée believe that his system of methodological signs enabled his scholars to quickly dispense with the basics and proceed to the study of higher, more ennobling ideas, he also considered his sign system to be a higher idea in itself. He took to heart Condillac's speculations about the possibility of using signed language as a sort of universal language. He saw his work in a much broader context than did his critics. In one of his letters to Heinicke he describes an experiment wherein five Deaf pupils were positioned so that they could not see each other's work. He then signed a ten-word proposition, and each student correctly transcribed the proposition into a different language: French, Latin, Italian, Spanish, and English. This exercise, he believed, pointed to the possibility of using methodological signs to create the sought-after universal language. He quotes Condillac's sentiment that standard methodological signs should be taught to students in every school in every nation. De l'Epée's writings indicate that he had no doubt that the acclaim his innovation had brought him was well deserved.

Heinicke remained unconvinced. But despite the emotion and occasional sarcasm evident in their letters, their disagreement was more a matter of degree. As mentioned previously, de l'Epée taught articulation to at least some of his older students. In fact, three chapters in his best-known work, *The Method of Educating the Deaf and Dumb; Confirmed by Long Experience,* address the topic of what is now called oral education, an educational philosophy that emphasizes training in speech and speech reading and the exclusion of signed language. The titles of chapters are "How We May Succeed in Teaching the Deaf and Dumb to Pronounce Vowels and Simple Syllables," "Necessary Observations Respecting the Reading and the Pronunciation of the Deaf and Dumb," and finally, "The Manner in which the Deaf and Dumb Are Taught to Understand by the Eye, Merely from the Motion of the Lips, without any Manual Sign Being Made to Them."[11] And just as de l'Epée was not above teaching speech and lip reading in addition to signed language, Heinicke used at least some signs in the course of instructing his students; he just placed more of an emphasis on speech than did de l'Epée. (Heinicke's position on the use of signs was probably never understood by de l'Epée, because Heinicke's letters, originally written in German, were translated into Latin for de l'Epée, and Heinicke's statements about his use of signs were mistranslated.)

Their most telling commonality, however, was that neither seemed to think it worthwhile to quote the opinions of Deaf individuals. De l'Epée called his students scholars; Heinicke boasted about the educational attainments of his students, but the ideas, the opinions, and the experiences of the Deaf with respect to the educational theories espoused by these two prominent hearing teachers were ignored. (It is worth noting that today many American schools for the Deaf have Deaf individuals on the staff, faculty, administration, and governing boards, a situation that guarantees that those who have received services designed to benefit the Deaf have input into how those same services are delivered in the future.)

Pierre Desloges

Had either Heinicke or de l'Epée wanted the opinions of Deaf individuals with respect to their educational methodologies, neither man would have had to have gone far. Both were surrounded by their own student-scholars. Or they could have asked Pierre Desloges, whose book, *A Deaf Person's Observations about an Elementary Course of Education,* already mentioned earlier in this chapter, was published a year or two before de l'Epée and Heinicke began their exchange of letters. Desloges, a self-taught tradesman, had followed the controversy over de l'Epée's new approach to the education of the Deaf, and he was a great supporter of the cleric, who surely must have heard of the book and its author. They lived in the same city, and they were interested in the same topic. But de l'Epée evinces no interest in the ideas and insights of his countryman.

Desloges's book should have made a difference in the debate between these two teachers. The author brought a unique sensibility to the discussion. He was familiar with signed language and the way it was used in a way that de l'Epée and Heinicke could never be. One did not have to agree with Desloges to acknowledge that his insights might prove to be useful, but neither his ideas or his opinions, nor the ideas or opinions of any other Deaf person, influenced this very public debate between de l'Epée and Heinicke. During Desloges's lifetime the Deaf were the raw material upon which well-intentioned hearing educators tested their philosophies and methodologies. They were beneficiaries or victims of those philosophies and methodologies, but they did not participate in the formulation of either.

Two centuries after Desloges's book was first published it is still worth the effort to examine Desloges's ideas about signed language and the Deaf and how his ideas differed from those of his hearing contemporaries. Later Deaf authors, many of whom have never heard of Desloges, continue, nevertheless, to give expression to many of the same perceptions and ideas that Desloges did. This pattern continues today.

Desloges addresses four issues related to signed language and its use in the education of the Deaf. First, he defends the signed language of the Deaf of Paris *as a language,* the equal of spoken languages. Second, he defends the methods of de l'Epée from the antisigned language criticisms of another French cleric involved in Deaf education, the abbé Deschamps. Third, he offers a few examples of the linguistic structures employed in the signed language of Parisian Deaf in order to demonstrate the existence of structure and grammar; his language, he assures the reader, is not a haphazard collection of gestures. (Today, his book, brief as it is, is the principal source of information about the indigenous signed language of eighteenth century Paris.) Finally, he shares his thoughts on the value of signed language to the general (hearing) population and its possible use as a universal language.

Signed language, Desloges emphasizes, is the language of the Deaf; it is a language of their own creation; it stands in the same relation to the Deaf as the German language stands in relation to the Germans. He writes forcibly that signed language—and he means the signed language used by the Deaf of Paris, not the system of methodological signs created by de l'Epée—is as expressive and as capable of conveying thoughts, both concrete and abstract, as any other language. The tone of the text is not strident, but it is insistent and uncompromising; "...we [the Deaf] usually do not learn sign language from hearing people."[12] and "... there is nothing in any part of speech that cannot be expressed in sign language."[13] This book is the first description of what in modern times has come to be called Deaf culture, and it is a description that is offered with style, reason, and insight.

From a more modern point of view it is unfortunate that so much of Desloges's brief work is taken up critiquing the writings of the abbé Deschamps, a critic of de l'Epée. In retrospect, Deschamps's criticisms were not especially cogent or influential. It is, however, in the course of his defense of de l'Epée against the criticisms of Deschamps that Desloges describes how de l'Epée studied the signed language of the Deaf prior to beginning his work. Although he acknowledges that de l'Epée found the indigenous signed language of Paris "defective," Desloges admits of no defects in his language. Neither does he criticize de l'Epée for his analysis—perhaps because de l'Epée was the first educator to use signs in a systematic, even celebratory, way in the education of the Deaf. De l'Epée does, after all, repeatedly emphasize that a language of signs is as capable of expressing higher ideas as any spoken language, an assertion that is very important to Desloges. And Desloges and de l'Epée both insist that signed language is the language best suited to the needs of the Deaf because it is their natural language. Desloges writes, "...we must conclude that the chief instrument in the education of the Deaf must be sign language and that, like it or not, we will always come back to this method for the compelling reason that sign is their [the Deaf's] natural language, the only one they can understand until with its help we have taught them another one."[14]

Desloges also appreciates the fact that de l'Epée does not teach his younger students speech, and his reason is both interesting and compassionate: Articulation lessons for a young uneducated Deaf person are, according to Desloges, not just tedious, a point upon which Deschamps, Desloges, and de l'Epée all agree, they are disgusting and from the young student's viewpoint pointless. At the time, teaching articulation sometimes required teachers to place their fingers inside the students' mouths, and sometimes the students had to place their fingers inside the mouths of their teachers. Deschamps and other early oralists advocated beginning these lessons as soon as possible—in particular, before the student had acquired sufficient language to understand the explanation for such a saliva-filled activity, and this was something that Desloges opposed. Desloges's emphasis on the students' point of view shows empathy for their situation, a trait that many of his hearing counterparts did not share.

By contrast with the slow and distasteful progress in articulation that even Deschamps acknowledged was part of the process of speech training, signed language was, according to Desloges, efficient and enjoyable, and if a student later received speech lessons accompanied by a coherent explanation (in sign) about the goals and methods of the lessons that was fine. What was important is that reasoned explanations prevail over the early brute force lessons favored by Deschamps, who acknowledged a need to sometimes teach speech forcibly and offer an explanation later when the student could appreciate it. (More than a century later Anne Sullivan, Helen Keller's teacher, shared Desloges's viewpoint and described the problem of teaching a Deaf child speech as a "first language" in these words, "The untaught deaf child who is made to articulate does not know what the goal is, and his lessons in speech are for a long time tedious and meaningless" and "[t]he acquiring of speech by untaught deaf children is always slow and painful. Too much stress, it seems to me, is often laid upon the importance of teaching a deaf child to articulate—a process which may be detrimental to the pupil's intellectual development.")[15]

With respect to the structure of Parisian signed language, Desloges contents himself with providing a handful of examples. His goal is to demonstrate the way that communication occurs via sign and to show how simple, usually iconic gestures can be combined to represent more abstract ideas. He even offers a test to show the utility of the language. Paris is large, he says, and finding a residence for the first time can be difficult. Nevertheless, he can, using only signs, direct a Deaf individual to a residence that the individual had never seen. His description of signing in the dark is also compelling. (Deschamps had written that signed language was useless in the dark.) Desloges writes that in the dark the Deaf simply guide each others hands to create the signs that they wish to convey, a method that is, according to Desloges, quicker and easier than fingerspelling into each other's hands. These are the kinds of insights and "proofs" that only someone who relied on signed language as a principal means of communication could offer, and they stand in stark contrast not only to the objections of the oralists of the time but also to the peculiar pride that de l'Epée takes in his students' transcriptions and in their ability to recite grammatically correct prayers.

Finally, Desloges shows he is aware of the interest shown by philosophers of his time in signed language as a possible universal language that would enable people of different linguistic backgrounds to communicate easily. He adds little new to the discussion and, instead, contents himself with quoting from other, more prominent writers on the topic: Count de Gébelin, abbé Copineau, and Condillac. The idea that his language is a more fundamental form of communication than any spoken language, and that it could have wider applications, evidently appeals to him as it would appeal to many of those interested in signed language for the next hundred years. [Today, researchers dismiss the idea of a universal "sign language." Instead, they often refer to *signed languages* and assert that, just as spoken languages are mutually unintelligible, so, too, are signed languages. (Not only, for example, is British Sign Language very different from Danish Sign Language, it is also quite distinct from American Sign Language.) But while there is certainly great variation in signed languages, it is also true that fluent signers from different countries can, in a few hours, establish enough of a common vocabulary and grammar to easily discuss a variety of topics, a feat that is much more difficult to accomplish using spoken language. The analogy between spoken and signed languages is a good one, but like all analogies, it has its limitations.]

In the end, however, it was not Desloges who profoundly influenced the development of signed language, it was de l'Epée, and from a modern point of view de l'Epée's contributions were especially significant in two ways. First, de l'Epée did not so much repair the language used by the Deaf of Paris as he did ruin it. Appending his extensive set of grammatical signs to the indigenous signed language of the Deaf probably made the resulting sign system incomprehensible to many native signers. (This has certainly been the result when, in more modern times, American educators created systems of methodological signs to convey English grammar in a way that was conceptually similar to what de l'Epée had done.) In fact, today de l'Epée's signing system is not considered a language at all but a method for encoding the French language. In this sense, his methodological signs have less in common with American Sign Language, or the signed language used by the Deaf of eighteenth century Paris, than it has with Morse code. In its day Morse code proved to be an effective way of encoding languages for transmission, but it was never more than that. In effect, it was the software that accompanied the hardware of the code key. Together they made it possible to transmit preexisting languages over wires and through the air, but Morse code is only a way of presenting a preexisting language, it is not a language itself. De l'Epée's system of methodological signs attempted to perform a similar function by enabling the user to visually represent the French language manually.

It is probably no coincidence that the various systems of methodological signs invented over the last two centuries have proved easier for hearing people to learn than for the Deaf, depending as they do on an intimate familiarity with the spoken language that they purport to represent. Methodological signs put the hearing teacher in charge. When the signed languages created by the Deaf are employed, the roles of Deaf student and hearing teacher, powerless and powerful, are often reversed: Hearing people generally have a harder time learning the signed languages favored by the Deaf than do the Deaf.

Second, de l'Epée's emphasis on the use of signs in the instruction of the Deaf tended to emphasize the existence of the Deaf as a social class. In fact, in the two centuries since de l'Epée opened his first school, there have been many who have claimed that de l'Epée's innovation *created* a new social class, the Deaf (with a capital "D"), united by a unique language. Desloges's book shows that such a claim is an exaggeration. The Deaf of Paris, at least, were a linguistic minority well before de l'Epée turned his attention to the field of education. Nevertheless, de l'Epée's work brought attention to the existence of this group and to the language that they had already created. The field of Deaf education was permanently changed by his work, but many of the resulting changes would surely have surprised him.

An excerpt from a written conversation between Laurent Clerc and Charles Sigourney, a member of the board of directors at the Hartford school, about the staffing at the school. Notice that although Clerc knew no language at all until the age of 12 and no English until his late 20s, his English in this conversation is perfect. Courtesy American School for the Deaf Archive.

The Natural Language of Signs

He frequented my school-room, and one day requested me to give him private lessons of an hour everyday. I could receive him but three times a week, in my room up stairs in the afternoon, and he came with punctuality, so great was his desire of acquiring the knowledge of the language of signs in the shortest possible time.
            —Laurent Clerc describing his early association with Thomas H.
                                                        Gallaudet in Paris[1]

On May 25, 1815, Thomas Hopkins Gallaudet (1787–1851) left the United States for Liverpool, England. Twenty-seven years old, a graduate of Yale College and the Andover Seminary, Gallaudet was sailing to England to learn a method for educating the Deaf. He hoped to learn as much as possible as quickly as possible and then to bring the information back to Hartford, Connecticut, in order to establish the first school for the Deaf in North America.

He did not pay for the trip himself. Gallaudet went at the behest of a committee of Hartford citizens organized by Mason Cogswell, a neighbor of the Gallaudet family. Cogswell's ten-year-old daughter, Alice, was Deaf. The family did not want to send Alice to England; they had decided, instead, to try to bring a little bit of England to Hartford. Gallaudet, who was also a committee member, was the committee's first choice to make the journey. He had always taken an interest in Alice's education and on occasion had made some simple and not very successful efforts to teach her language. He was not, however, especially enthusiastic about making the trip. In fact, he had initially refused their offer but soon acquiesced. Perhaps he considered their proposal a sign from God. His son, Edward Miner Gallaudet, later wrote that after graduating from the seminary Gallaudet returned to the family home to think about how he might best serve God. He had been waiting for a sign from heaven. Perhaps this was it.

A faded green box at the Library of Congress in the Division of Rare Books and Manuscripts is the current resting place of the water-stained journal that Gallaudet kept during his European trip. He gave it a name: *A Journal of Some Occurrences in my Life Which have a Relation to the Instruction of the Deaf and Dumb*. More than half the pages of the journal are blank. Most of the rest is a carefully documented, immaculately written account of his failure to accomplish his original goal. Deaf education in Great Britain was a business during the early years of the nineteenth century—a monopoly, in fact—controlled by a family named Braidwood, and the family members had no interest in sharing their techniques and insights in the field of deaf education. Gallaudet had not anticipated this problem, and it is clear from his journal and subsequent accounts that he had a great deal of difficulty accepting the situation.

Gallaudet's first stop was a school for the Deaf in London run by the Braidwoods, but they refused to let him observe the classes, citing the distractions that his presence would cause the students. Gallaudet met with the governing board of the school to explain his goals. They formed a subcommittee to study his proposal. He presented letters of recommendation; he met with the teacher; he tried everything that a well-educated, nineteenth century gentleman could try. In the end, they offered him a three-year, six-day per week contract to work as an assistant. This, they explained, would be the best way to learn the Braidwood methods. The hours were long—he would begin at seven in the morning and finish at eight at night—and the pay was low; the work was repetitive and not especially stimulating. Gallaudet, a New England aristocrat, was offended by both the offer and the inquiries school officials made about the possibility of extending their business into America. He gave up hope of learning what he needed to know at the London school.

But something important had already occurred. While in London Gallaudet saw a demonstration of signed language as a medium of communication. The demonstration was one of several that the French cleric Roche Amboise Sicard, Charles-Michel de l'Epée's successor at the Paris school, and two of his senior students, Laurent Clerc (1785–1869) and Jean Massieu, had presented during their stay in England. Sicard was a royalist. He had fled to London during Napoleon's "Hundred Days" return to power. He returned soon after Napoleon's defeat. Gallaudet and Sicard spoke briefly at the presentation, and Sicard invited the American to visit the Paris school, but Gallaudet had other plans.

In late August 1815, Gallaudet left London for Scotland. He would spend the winter unsuccessfully attempting to study deaf education at a school in

Edinburgh. This school, too, was controlled by the Braidwoods, and school officials operated under a contract that specified a large financial penalty should they reveal the methods used at the school without prior permission from Thomas Braidwood. Gallaudet appealed directly to Braidwood to no avail. He sought to convince school officials that the contract did not apply to him as an American; they did not agree. He spent the better part of the Scottish winter writing letters to Mason Cogswell, Alice Cogswell, to his family and friends, and reading a book on deaf education by the abbé Sicard.

The last five pages of Gallaudet's journal contain a brief description of his time in France. He arrived in Paris in March 1816. In the manner of his predecessor, de l'Epée, Sicard welcomed visitors. He sought to educate not just students but instructors as well. Gallaudet asked many questions. He studied with both Laurent Clerc and Jean Massieu. Both Deaf men had studied under Sicard and remained at the school as teachers. Soon Gallaudet was studying signed language with Clerc, a man two years his senior. Feeling the pressure of time, he asked Clerc how long it would take to become fluent in Clerc's signed language. Clerc told him that it would take at least six months to learn—a year to become skillful enough to teach others. His patience wearing thin after almost a year in Europe, Gallaudet decided to offer Clerc a position as teacher at the Hartford School, and over the objections of Sicard, who pleaded with Clerc to stay and who offered him a raise in pay, Clerc agreed to go.

Clerc's mother also presented a potential obstacle to the trip. Gallaudet wrote her a letter promising that should Clerc accompany him to America, he would remain Clerc's "constant and faithful friend." During Clerc's time in America, Gallaudet promised the mother that her son would "receive a reward," "perfect his English," and "acquire a reputation." To his credit, Gallaudet remained true to all of these promises. Although Clerc was a teacher at the Hartford school and Gallaudet the principal, Gallaudet had no objection when Clerc later asked for a raise in pay that would make his salary larger than Gallaudet's. And during the voyage back to the United States, a voyage that, because of bad weather, lasted nearly two months, Gallaudet gave Clerc daily English lessons even as Clerc taught him sign. (Clerc demonstrated a remarkable facility with languages and his written notes indicate that he quickly mastered English.) Finally, it was Clerc, not Gallaudet, who successfully lobbied President James Madison and members of Congress, including Henry Clay, for help in funding the Hartford school. The federal government gave the school a large land grant in Alabama, which was later sold to raise money. The land grant was awarded three years after the school opened. On April 15, 1817, the first school for the Deaf in the United States, now known as the American School for the Deaf, opened in Hartford.

Throughout his life Gallaudet spoke highly of Clerc. Publicly and privately he remained Clerc's constant and faithful friend. In his papers and speeches he referred to Clerc as "the intelligent laborer," and he offered Clerc assistance whenever possible. Clerc, for example, enjoyed the company of his students. For awhile he may have been the only well-educated Deaf person fluent in this signed language in the Western Hemisphere. He must have felt isolated, and so he developed the habit of welcoming groups of students over to his home after class for conversation. It was a custom that he maintained well into retirement. Early in his career at Hartford, however, Clerc's after-class meetings were a source of concern, because groups of students of both sexes stopped by for conversation. In the Library of Congress collection is a letter, dated 1817, wherein Gallaudet wrote a four-page response to a complaint from a Mr. Terry about Clerc's after school get-togethers. In the letter Gallaudet reminds Terry of Clerc's "peculiar situation" and then Gallaudet writes that Clerc

> is entitled to our kindest regards...his reasonable wishes should in every way be consulted. It is no small gratification to him, surely a very innocent one, to have an opportunity out of school hours, of enjoying the pleasures of social conversation with the young ladies. They esteem this, too, a peculiar privilege, and I may add, also that it is a singular advantage to them, in as much as their chief business here is to acquire language, and *his* language of signs is the foundation of all their improvement... Shut out as they are from the usual sources of enjoyment, they look to their instructor, not only for improvement, but for entertainment. Shall this be denied them! It would almost be cruel to do it...I know his disposition well. He is as far aloof from any petty jealousy or retaliation as any man I was ever acquainted with. (Gallaudet's italics)

But Gallaudet was no mere imitator. It is true that he learned most of his signed language from Clerc, just as Clerc learned much of his English from Gallaudet, but Gallaudet was determined to understand Clerc's signed language *as a language,* and this was important because there were many in his time—as there are in our own—who failed to appreciate that the signed language used by American Deaf is, in fact, a fully formed language. It was this language in which Gallaudet had an interest. By contrast, de l'Epée had looked toward the language of the Deaf of Paris for inspiration only. He preferred to create his own signed language or at least his own signing system. Gallaudet, on the other hand, studied the language of Clerc, the language of his students, and the signs and gestures of other Deaf individuals in an attempt to identify certain features that he believed to be common to all gestural languages. He was not content to simply become proficient in the use of this signed language. Almost as soon as he developed facility in the new language, a language that would continue to fascinate him for the rest of his life, he began to theorize and experiment with it.

Initially, Gallaudet's views on sign were quite conservative. He accepted, more or less, what he had been taught in Paris. In an 1819 article for the *Christian Observer*[2] Gallaudet claims that his teaching methods were in general accord with the methods of the abbé Sicard, Laurent Clerc's teacher at the Paris school. He acknowledges that some criticize Sicard's system of signs, which was a variant of that of de l'Epée's methodological signs, as "unnecessarily prolix, and savoring too much of metaphysical subtlety." Nevertheless, he claims that the general principles of Sicard's methods, which were similar in concept to those of de l'Epée, correspond to the "laws of the mind," and, indeed, the students at the Hartford school were initially taught via methodological signs. But Gallaudet's opinion of Sicard's system of signs changed as did those of his colleagues—so much so, that by 1847 Luzerne Rae, a teacher at the Hartford school and a serious student of signed language, was able to write the following words about Sicard without engendering any apparent controversy among his colleagues at the Hartford school:

> The French successors of Sicard, if you ask their real opinion, will whisper in your ear that this distinguished man, with all his merits, was very much of a charlatan; a judgment from which those will hardly dissent who believe, as I do, that his system of "Methodical Signs" is a complete piece of charlatanry, from beginning to end...I have little doubt that the time will come, and at no distant day, when all our American schools for the Deaf and Dumb, will follow the wise example of the Paris Institution and that of most of the others in France, by entirely discarding methodical signs from their course of instruction.[3]

There is little in the record spanning the years 1820–1830 that indicates the way Gallaudet's ideas about signed language evolved and how he came to reject the methodological signs of de l'Epée and Sicard in favor of what he called "the natural language of signs," a conception of signed language that was the dominant model at American schools for the Deaf for decades. There is, however, an interesting 1820 article in the *Christian Observer* by someone identified only by the letter K, who seems to have been a teacher at the Hartford school.[4] In the article the author describes the modes of communication used at the school for the instruction of the students. K identifies four types of communication: the natural language of signs, the methodological signs created by de l'Epée and enlarged upon by Sicard, the manual alphabet, and writing. (The writer dismisses the teaching of speech to the Deaf as a waste of time. It requires, he asserts, large amounts of time without introducing "any original knowledge to the mind of the pupil.")

First, K asserts that the natural language of signs is the foundation of all attempts to educate the Deaf. Interestingly, he claims that the natural language of signs was originally used by the Deaf and that it is "singularly" adapted to their needs. He notes that when two Deaf individuals meet for the first time, they use the natural language of signs to communicate and that it is through this medium that they are able to discuss "all common topics." The idea that what is here called the natural language of signs is a language that is not only for the Deaf but also *of* the Deaf passes with little comment. (It is also interesting to note that K asserts that the faculty of the Hartford school "hope very soon to become masters of their profession, and thus to secure its advantages beyond the danger of loss," and that they are learning the language of signs via daily lectures "given by their ingenious and experienced associate, Mr. Clerc...")[5]

Second, Sicard's signing system had evidently not yet been jettisoned at the Hartford school at the time that K wrote the article, because he describes Sicard's signing system as a standardized version of the natural language of signs, "divested of certain peculiarities of dialect, which have grown out of the various circumstances of life under which different individuals have been placed...," a description that clearly shows that some on the Hartford faculty acknowledged the existence of dialects and the not-quite-universal nature of the natural language of signs. K praises the use of Sicard's methodological signs, because, he believed, it emphasized connections between signed and written language—presumably English. Paradoxically, and in the same sentence, he compares methodological signs to Chinese characters, and it is in these few remarks that it becomes apparent that a new concept of signed language is being formulated. K asserts that the principal difference between Sicard's methodological signs and Chinese characters is that the former is communicated via gestures, body language, and facial expressions, while the latter is communicated via pen and paper. This emphasis on gestures and body language is a marked shift in emphasis from the thinking of de l'Epée and Sicard, who emphasized well-formed manual gestures to the exclusion of other aspects of visual communication in the representation of spoken French and who cared little about the nonmanual aspects of sign.

Third, K emphasizes the distinction between the manual alphabet and signed language, a distinction that was at least as important to nineteenth century researchers as it is to twenty-first century researchers. They asserted—and contemporary researchers agree—that the manual alphabet is not, strictly speaking, a language at all. It is simply a different way of encoding English. One reason it is valuable is that it enables Deaf individuals to converse with their hearing friends more quickly than would be possible by pen and paper. And because the manual alphabet enables one to create a visual and relatively easy-to-recognize representation of the English language, a hearing person would not need to know the natural language of signs to use it. Communication via the manual alphabet, he asserts, evinces the same arbitrariness of representation that is found in spoken and written English, and in that sense it is inferior to the natural language of signs, which, he believed, was iconic in nature. Nevertheless, fingerspelling does, according to K, serve as an important bridge between spoken and visual language, and this is its great advantage.

The fourth and, according to K, the final method of communication important to the Deaf is writing. K explains that the main aim of the program at Hartford is to educate students so that they can spontaneously produce grammatically correct writing. It was through the written word that the graduates of the program at Hartford were to enter larger society. There is not much text devoted to discussing the importance of writing and reading, but a considerable portion of the remaining article is a defense of the decision of the faculty at Hartford to forgo training in speech. K acknowledges that the decision is controversial but asserts that speech training requires too much time, and the results are rarely commensurate with the effort. Those who emphasize the importance of speech training confuse, according to K, the gift of speech with the gift of reason. Given the limited time that the students spend in school, K asserts that it is far more productive to "unfold silently the latent capacities of the understanding" than to teach the Deaf to speak, although the latter "will always appear to the multitude a far more wonderful feat of ingenuity."[6]

These two articles in the *Christian Observer,* the first from 1819 by Gallaudet and the second from 1820 by K, provide early and rare insights into the signed language philosophy of the early American teachers of the Deaf.

But Gallaudet's understanding of signed language continued to evolve. In a manuscript[7] entitled *Essay on Signs,* which the Library of Congress has dated ca. 1830, Gallaudet describes some experiments that clearly helped shape his ideas about sign. He writes how in 1818 a Chinese man, with virtually no knowledge of English, was passing through Hartford. Gallaudet invited the man to spend an evening at the school—or the "asylum" as it was then called—for the purpose of introducing him to Clerc. It was one of the first of many similar experiments. Clerc, who never used his voice to communicate with anyone—he preferred to write notes or to sign—did not know Chinese. Gallaudet watched the two of them interact. He hoped to discover "to what extent Mr. Clerc, who was entirely ignorant of the Chinese language, could conduct an intelligible conversation with the foreigner by signs and gestures merely."[8] At first the Chinese man was bewildered by the unusual nature of Clerc's language, but "before one hour had elapsed" the two of them were signing back and forth. Clerc learned about the man's hometown, his parents, his family, his "former pursuits in his own country," his home in the United States, and his ideas concerning God and the afterlife. (Religious topics were always foremost in the thoughts of Gallaudet and Clerc.) Gallaudet writes how the man "caught the spirit of his new deaf and dumb acquaintance," and how he began to use "the language of the countenance and gestures, with considerable effect, to make himself understood." By the end of the evening Clerc had learned about 20 Chinese words. From the description it is apparent that Gallaudet considered the experiment very revealing.

In the same manuscript Gallaudet also describes how he visited a missionary school in Cornwall, Connecticut, where 20 "heathen" youth were receiving an education. Several students, Native Americans of different tribes as well as students from the "South Seas," were gathered for an evening of conversation with Gallaudet. The conversation was carried out in signed language. Again, the topics included the history of each individual, the histories of their families, "the state of manners and morals in their respective countries," and their religious insights. The youths "appeared to take a deep interest" in the conversation "and to have a peculiar aptitude both in comprehending the signs which were proposed to them and in inventing those which were necessary for a reply."[9] But there was something else—something which Gallaudet regarded as equally significant: Some of the signs used by the South Sea Islanders in their native lands were "precisely the same" as the ones used at the asylum in Hartford.

In this essay and in later writings Gallaudet emphasized his belief that signed language is more than a collection of manual gestures. He recognized in a way that Sicard and de l'Epée did not that a great deal of what contemporary researchers call linguistic information is (in signed language) conveyed via nonmanual signals, e.g., facial expressions, the direction of the signer's gaze, the attitude of the body, etc. To demonstrate how much information is conveyed nonmanually, he undertook the following experiment:[10] A third party—Gallaudet identifies him only as "an eminent painter of our country"—chose a story that Gallaudet was to convey to his more advanced Deaf students "without any words on his fingers, or using his arms at all in making gestures." Gallaudet was to rely exclusively on the nonmanual aspects of the natural language of signs. The painter chose the story in which Brutus orders the death of his sons. [Junius Lucius Brutus (fl. sixth century BCE) deposed the king, Lucius Tarquinius Superbus. When his sons join in a plot against their father to restore the Tarquins to the throne, Brutus sentences his sons to death.] In describing the experiment Gallaudet acknowledges that the students had encountered the story before but only "two or three years previous." No hints were given and Gallaudet confined himself to "expressions of the countenance, motions of the head, and attitudes of the body." The students

understood the story and this proved to Gallaudet how important these nonmanual aspects of signed language are to signed communication. They were, he
believed, an integral part of signed language.

Similarly, Charles P. Turner, a prominent nineteenth century educator of the
Deaf, recounted an experiment in which an unidentified instructor successfully
conveyed the biblical story "The Offering of Isaac" without the slightest motion
of hand or arm.[11] These types of experiments and their interpretation by Gallaudet and his colleagues demonstrate how they studied the natural language of signs
and how they came to perceive it. (It was only during the latter years of the twentieth century, after a hiatus of more than a century, that researchers returned to
these ideas and again identified signed language as a "dual channel" system of
communication, by which they meant that much of the information conveyed
in signed language is not conveyed manually.)

Gallaudet was interested in all types of signed and gestural communication,
and he made little distinction between the two. Manual and nonmanual signs,
formal signs, and pantomime were, he believed, all aspects of the natural language
of signs. The foundation for his beliefs rested on the success of his experiments,
and he sought many opportunities to test his ideas and his communication skills.
For example, while the men who captured the slave ship *Amistad* were impris-
oned in American jails, Gallaudet met with them to learn their story. They knew
no English; Gallaudet communicated with them via the natural language of signs.

It was Gallaudet's belief that the natural language of signs provided a common
language for individuals of widely different cultural and linguistic backgrounds.
The level of communication repeatedly achieved between linguistically disparate
parties reinforced his belief in the essential correctness of his ideas. And in another example, taken from his best-known work on the natural language of signs,[12]
Gallaudet recounts how he and a "fellow-laborer" visited an 80-year-old, illiter-
ate, Deaf man, who knew no formal signs and who wanted to make a will. The
man's sole medium of communication was what Gallaudet called "natural signs,"
and in this case he meant a makeshift system of informal gestures that the elderly
man had, over the years, devised to communicate with those around him.
"Exhibiting a great deal of ingenuity" on the part of all three, the old man was
able to convey how he wanted his property divided upon his death. Gallaudet
and his companion were certain that they had understood the man's desires.

Gallaudet and the other faculty members at the American Asylum believed
that they had discovered something that was both new and simultaneously
ancient—new, because the language of signs that they had learned had, in part,
arisen out of the educational system founded by the abbé de l'Epée, and ancient,
because they believed that signed language is a language of near-universal images,

a mode of communication that intimately reflects how every human perceives the world. His belief in the universality of signed language explains why he was so anxious to sign with people from different cultural and linguistic backgrounds. If he was correct in his beliefs about the natural language of signs, then his efforts would be rewarded with meaningful communication. That he experienced some success in communicating with Deaf individuals from different regions and different educational backgrounds as well as some success in communicating with hearing individuals from different cultural and linguistic backgrounds was proof, he believed, of the universality of the natural language of signs.

It is often asserted by modern writers that there is no universal signed language, and, in fact, contemporary linguists and others interested in the subject generally speak of signed languages rather than a single signed language. They cite many examples of the way different signs are used by different peoples to represent the same concept, and they cite experiments that show that Deaf people from different geographic areas—Deaf individuals whose first language is a signed language—encounter the same sorts of problems when they attempt to communicate via signs that hearing individuals from different linguistic backgrounds experience when they first attempt to communicate with each other via words. Signed languages, they assert, are no more universal than spoken languages, and Gallaudet's ideas are summarily dismissed.

To be sure, Gallaudet's writings are not the final words on the nature of signed language, but contemporary writers often mischaracterize Gallaudet's ideas. Of course, Gallaudet understood that people from different cultural backgrounds often used different signs to represent the same object or concept. He had taken time to meet Deaf individuals from a variety of backgrounds and with varying levels of education, and he frequently remarked on the variability of signs. He had observed and attempted to communicate via signs with Native Americans from the Great Plains, who had created their own signed language to facilitate communication between different linguistic groups. He knew that Deaf individuals from different geographic areas might initially encounter difficulties in communicating with each other. He had remarked on this. And it would have come as no surprise to him to be told that the Deaf of different countries in Europe used signs different from those used in Hartford. He and Clerc had altered some of the French signs to make them more appropriate for American usage. All of these assertions about the nonuniversal nature of signed languages are apparent to even the most casual observer, but they do not by themselves invalidate Gallaudet's understanding of signed language.

To Gallaudet, properly made signs bear the same relation to objects (and concepts) that shadows bear to the objects that cast them. Of course, an object can cast a variety of shadows. The precise shape of a shadow depends, for example, on the angle at which the light strikes the object. There is a one-to-many relationship between an object and the shadows that it casts, but not every shadow can be a representation of a particular object, and some shadows are more representative of the object that casts them than are others—at least in the sense that they are more easily recognized as symbols of the original object. The goal of a skilled signer is, therefore, to express oneself via the most iconic, easy-to-recognize signs possible. Signs are, in this view, the physical expression of the relationships that exist between the speaker's mind and soul and the exterior world—relationships realized in the motion of the body, the expressions of the face, the tilt of the head, and a rich vocabulary of manual gestures. Signed language is unique and universal, Gallaudet believed, because it is language—or, more precisely, is *thought*— made visible.

In what may be his earliest writings on the nature of signed language,[13] Gallaudet endorses the views of an anonymous author of an August 1818 article in the *Christian Observer*. That author wrote "...so far as intellectual processes bear any analogy to the motions of matter, it [signed language] shadows forth this analogy in very striking and significant emblems."[14] Although this view of signed language did not originate with Gallaudet, he and his Hartford colleagues were more specific about the nature of these relationships than their predecessors, and they sought evidence for the existence of these relationships in experiments. It was their opinion that their experiments confirmed their beliefs.

Between 1820 and 1847 there is not much in the record that describes how ideas about signed language were changing, but in 1847 the Hartford school began publishing the *American Annals of the Deaf and Dumb,* a scholarly journal, now known as the *American Annals of the Deaf,* the first English language scholarly journal devoted to those topics of most relevance to the Deaf and their education. The introductory remarks, written by Luzerne Rae, describe a journal with a very broad mission. Among other topics Rae writes that the journal hopes to publish articles about the history of the deaf, because "[t]hey have a history peculiar to themselves, extending back for many centuries into the past, and sustaining relations, of more or less interest, to the general history of the human race."[15] The journal, Rae continues, is also interested in publishing statistics of every kind relating to the Deaf, and "a careful exposition of the philosophy of the language of signs." Other potential topics are described as well.

In the first issue of the *Annals,* Gallaudet writes the first of a two-part article about the natural language of signs. (The second part was published in the next issue.) These two articles, taken together, contain his fully formed theory of what the natural language of signs is and how it should be used.[16] By 1847 Gallaudet had completely abandoned the signing system of Sicard and directed his attention to delineating the properties of the natural language of signs. A review of other contemporary writers shows that Gallaudet's theory also reflects the thinking of his colleagues, individuals who thought a great deal about signed language and the best way to use it. Gallaudet's two articles are especially important, however, because they form the basis for how Americans interested in the nature of signed language would understand the subject for the next century.

Gallaudet believed that the natural language of signs holds a special place among all human languages, because it is nonarbitrary in the following sense: The words of a spoken language are, according to Gallaudet, arbitrary symbols of the objects (and concepts) that they represent. By contrast, properly made signs are "actual portraits of the objects."[17] In "Essay on Signs" Gallaudet writes, "Signs and gestures have a peculiar significance from their resemblance to the object which they are intended to denote, and this is true even of those which are employed to denote intellectual objects." To Gallaudet, the representational nature of a well-crafted sign was part of its beauty and its utility, because signs, when executed by a skillful signer, had the potential to transcend linguistic barriers. A well-made sign would, in general, be easy to recognize, in the same way, and for the same reason, that a well-made, representational portrait renders its subject in a way that is often described as "realistic"—realistic in the sense that the viewer can quickly associate the subject with its image.

It is important to emphasize that in Gallaudet's characterization of signed language there exists no hint of the existence of a one-to-one correspondence between signs and objects as is sometimes claimed by contemporary critics of Gallaudet's philosophy of signs. Gallaudet merely asserts that to sign properly one should choose signs that best represent the objects or concepts to which one is referring. Signing, in this view, has much in common with pantomime, and these early signers took no offense at the comparison. In fact, they sometimes described their own efforts in terms of pantomime, although they had in mind the art of the Roman pantomimists, to which references can be found in a number of articles by several authors, rather than any parlor game.[18] The most prominent of the Roman pantomimists, Roscius, is said to have engaged in a public contest with the orator Cicero to determine who could express a thought more forcefully. Roscius was restricted to gestures and Cicero was restricted to words. This contest, the idea of pantomime as an ancient and respected art form, and the connections that exist between "formal" signs and pantomime were very important to these early thinkers. Gallaudet described natural language in this way:

The natural language of signs is abundantly capable of either portraying or recalling
...objects and circumstances. The life, picture-like delineation, pantomimic spirit,
variety, and grace with which this [signing] may be done...constitute a visual language which has a charm...that merely *oral* language does not possess.[19] (Gallaudet's italics)

The assertion that signed language was more expressive than spoken language was
an oft-repeated refrain of many of these early sign scholars.

But choosing the correct signs is, in this view, only one aspect of effective
signed language communication. The signs must be made expressively, and they
must be ordered in a way that best conveys the signer's intent. In "Essay on Signs"
Gallaudet gives a description of expressive signing that emphasizes its connections
with pantomime. Gallaudet imagines a missionary in a foreign land, placed
among people who do not speak his language and whose language he understands
only a little—in particular, the missionary is assumed to know the foreign word
for water. How, Gallaudet asks, could one learn the word that signifies *boiling?*
With words, he asserts, this is difficult *because* words are arbitrary signifiers of
objects and concepts, but by using the natural language of signs the concept of
boiling is easy to convey. In the following quotation, Gallaudet describes how
he might communicate the concept of boiling. Today some would characterize
Gallaudet's example as a combination of formal signs and pantomime, but Gallaudet would have said—and without qualification—that he was simply employing *the natural language of signs:*

He describes a kettle by signs, [and via pantomime] he places the wood beneath it, he
fills it with water, he kindles the fire, he portrays the bubbling of the water, dips his
finger into it and draws it out suddenly as if it were burnt. He has before learned
the name of water, and what do you call this bubbling water he inquires, this water
which burns my finger?[20]

(Gallaudet often wrote that missionaries in foreign lands might profitably use the
natural language of signs to quickly establish a common language with their
potential converts.)

Effective sign, then, involved the use of formal signs, facial expressions, body
language, and what he called pantomime as opposed to the sort of signs that
one might find in a dictionary of signs. But Gallaudet's broad—and realistic—
concept of what is involved in signed language communication created its own
difficulties. If one perceives signed language as a fluid, complex, and sometimes
simultaneous mixture of facial expressions, pantomime, body language, and formal signs, how can one describe it analytically? How can one reduce the problem
of characterizing the natural language of signs into a series of tractable subprob-
lems? It is often said that every language has three characteristics—a vocabulary,

a grammar, and a phonology or system of pronunciation—but where modern scholars see a hierarchy of individually solvable problems, Gallaudet saw a unified whole, a beautiful mode of self-expression that resisted the methods of analysis.

One consequence of Gallaudet's holistic view of signed language was that the natural language of signs could not be recorded as spoken languages are. In contrast to de l'Epée, who created his own signed language dictionary—a task that was, for him, simple in concept, because he had also invented many of the signs—Gallaudet dismissed the possibility of ever creating a signed language dictionary. He believed that the only way to learn signed language was to model one's own signs (in the most inclusive sense of the word) on those who were already proficient. Also in contrast to de l'Epée, Gallaudet often looked toward the Deaf themselves as the best models of signed language technique and expressiveness:

> For, the language of signs is not to be learned from books. It cannot be delineated in pictures, or printed on paper. It must be learned in a great degree, from the living, looking, acting model. Some of the finest models, for such a purpose, are found among the *originators* of this language, the deaf and dumb.[21] (italics added)

Although Gallaudet's approach to signed language obviated the need to consider the language analytically, Gallaudet did occasionally describe and analyze individual signs and write about what he had discovered. Like other members of the Hartford faculty, he delighted in finding signs in other signed languages that were similar or identical to those with which he was familiar, and he described them in ways that indicated an interest in their etymology. For example, Gallaudet wrote about the signed language used by Native Americans.[22] His source was Major Stephen H. Long's *Account of an Expedition from Pittsburgh to the Rocky Mountains in 1819*. Gallaudet writes that the Native American signs for *love, truth, now* (or *at present*), *theft*, and *seeing*, though developed independently and in very different cultural circumstances from those that he and others had learned from Clerc, were, in fact, similar to those used at the Asylum. (The signs that Long described in his report are similar to signs used today for the same concepts.)

Long's account, which contains his ruminations about the existence of a universal signed language, was very popular with the faculty and graduates of the early Deaf schools. It was sometimes quoted in articles, and Edwin John Mann, a former student at the Hartford school and the author of the first book written by a Deaf person in the United States, included Long's report in his book, *The Deaf and Dumb: or, A Collection of Articles Relating to the Condition of Deaf Mutes; Their Education, and the Principal Asylums Devoted to Their Instruction*. In his account Long wrote as follows:

Philosophers have discussed the subject of an universal language, but have failed to invent one, while the savages of America have adopted the only one which can possibly become universal. The language of signs is so true to nature, that the deaf and dumb, from different parts of the globe, will immediately, on meeting, understand each other. . .

If we examine the signs employed by the Indians, it will be found that some are peculiar, and arise from their savage customs, and are not so universal as sign language in general; but others are natural and universally applicable, and are the same as those employed in the schools for the deaf and dumb, after the method of the celebrated Abbé Sicard.[23]

Here again, it is apparent even from this brief excerpt that the concept of universality rested on something deeper than a common, cross-cultural lexicon, since Long, too, acknowledges that the signs of the Native Americans and the Deaf Americans educated at Hartford and other schools were not identical.

During the next few decades the *American Annals of the Deaf* published a long series of articles on the nature of signed language. The authors were mostly teachers of the Deaf who subscribed to the idea of signed language as a "natural" and "universal" language—ideas that had been so eloquently championed by Gallaudet in his early writings for the *Annals*. In fact, many of those writers had either received their training at Hartford or had been trained by others who had learned about signed language and educational theory at Hartford. For about 50 years the school at Hartford was the most influential institution of its kind in North America.

The articles that appeared in the *Annals* for the first few decades of its existence are important because they amplify and clarify ideas originally raised by Gallaudet in his description of the natural language of signs, but they do not conflict with any of Gallaudet's fundamental premises. These attitudes, ideas, and theories taken together yield an elaborate, carefully reasoned theory of visual communication. But in retrospect their efforts also represent something of an intellectual dead end. The views of Gallaudet and his followers on the linguistic characteristics of the natural language of signs did not change over time, and this is peculiar because there were other ideas about signed language of which they were surely aware—some of the most influential writers of the time were friends and admirers of Clerc—and while Parisian perceptions of signed language continued to evolve for a few decades after the departure of Clerc to the United States, these ideas did not find their way into American thinking.

Especially important in this regard were the writings of Roch-Amboise-Auguste Bébian. Bébian was born in Guadaloupe; he was the godson of Roch-Amboise Sicard, who was head of the Paris institution; he was a friend of Laurent Clerc and an instructor at the Paris institution himself. As a youth Bébian was sent to Paris for his education and while in Paris he lived at Sicard's school. By 1817 Bébian had identified the same shortcomings in Sicard's methodological signs that are identified by many today in similar systems.

> He [de l'Epée] gave these signs to his pupils, rather than getting them from his pupils ...Ultimately this [de l'Epée's system of methodological signs] was merely a kind of syllabic spelling of French words in gestures instead of the direct translation of thought and its living image.

He goes on to criticize de l'Epée because he made

> great efforts to bend them [signs] to that language [French]. But as sign language is quite different from all other languages, it had to be distorted to conform to French usage, and it was sometimes so disfigured as to become unintelligible.[24]

Bébian sought to understand signed language as it was used by the Deaf, a goal that was in stark contrast to that of de l'Epée and of his successor Sicard. (Sicard, Bébian asserted, had only completed the program of methodological signs that his mentor had begun.) Furthermore, Bébian wanted his description of signed language to be intrinsic to signed language—that is, Bébian did not want to write *about* signed language, he wanted to write the language itself. This is what makes Bébian's "Essay" so important: In it he considers the possibility of developing a system of sign writing. He called his system mimography, and his writing indicates that he understood the problems inherent in writing signs at a level that would not be attained again until the latter half of the twentieth century.

Bébian reasons by analogy. He notes that despite the rich vocabulary of spoken languages, they can be recorded on paper using a relatively small number of symbols. He argues that it should be possible to do something similar with signed language. The key hurdle to overcome, according to Bébian, is to identify the (presumably) small number of fundamental gestures and facial expressions out of which all signs are comprised and then to represent each such fundamental unit with its own schematic diagram. Finally, these schematic components would be combined in various ways to represent signs and eventually complete signed language sentences. (Each spoken language also has its own fundamental—and characteristic—set of sounds; these are combined in a variety of ways to yield the set of all spoken words in the language. English, for example, has about 45 such sounds, which in the jargon of linguistics are called *phonemes*.)

It is significant that Bébian recognized that there exists a visual analogue to the phonology of spoken languages and that of these fundamental signed units some were produced manually and some were communicated (enunciated) via facial expressions. Bébian's ideas were a great triumph of imagination and insight, but they had little effect on his contemporaries. Even educators and educational theorists at Hartford and their colleagues at other institutions for the Deaf in other states, people who spent a great deal of time thinking and writing about the nature of signed languages and who must have been aware of the work of Bébian, Clerc's old friend, did not consider Bébian's ideas worthy of comment.

But in Paris, Ferdinand Berthier, a Deaf scholar and teacher, the first Deaf person to receive the Legion of Honor, and an admirer of Laurent Clerc, agreed with Bébian about the importance of developing a method for writing signed language.[25] Berthier, too, recognized the importance of finding a way to write (French) signed language, and he quotes Bébian's ideas, but he does not seem to see quite as far into the problem as Bébian. He merely asserts that the key to writing signs is to create a symbol for each arm or face movement. He seems to think that the problem is easily solvable, but this has not proved to be the case.

Part of the problem in writing signs is to identify those gestures and facial expressions (or those components of gestures and those components of facial expressions) that are fundamental to the transmission of information in the sense that if such a gesture or expression was omitted, the meaning of the utterance would change. Simply asserting that the development of a written form of signed language requires one only to place a symbol in correspondence with each gesture or facial expression and then to combine them accordingly is to misunderstand the nature of the problem.[26] Not every gesture conveys meaning, and not every hand shape or expression is linguistically significant. Berthier wrote that he was working on the problem, but neither he nor Bébian finished developing a system.

These men, both of whom saw more deeply into the nature of signed language than their contemporaries, had no influence on the evolution of signed language in Europe or America. The French educational system eventually abandoned the use of signed language as a language of instruction. In the United States, too, signed language would soon fall out of favor as a language of instruction at many schools for the Deaf. The ideas developed by Gallaudet and his contemporaries would soon attract more derision that intellectual interest, and research into the nature of signed language(s) would end. The hiatus lasted almost a century.

Why Signed Language?

A topic closely related to early conceptions of signed language, one that often occupied the minds of Gallaudet and his colleagues, involved their attempts to understand the thoughts of the Deaf before they learn language. This question does not have the same force when asked of a hearing person. Hearing children begin to internalize the language of their parents soon after birth. By contrast, many Deaf children of hearing parents never become fluent in the language of their parents. Moreover, during the first half of the nineteenth century most Deaf children spent most of their childhood without formal instruction—the Hartford school was typical of the time in that they did not generally admit children until they were about 12 years old—and, as a consequence, Deaf children learned about their environment without the interposition of words. Theirs was often a world of uninterpreted images and undescribed feelings. Under these circumstances, how does one understand the world? In the absence of language, what, in fact, does "understand" mean?

Clerc's own description of life without language—he began his formal education at the age of 12—is sometimes harsh and sometimes humorous. He writes that those without language live in a vegetative state and that education enables them to "pass from the class of brutes to the class of men."[27] Of his own childhood he wrote the following:

> I was about twelve years old when I arrived at the Abbé Sicard's school. I was endowed with considerable intelligence, but nevertheless I had no idea of intellectual things. I had it is true, a mind, but it did not think; I had a heart, but it did not feel.
>
> My mother, affected at my misfortune, had endeavored to show me the heavens, and to make me know God, imagining that I understood her, but her attempts were [in] vain; I could comprehend nothing. I believed that God was a tall, big and strong man, and that Jesus Christ having come to kill us, had been killed by us, and placed on a cross as one of our triumphs.[28]

As his hearing colleagues did, Clerc often described the condition of deafness as a misfortune, and, like them, his remarks on life without language tend to concentrate on the way his lack of language affected his understanding of God. Upon this topic a number of long and thoughtful articles were written.[29] Of special interest was the question of whether an uneducated, prelingually Deaf individual had an innate idea of God and, if so, what that idea was.

Ferdinand Berthier, the Deaf instructor at the Paris institution and prominent writer on Deafness and signed language mentioned earlier, wrote as follows:

> It is possible that some deaf-mutes may attribute certain effects, as storms, wind, and hail, to a certain cause, and may figure to themselves one or more extraordinary beings commanding the rain, the lightning, and other natural phenomena; but a deaf and dumb person, without instruction, will never have a notion, even vague and confused, of a superior existence, whom it is his duty to love, revere, and obey, and to whom he must give an account of his thoughts and of his actions.[30]

Clerc, Berthier, and others described a general lack of awareness experienced by a Deaf individual prior to the acquisition of language. Their remarks were undoubtedly informed by their personal experience. Hearing writers of the time had a decidedly more upbeat assessment of life without language. Harvey Peet, a prolific nineteenth-century writer and educator of the Deaf, expressed his belief about life without language this way: ". . . [Deaf] children, cut off from intellectual commerce with mankind, must have an instinctive language and innate ideas of religion." And Roch-Amboise-Auguste Bébian came close to praising life without language: "it is unproven that complete ignorance is any further from true science than much knowledge riddled with errors and prejudices. And it is similarly unproven that we would not be gaining by losing everything we know, on the condition that we also lost everything that we merely think we know."[31]

It is, however, in their ruminations about life without language by American instructors of the Deaf that one finds the clearest explanations for what they expected their students to acquire when they learned the natural language of signs. As with most of their predecessors and most of their successors, nineteenth-century hearing Americans perceived the condition of deafness as a problem to be solved, and the principal problem that they associated with deafness was the problem of communicating with God. Because nothing was more important (and nothing else was as important) as one's relationship with God, they considered the "problem" of Deafness essentially "solved" when one learned how to pray. Briefly, signed language enabled the Deaf to pray.

At most schools for the Deaf during the first half of the nineteenth century a great deal of time was devoted to the subject of religion. In addition to classroom instruction, for example, Peet's school, the New York institution, began the school day in the chapel with prayers; the school day ended in the chapel with prayers; the Bible was studied each Saturday morning, and worship services were conducted on Sunday. In fact, for many years at all the large educational institutions for the Deaf, religious instruction was the principal vehicle for all instruction. (In the early days of the Hartford school there were only two subjects, religion and communication, and the school day lasted eight hours.)

All religious instruction was perceived by the faculty of these early schools as nondenominational, because none of the educational institutions were affiliated with a particular brand of evangelical Christianity—just the opposite: such ties were explicitly rejected. Students were encouraged to pursue ties with the denomination of their choice, although it is clear from contemporary accounts that most writers were evangelical Protestants, and "church" generally meant a Protestant church. Nevertheless, Clerc, a Catholic, seemed to have felt that his religious beliefs were respected by those with whom he worked, and so it appears that in his case the tolerance expressed by these early educators extended as far as the Catholic faith. From the writings of these authors, however, one would not know that there were religions other than Christianity.

The emphasis on religion by these writers also had a practical side. Adolescents devoid of language are, they often claimed, difficult—difficult to control, difficult to warn, difficult to compliment. None but the simplest sentiments are likely to be understood. Prelingually Deaf adolescents, according to these authors, often lack impulse control. Religion—communicated via signs—was perceived as the ideal vehicle to introduce the concepts of discipline, truth, "enlightened self-interest," hope, ambition, and fear.[32] It was through religion that "[t]he moral influence of the government and discipline of the institution over the objects of its care is thus secured." The sooner this goal could be secured the better, and that was part of the beauty of the natural language of signs: It was the most efficient medium of instruction. Gallaudet described his goal in this way:

> he [the Deaf student] easily and quickly becomes acquainted with this improved language by his constant, familiar intercommunication with the teachers and his fellow-pupils. By means of it his government and discipline, through a kind moral influence, can at once be begun; for he has a language common to him and his teacher. Every day he is improving in this language; and this medium of moral influence is rapidly enlarging. His mind becomes more and more enlightened; his conscience more and more easily addressed...He recognizes his relation to God and to his fellow men. He learns much of the divine character, and of his own obligations and duties.[33]

Religion was the key to responsible student behavior, and this explains, in part, the lack of emphasis that these early educators placed on articulation. God, they were sure, understood every language, and God has no linguistic favorites. The best language choice for the students was, therefore, the language that was easiest to learn. Signed language provided a medium for the Deaf to express their thoughts in a way that was beautiful, elegant, and powerful, and the natural language of signs was, for the Deaf, easy to learn. The natural language of signs enabled them to begin communicating effectively with their God at the earliest possible time.

Gallaudet and his colleagues never hesitated to point out that speech was difficult, time-consuming, and often impossible for the Deaf to master. Speech reading was even harder, and it took even longer to make progress, when progress was made at all. To put so much emphasis on the medium in which one communicated rather than on the message that one wished to communicate was wrong, they believed, because it took away valuable time that one could spend learning, discussing, and praying. The acquisition of a primary language, Gallaudet and his colleagues argued, should not be delayed. A primary language needed to be acquired as soon as possible, because to live without language was to live estranged from God.

Signed language also enabled the Deaf to join in "social religious exercises."[34] Sermons, for example, could be presented in sign before a large group and understood by all. (By contrast, speech reading a sermon from the back of a small chapel is impossible.) There was no question in Gallaudet's mind that the natural language of signs was the right choice.

While Gallaudet's principal argument for the adoption of signed language has lost much of its force with many contemporary educators, he also recognized that there were other secondary advantages to signed language. These secondary advantages are today often cited as the principal advantages of using signed language in an educational setting. Gallaudet and his colleagues often noted that the natural language of signs enabled the Deaf to socialize more easily and to enjoy the pleasure of each other's company. There was a freedom and sense of satisfaction enjoyed by the Deaf in the creative use of signed language that should not be dismissed. Not only did the Deaf spontaneously begin to develop some aspects of signed language as children—this was the natural part of the natural language of signs—their ability to quickly understand and use sign was, he believed, a sort of compensation for their disability, a gift from the "God of Nature and of Providence." To interfere with a Deaf child's use of signed language, to discourage or otherwise interfere with the child's attempts to learn a language so uniquely suited to his or her situation, was, according to Gallaudet, cruel. To attempt to suppress their natural inclination to use this visual language was like "tying the wings of the young lark that is making its first, aspiring essays to fly upward."[35]

Gallaudet's October 1847 and January 1848 articles in the *Annals* mark the beginning of a long series of works on the nature of signed language in that journal. It would be just as accurate, however, to describe Gallaudet's work as the end of the first serious attempt by American educators and intellectuals to develop a comprehensive theory about the nature of signed language. The many other articles that would be published in the *Annals* over the next few decades were amplifications and clarifications of ideas that can be found in the writings of Gallaudet. These articles are interesting and well written, but none of them pointed in new directions; none introduced new concepts. The points raised and the insights gleaned in those later works would have been familiar to Gallaudet, and it is likely that he would have agreed with them. These individuals had their theory of sign; they had put it to the test, and they were satisfied with the results.

In some ways it is not difficult to understand why they were satisfied with their results. The results of their efforts, as reflected in the actions of the early graduates, were extremely impressive. Prior to the establishment of these early schools, the Deaf had been largely shut out of American life. The early graduates of these schools organized themselves and worked to create a better environment for the Deaf. They published books and periodicals. They came together formally and informally. They worked, and they celebrated their accomplishments. Clerc, Gallaudet, and their colleagues had developed a new American social class, the Deaf.

But these accomplishments were soon to be disparaged. A new generation of American educators and educational theorists would soon challenge virtually every assertion made by Gallaudet about signed language and its value to the Deaf. These educators and educational theorists would do their best to eliminate signed language among the Deaf, and they were partially successful. Although the thoughts expressed by Gallaudet were not forgotten, their influence on the education of later generations of American Deaf was not great. The new prospeech/antisign philosophy that arose in the United States soon after the conclusion of the Civil War formed the basis for American educational policies as they applied to the Deaf for the next 100 years. Signed languages were not seriously analyzed as a linguistic phenomenon again until the 1960s.

Three

Experiment in Television *and the Last of the Great Anti-American Sign Language Debates*

I heartily agree with all that experienced teachers of the deaf have urged concerning the beauty and great interest of this gesture-language. It is indeed most interesting to observe how pantomimic gestures have been abbreviated to simple signs expressive of concrete ideas; how these have been compounded or have changed their meaning to indicate abstract thoughts; and how the sequence of sign-words has to a certain extent become obligatory, this forming a sort of gesture syntax or grammar...

You may ask why it is that with my high appreciation of this language, as a language, I should advocate its entire abolition in our institutions for the deaf.
—Alexander Graham Bell, in "Fallacies Concerning the Deaf," *American Annals of the Deaf,* January 1884, Volume 29, pp. 32–69.

Even in the late 1960s there were those on the staffs of America's three major television networks who saw a place for high art on commercial TV. There were not many, of course, but they existed, and occasionally they produced programs that reflected their tastes. At the National Broadcasting Company (NBC) those who hoped to find a place for thoughtful, introspective art on commercial television produced a program called *Experiment in Television*. The show ran for several seasons and featured innovative art and innovative artists ranging from the already-famous Federico Fellini to the then-unknown Jim Henson. The programs usually received good reviews, and although *Experiment in Television* never made much money, it never lost much, either. It could not. Even by the standards of the day *Experiment in Television*'s budget was tiny—so small, in fact, that a number of episodes were produced overseas in a bid to save cash. Sponsors were few and fickle, and the audience was neither large nor loyal. In 1969 in an article

Audree Norton, one of the lead performers in the original cast of the National Theatre of the Deaf, together with Joseph Velez, another early cast member, in the production of "Tales of Kasane." Courtesy of Audree Norton.

for *Time* magazine Tom McAvity, general program executive for the series, described his viewers in these words: "A good bowling match will kick the hell out of us." Still, at a time when there were only three broadcast networks and no alternatives, *Experiment in Television* was part of The Big Time, and for those lesser-known artists chosen to perform, it represented an enormous opportunity to demonstrate their talents to a national audience in a supportive, high-quality environment.

In February 1967 NBC taped a performance at the Eugene O'Neill Theater Center in New London, Connecticut, by the recently established National Theatre of the Deaf for broadcast on *Experiment in Television*. The performance included scenes from *All the Way Home, Guys and Dolls, Hamlet, Kismet,* and *South Pacific,* and although the names of the plays and musicals were familiar to most of the viewing audience, the presentation was not. The National Theatre of the Deaf was creating a new art form by presenting theatrical productions in two languages simultaneously. English and American Sign Language were the languages, and although the performance was bilingual, most members of the audience would follow the dialogue in only one or the other of the two languages—not both, at least not simultaneously. That was part of the challenge: to create a unified two-language art form rather than a simple translation of an English language theatrical work.

For the cast, however, the performance was about more than theater. They were keenly aware that they were performing for two separate nationwide audiences, one Deaf and one hearing, and cast members had expectations for each audience that went beyond the performance. With respect to the Deaf audience, it was the hope of many cast members, most of whom were themselves Deaf, that the performance would be a source of pride. Audree Norton, a principal member of the cast at the time, wrote that, with respect to the Deaf audience, "We, deaf actors, felt that our mission was to stimulate, celebrate, and enhance the beauty of American Sign Language and deaf culture through the shared experience of NTD [National Theatre of the Deaf] as a professional theater."[1] She also hoped that a professional theatrical group would cause Deaf people to view their potential in new ways. "The other value was that NTD symbolized a breakdown of trite vocational programs...NTD encouraged the deaf to enter professional theater as a stepping stone to various careers and advanced education."

With respect to the hearing part of the audience, cast members hoped that their performance would heighten awareness of the language and culture of their Deaf neighbors. Bernard Bragg, one of the founders of the National Theatre of the Deaf, a former student of Marcel Marceau, and one of the troupe's most prominent actors (he had already starred in his own California television program

The Silent Man) expressed it this way, "We show to the public that we are a people having our own language, culture, artistic talent, let alone pride and respect."[2] Audree Norton wrote, "Many of us (actors) were thinking about what we valued most in our lives, about what our purpose was then, about how we valued our freedom, and what the history of deaf culture had been and what we wanted our future to be. We dreamed of a professional deaf theater to share our language and culture with the public."

One reason it was so important to cast members to share their language, American Sign Language, with the broader, nonsigning public was that for a long time American Sign Language had been hidden. This was no accident. During the century preceding the 1967 broadcast many American educators and educational theorists had sought to suppress public displays of American Sign Language as a first step toward abolishing it entirely. Although in 1967 the general public was largely unaware of the difficulties that many Deaf citizens had encountered in learning and using signed language, there were few Deaf members of the audience or of the cast who had not seen their language denigrated by those same educators who sought to eliminate it. Many on the cast felt that the best defense against those who sought to suppress their language was to demonstrate its utility and beauty. Bernard Bragg expressed his motivation this way: "Nationwide exposure to our creative talents and the power, grace, and beauty of our sign language was much needed at that time to establish that we Deaf people do have a place of our very own in the sun." The National Theatre of the Deaf offered its audiences more than an opportunity to watch theater; it offered an opportunity to obtain a positive view of the accomplishments, the language, and the potential of the Deaf. By 1967 these opportunities had been almost ten years in the making.

The National Theatre of the Deaf traces its origins to the late 1950s' lobbying efforts of the actress Anne Bancroft, star of *The Miracle Worker*, and psychologist Edna Levine. Together they recruited Arthur Penn, director of the Broadway version of *The Miracle Worker*, and Gene Lasko, director of the television version of the same play. Their goal was to obtain federal funding for a Broadway play that would be performed in signed language but aimed at a general audience. They were hoping to create a new kind of theater, one that would use signed and spoken languages simultaneously and yet appeal aesthetically and intellectually to the theatergoer who could follow only one language at a time. They were unsuccessful; their proposal was denied. But Bancroft and Levine were undeterred. They submitted a second grant proposal. Again they were unsuccessful, but their efforts were attracting the interest and support of a growing number of Deaf and hearing individuals, some of whom where connected with the theater and some with the government.

After the second proposal was rejected, Bancroft turned her attention to other projects, but Levine wrote a third proposal, and in 1966, seven years after her first proposal was turned down, the federal government awarded The National Theatre of the Deaf a grant of $16,500. The money was used to finance a production of Euripides' *Iphigenia in Aulis* at Gallaudet College in Washington, D.C. As the original 12-month grant drew to a close, the National Theatre received a $331,000, three-year grant. With this money the Theatre hoped to produce a high-quality artistic work with broad appeal. Its goal was to establish a permanent traveling reparatory theater *of* the Deaf—but *for* a much broader audience—and the NBC performance was its first opportunity to prove that such an audience existed.

The National Theatre of the Deaf's national debut was eagerly awaited by many Deaf people around the country. There were then—as there are now—a number of newspapers printed especially for a Deaf readership. Stories about the National Theatre featured prominently in these periodicals. They described a 1966 playwriting contest—first prize $500—for the newly established reparatory theater, and they reported on the theater group's progress in recruiting actors and support staff. The December 1966 issue of *The Deaf American,* for example, featured an article that described the writing contest, a history of the National Theatre of the Deaf that included extensive quotations from the third grant proposal, information on plans for a future drama school, and a progress report on plans for the first tour. The article was very thorough. In addition to the predominantly adult readership of this and other similar Deaf publications, many students and faculty at Gallaudet College, and students and faculty at many primary and secondary schools for the Deaf, looked forward to the performance. The National Theatre of the Deaf's performance on *Experiment in Television* marked the first time that an American Sign Language performance of any sort would be shown to a national audience.

With so much anticipation it is easy to understand why so many reacted so emotionally when another group, claiming to represent the best interests of the nation's Deaf children, began to strenuously lobby NBC to cancel its plans to show the National Theatre of the Deaf's performance. George W. Fellendorf, Executive Director of the Alexander Graham (AG) Bell Association, one of the nation's oldest, wealthiest, and most influential organizations in the field of Deaf education, sent a letter to NBC asking that it drop its plans to air the program. In a letter dated November 23, 1966, and sent to Julian Goodman, President of NBC, Mr. Fellendorf wrote, "Continuing to display sign language on nationwide

TV destroys the efforts of thousands of parents of deaf children and teachers of the deaf who are trying to teach deaf children to speak. This program will evoke unfavorable reaction from educators and parents and the informed public."[3]

Mr. Fellendorf did not act alone. He asked for and received enthusiastic support from a number of parents, teachers, and principals at some of the nation's oldest and most prominent schools for the Deaf. In a letter dated February 3, 1967, Josephine Timberlake, also of the AG Bell Association, wrote David Hays, director of the National Theatre of the Deaf, and Julian Goodman of NBC, "I deeply deplore the proposed plan to give recognition and dignity to the sign language...Any exposure to or use of the makeshift language of signs, no matter how artistically presented, interferes with his [the deaf child's] learning to understand and to use the English language by means of speech and lip reading."[4] And from the Research Department at the Clarke School for the Deaf, Northampton, Massachusetts, one of the nation's most prominent schools for the Deaf, Ruth Hudgins wrote, "By repeated display of the manual language on a nationwide network you will prejudice public thinking in regard to the education of deaf children."[5] There were many more—and more emotional—letters of protest directed at both Hays and Goodman.

The many disparaging remarks about signed language and the notion that the actors, most of whom were Deaf, would contaminate the minds of Deaf children by performing scenes from *Hamlet* and *South Pacific* in American Sign Language caused offense to many cast members. The Bell Association's letter-writing campaign was also a source of deep concern. Cast members knew that the Bell Association had a long and remarkable history of successfully lobbying against signed language. By today's standards some of its demands were outrageous, but it was often successful. (Many years earlier, for example, when Gallaudet College, the nation's liberal arts college for the Deaf, was preparing to establish its own teacher-training program, Alexander Graham Bell himself lobbied Congress to withhold funds from the college if the college did not explicitly exclude Deaf applicants from the program, and for many years Deaf applicants were explicitly barred from admission to Gallaudet's teacher-training program. Many similar affronts followed.) Members of the cast of the National Theatre of the Deaf understood that there was a real possibility that NBC would acquiesce to the Bell Association's demands and that the performance would be canceled. Bernard Bragg described their feelings this way: "We were all upset, worried, and sick to the stomach." After years of attempting to establish a reparatory theater of the Deaf, the cast faced the very real possibility that their first nationwide performance would be canceled, and in the alleged best interests of the nation's Deaf children the National Theatre of the Deaf would be kept off of national television.

The fear of the Bell Association and its supporters was that favorable publicity for American Sign Language would, over the long term, lead to the marginalization of the nation's oral schools for the Deaf and for the Bell Association itself. In a memo dated January 17, 1967, and addressed to "Directors of the AG Bell Association, Committee Members, and All Oral Deaf Adult Section Members," Mr. Fellendorf asked for support in these words: "It is imperative that letters be directed to Mr. Hays with carbon copies to Mr. Julian Goodman, President of the National Broadcasting Company, so that we can effectively counteract this effort to make the sign language of the deaf to be an artistic art form to be encouraged in the theater, televised into the homes of parents and employers, *and quite likely emulated in educational and parental circles.*"[6] (italics added)

It is important to understand that one cannot effectively do a play before a Deaf audience if members of the audience attempt to employ only speech reading techniques to follow the dialogue. It is simply too hard to speech read from a distance—especially when the actor is not directly facing the Deaf person in the audience or when the lighting is not ideal. Signed language was an integral part of the presentation. The National Theatre of the Deaf did not just celebrate American Sign Language; it demonstrated that signed language was necessary to communicate with the Deaf members of the audience. There was no alternative, a fact that both highlighted the limitations of speech reading as a communications technique and effectively demonstrated the utility of signed language for the Deaf.

The belief that favorable reviews of the production would make signed language more interesting to the public and make employers less averse to hiring the Deaf was shared by both sides. Edna Levine also described the impact of a theater of the Deaf on potential employers in her grant proposal. In addition to describing the artistic impact that a theater of the Deaf would have on its audience and the way this new form of theater might enrich the theatrical arts in general, she wrote, "Once these audiences, including potential employers, have been exposed to the talents and abilities of the deaf, there is no doubt that their attitudes will undergo significant improvement, and that this in turn will make for deeper interest in the problem of deafness and for broader vocational acceptance." *Both sides in the dispute agreed on the possible outcome of a successful performance;* the argument between them centered on the desirability of the outcome.

Here was a disagreement about the place of American Sign Language in American culture: The National Theatre of the Deaf wanted to celebrate it; the Alexander Graham Bell Association wanted to suppress it. The argument may appear similar to the disagreement between Charles-Michel de l'Epée and Samuel Heinicke about the role of signed language in the education of the Deaf that occurred almost two centuries earlier, but that is not the case. The Alexander Graham Bell Association's position on American Sign Language was (and is) more extreme than that advocated by Heinicke, who emphasized the importance of teaching speech as part of the education of Deaf children, but who willingly acknowledged that he used signs as well. By contrast, the Alexander Graham Bell Association saw no place at all for signed language in the education of the Deaf. It regarded the introduction of signed language into the United States as a historical aberration and the continued presence of the language on the American cultural scene as regrettable, even harmful to the best interests of the Deaf.

Unlike the debate that occurred between Heinicke and de l'Epée, this time the Deaf successfully inserted their ideas and opinions into the dispute about the recognition to be accorded signed language. Deaf cast members were very much involved in all aspects of the National Theatre of the Deaf. In addition to their roles as actors, Deaf individuals were involved in the recruitment of talent, in production, and in formulating policy. (George W. Fellendorf's attempt to pressure NBC via a letter-writing campaign was effectively countered by the National Theatre of the Deaf's own appeal for support from the superintendents of other schools for the Deaf, a suggestion of Bernard Bragg's.) This was a theater *of* the Deaf not *for* the Deaf, a distinction of which everyone in the troupe was aware.

Experiment in Television carried the performance on schedule. The reviews were positive. The National Theatre of the Deaf became an important, long-term contributor to American theater. Its influence on the American theater and the efforts of its alumni have been well documented: It was the first American theatrical troupe to tour the People's Republic of China; Phyllis Frelich, a National Theatre of the Deaf alumna, received a Tony Award for her starring role in the Broadway production of *Children of a Lesser God;* the National Theatre of the Deaf has cultivated a worldwide audience, and many alumni—including Audree Norton and Bernard Bragg—went on to perform in movies or television as well as on stage.

In describing the first nationally televised performance of the National Theatre of the Deaf, Bernard Bragg wrote, "Our first nationwide TV show proved to be a great impetus to a better understanding and appreciation of our language on the part of the public. . ." Fellendorf's fear that a positive portrayal of American Sign Language might be "emulated in educational and parental circles" was Bragg's hope. In 1978 the Alexander Graham Bell Association hired a signed language interpreter for its convention for the first time in its 91-year history. It remains, however, firmly committed to the primacy of oral education.

Why Not Signed Language?

Today the attempt by George W. Fellendorf and others to quash the network debut of the National Theatre of the Deaf impresses many as intolerant. Indeed, I could find no one willing to defend it—even at the AG Bell Association. Even Mr. Fellendorf, nearly 40 years later, in correspondence about the incident, simply noted, "Today I have no personal problems with sign language....AG Bell [Association] was and is an educational institution, not an artistic one, so all decisions [about opposing the National Theatre of the Deaf's performance] were connected with what was considered best for the education of children with severe to profound hearing impairments."[7] End of story.

But it would be a mistake to view Mr. Fellendorf's actions on behalf of the AG Bell Association by today's standards; much has changed during the intervening decades. In fact, in 1967 there were many people—some Deaf, most hearing—who agreed with the position taken by the Bell Association's Executive Director, and regardless of their position on the issue, few Deaf were surprised by the Bell Association's actions. Even Deaf individuals who disagreed with Fellendorf's position could have easily paraphrased his arguments before he made them. In fact, irrespective of where in the United States or Canada a Deaf person grew up and irrespective of the method under which he or she had been educated, in 1967 virtually every Deaf adult was intimately familiar with attempts by well-educated, predominantly hearing groups of educators and educational theorists to denigrate and suppress the use of American Sign Language. Throughout their lives the Deaf had witnessed American Sign Language deprecated—even banned—in the "best interests" of orally educated Deaf children. It was part of the Deaf experience. What was less familiar—or at least less frequently discussed—were the reasons that signed language was considered harmful. What exactly were the best interests of the Deaf that Fellendorf and others fought so hard to protect? How did the suppression of signed language further those interests?

Today many supporters of oral education express their goals in the language of mainstreaming. One should, the argument goes, do as much as possible to "mainstream" the Deaf into social and educational settings, but today the philosophy of mainstreaming is usually unexamined. It is, instead, often presented as an amorphous but desirable goal that is somehow connected with integration, a goal that one should work hard to attain. But without further examination how can one know whether one has attained the goal? Who, in fact, is mainstreamed and who is not? Among adults how can one identify someone who is mainstreamed? Were the Deaf cast members of the National Theatre of the Deaf, who in 1967 performed on national television, the most mainstream of all entertainment media, and who claimed American Sign Language, a decidedly minority language, as their own language, mainstreamed? Are successful Deaf publishers of Deaf newspapers and periodicals mainstreamed? Are Deaf teachers of Deaf students mainstreamed? If the answer is no, is this bad? And among children, is a single Deaf child in a large hearing school mainstreamed if he or she is unaware of the morning announcements detailing the activities of various school organizations and clubs? Is a child mainstreamed simply by being present in the same room with hearing children? If the answer is no, what does mainstreaming entail? If the answer is yes, why is mainstreaming desirable? Today, these questions generally go unasked, but it was not always so. At one time oralists were very keen to debate exactly these types of questions, and they found answers that they regarded as satisfactory, but the word that they preferred to use instead of "mainstreaming" was "integration." Early oralists sought to *integrate* Deaf of all ages, and there was general agreement about what the word "integrate" meant in this context— precisely because they spent so much time discussing the concept. It is in the words of early oralists that one can find the origin of the antipathy toward signed language that for so long pervaded American culture, and the most articulate and influential of all early oralists was the great scientist and inventor, Alexander Graham Bell.

George Fellendorf's 1967 proposal to cancel the performance would have sounded reasonable to Alexander Graham Bell. In fact, Bell had spoken out specifically against theatrical plays by the Deaf, because he believed that such plays were against the best interests of the Deaf.[8] More generally, Bell worked hard throughout his life to shape educational policy with respect to Deaf children, and he also worked hard to affect how adult Deaf lived their lives. His efforts, research, and opinions on these issues influenced societal attitudes toward the Deaf, toward signed language, and toward Deaf cultural institutions for many decades after his death. His influence was so long lasting that 45 years later Fellendorf and many others un-self-consciously expressed ideas about signed language and oral education that were virtually identical with those of Bell. Had Bell been alive in 1967 he undoubtedly would have used his considerable prestige and his many social and political contacts to keep the National Theatre of the Deaf off the air. He, too, believed that signed language was harmful and that it was in the best interests of everyone if no Deaf person ever learned it. As his successors at the Bell Association did, Alexander Graham Bell interpreted the phrase "best interests" in the broadest possible sense, and it is in Bell's own words that one finds the best explanation for the antisigned language bias that was for so long a part of American culture.

Deafness and the Deaf loomed large in the life of Alexander Graham Bell. Despite his many inventions—the telephone was the most famous, but he held numerous patents—deafness and Deaf education were the only topics in which he maintained a lifelong interest. It is easy to see why: Bell's mother, Eliza Grace Symonds Bell, who lost much of her hearing during childhood, taught him at home until he was 10 years old. She was a talented artist and a piano player. She retained the use of speech throughout her life, and it was through speech that she communicated. Eliza Bell did not sign.

Alexander Graham Bell's father, Melville Bell, spent a lifetime studying elocution and the mechanics of human speech. The father's book *Standard Elocutionists* went through almost 200 English language editions. Melville Bell's principal discovery is called "visible speech," a series of ideograms created to represent all the positions of the lips, tongue, and soft palate required to express any sound a person can make. The goal was to create a compact system of notation that would make the mechanism of pronunciation visible. Alexander Graham Bell likened visible speech to the symbols used in chemistry with which one can describe all manner of chemical compounds via a small number of letters and numbers combined according to definite rules, e.g., H_2O. Similarly, using the principles of visible speech one could convey to a Deaf person, who cannot, of course, hear his or her own voice, both the standard pronunciation for any word as well as how he or she might be (mis)pronouncing it.

In testimony to a British Royal Commission investigating the education of the Deaf in America, Bell proudly recounted how a "Hindustani scholar" demonstrated to his father, Melville Bell, the pronunciation of Hindu words that contained what Bell describes as "some very curious sounds." The scholar had unsuccessfully labored to teach his students the correct pronunciation of these words. (Alexander Bell was out of the room at the time of this conversation.) The father represented these sounds in a series of visible speech ideograms. When the son returned he examined the ideograms and successfully pronounced the words without ever having heard them, much to the surprise and delight of the scholar. To Bell this was a powerful demonstration of the utility of his father's invention.[9] The system was never very popular, however—it was apparently too difficult and time-consuming for most people to learn—but both father and son were very proud of it, and both were experts in its use.

Mabel Hubbard Bell, Alexander Graham Bell's wife, was also Deaf. She became deaf in 1861 at the age of four. In 1867 her parents, determined that she should receive the best education possible, founded the Clarke Institution for Deaf Mutes, now known as CLARKE—School for the Deaf/Center for Oral Education (and hereafter referred to simply as the Clarke School) in

Northampton, Massachusetts. Gardiner Greene Hubbard, Mabel's father, was the institution's first president. In 1870 the Hubbards traveled to Germany, the nation most heavily invested in the oral education of the Deaf, so that their daughter might receive further instruction in speech. Her teachers in Germany did what they did best: They proceeded to teach young Mabel how to speak the German language. The Hubbards remained in Europe for two and one-half years before returning to the United States. Still striving to improve her speech Mabel Hubbard met "Alec" Bell for the first time in his capacity as a tutor. They were married in 1877. Mabel Hubbard Bell was always active and opinionated and she led a full and vigorous life. She did not, however, learn to sign.

Broadly speaking, Bell's interest in the field of deafness centered on two topics that he perceived to be closely related: The first topic that he studied was the education of the Deaf. With respect to Deaf education he was interested solely in those aspects of the subject that were peculiar to that discipline: the teaching of speech, speech reading, and the use (or not) of signed language. Second, Bell was fascinated with the hereditary nature of deafness, and he spent a great deal of time and energy attempting to understand and control all factors that contributed to the birth of deaf children. The connections that Bell thought he saw between these two disparate fields made his work controversial. It is no exaggeration to say that he studied both topics with an intensity and a thoroughness evinced by no other researcher either before or since. Despite his fame as an inventor, deafness was Bell's life.

In the area of education, Bell was interested in both the theoretical and practical issues associated with educating the Deaf—especially the very young—and as any good scientist would, Bell continually gathered information to compare theory with practice. He dutifully corresponded with principals and other school officials throughout the United States and Canada. He knew many personally. He used these connections to collect statistics from those schools on the methodologies they used in the instruction of the students, student performance, student backgrounds, and the etiology of deafness. From these statistics he sought to deduce theories that might lead to better educational practices, but for Bell the term "better educational practices" often meant more emphasis on teaching speech. "Articulation," the term preferred by Bell and other researchers at the time, was something to which he was completely committed. With the help of his father's visible speech or some other conceptually similar method—Bell was flexible on the details of the methods employed to accomplish his goals—he believed it was possible to train young Deaf children to enunciate at a level "as perfect as our [hearing people's] own."[10]

To teach Deaf children to articulate clearly, he often asserted, training had to begin as early as possible. This was critical for two reasons. First, teaching speech to someone who cannot hear his or her own voice is exceedingly difficult and so, Bell believed, the earlier one begins, the better one's chances are of completing the task before the student graduates from school. Second, and more fundamentally, Bell wanted Deaf children to *think* in words (as opposed to signs), because, he believed, a student who thinks in words is integrated into society *from the inside out*. Signed language, in Bell's eyes, interfered with the integration of the Deaf into mainstream American culture. "That language [signed language]" he said, "is not of any value whatever in promoting social intercourse with the hearing,"[11] and that was reason enough for him to reject it entirely. Never mind that the Deaf might have a particular interest in communicating with each other (and with those hearing individuals who had taken the time to learn to sign) via a visual language especially designed for the purpose. To Bell this was not relevant. The existence of a community of expert signers was, in fact, a further argument against the use of sign. Signed language, he believed, enabled the Deaf to exist as a separate cultural and linguistic group within American society, and he saw the existence of such a group as bad for everyone. Bell wanted to free the Deaf *from* sign—as opposed to those who wanted to free the Deaf *to* sign—and he advocated his position thoughtfully and continually. Throughout his life Bell clung to the idea that although the Deaf could never be made to hear, they could, at least, be trained to act and think as hearing persons do.

These opinions were not unique to Bell. They were shared by many teachers of the Deaf throughout the latter half of the nineteenth and the first half of the twentieth century, but unlike so many of his contemporaries, Bell worked hard to see all sides of the issue. His writings and speeches were not simple polemics as were those of many oralist educators. He acknowledged, for example, that manually educated, prelingually Deaf students—that is, students who are born deaf and those who lost their hearing before learning speech—generally tended to read better than their orally educated counterparts,[12] a unique observation among the oralists of the time. But that difference, he believed, did not reflect badly on oralism as a philosophy. He asserted that the difference could be eliminated with better teaching techniques on the part of oral educators. Nor did Bell's intolerance of signed language stem from an ignorance of the language itself. While neither his mother nor his wife signed, Bell was an expert at fingerspelling, and for a year he dutifully took lessons in sign. (There is an important distinction between fingerspelling, where every letter of a word is represented by a unique hand shape, and signed language, where single gestures are used to represent ideas in the same way that words are used independently of their written form.) Even as he advocated the abolition of the language, Bell did not hesitate to describe it as fascinating and beautiful.[13] He worked to understand both sides of every issue concerning the Deaf, and at some level he was successful. He was generally able to accurately summarize all sides of most relevant issues, and after the summary he would speak out against the use of signed language.

While Bell believed that every Deaf child could and should be taught to speak —and that none should be taught to sign—he freely acknowledged that speech reading was not for everyone. He stated that there were many intelligent Deaf students, who, despite everyone's best efforts, would never become very good at speech reading. (By contrast, many of his contemporaries in the field of oral education characterized students who were unsuccessful at speech reading as "oral failures," students who were not bright enough to succeed.) For Bell, these students were not a source of special concern; although he knew that, at best, when provided with the proper training in speech (and methodically deprived of signed language skills), they would forever be able to hold only half a conversation. This situation did not indicate to Bell a shortcoming in his method or a reason to advocate for the use of signed language. To him it was simply the way things were.

Bell was also remarkably well versed in the practical techniques and practical difficulties associated with speech reading. He studied the frequency with which words appeared in various contexts; he had a thorough knowledge of what sounds and words (called homophenes) looked identical to the speech reader but sounded different—for example, bat, mat, and pat are homophenes—and from this information he was able to estimate how much information, under ideal conditions, could be reliably gleaned by observing the mouth of the speaker and how much information had to be deduced, or guessed, from the context in which the unknown homophene appeared. Unlike many of his pro-oralist contemporaries, Bell generally refrained from making extravagant claims about the value and utility of speech reading as a communication tool.

Bell's enthusiasm for studying the mechanisms of speech as well as the techniques and limitations of speech reading reflected his practical side. As one might expect from one of the nineteenth century's most important inventors, theoretical insights were not enough for Bell. He often tested his ideas in class—even to the extent of establishing experimental schools. He created a teacher-training program for articulation teachers in order to put his ideas into practice. When he observed that his soon-to-be teachers were short on practical experience, he established free classes for adult Deaf so that his teachers could gain the instructional experience they needed before graduation; Bell also taught at the Horace Mann School in Boston; he taught the mechanics of speech at Boston University; he established an experimental private school in Washington, D.C., for four young Deaf children; he instructed a Deaf child himself and wrote about the experience, he taught teachers at the Clarke School, and he rarely passed a school for the Deaf without stopping to visit and speak with principals, teachers, and students. He was especially fond of sitting with the younger students and engaging in written conversations as a way of testing their mastery of written English. He never stopped.

It is difficult to appreciate just how committed Bell was to the education of the Deaf. It helps, however, to know that he created the telephone as a device to aid in the teaching of articulation to the Deaf[14]—it was originally envisioned as an early version of a hearing aid—and years after the completion of his most famous invention, in testimony before the Royal Commission of the United Kingdom on the Condition of the Blind, the Deaf and Dumb, he repeatedly refers to his work on the telephone as something that took his attention *away* from his work with the Deaf. The phone, it seems, turned out to be something of a distraction from his life's work. Note one more example: In recognition of Bell's great invention the French government awarded him the Volta Prize, an award that included a very large sum of money. Bell used this money and more to establish the Volta Bureau, an organization dedicated to "the increase and diffusion of knowledge relating to the deaf." (The Volta Bureau has become today's Alexander Graham Bell Association for the Deaf and Hard of Hearing, the organization that so vocally opposed the broadcast of the first nationally televised performance by the National Theatre of the Deaf.)

All of Bell's research and his experiences with the Deaf and his unwavering belief in the importance of speech and the necessity of abolishing signed language led him to a remarkable conclusion with respect to the education of Deaf children: The ideal environment in which to educate a Deaf child would consist of one Deaf child per school.[15] In such a situation it would be virtually impossible for the child to use or even to learn signed language. The value of articulation lessons would, under the circumstances, be apparent to even the most skeptical Deaf student, and any speech reading skills that the student managed to acquire would prove invaluable. Integration under such circumstances would, he believed, be almost unavoidable, and the full weight of the institution—and of Bell's theories—could be brought to bear on the isolated young child. There could be no escape.

To be sure, Bell realized that it would sometimes be impossible to achieve a one Deaf student per school ratio. Undeterred, he envisioned a whole spectrum of fallback scenarios. Each situation surrendered slightly more control over the speech environment of the student, each situation represented a slight increase in the Deaf student's opportunities to meet and associate with other Deaf, and each increment represented an increase in the probability that the Deaf student might be exposed to signed language. Bell surrendered these increments only with the greatest reluctance. Signed language, he believed, was "foreign"; it hindered the Deaf student's acquisition of English, which he identified as "the language of the people," and it caused the Deaf to "associate together in adult life, and avoid the society of hearing people."[16]

The struggle to educate the Deaf was, from Bell's point of view, won or lost well before the child was ready to begin high school. From the student's point of view, of course, "the struggle" had barely begun. At 14 years of age one has barely scratched the surface of one's education; most important ideas remain to be explored and youthful ambition remains to be reconciled to everything from the laws of economics to the laws of physics. None of this interested Bell. He wanted to control not what Deaf children thought, but *the way they thought it.* It was not enough that one had interesting, beautiful, or productive ideas—from Bell's point of view this hardly counted as an issue in Deaf education—what was important to him was the language in which the Deaf *thought.* It had to be English; it could not be a language of signs, and to effectively control the language of thought, Bell knew that one could not begin too early.

To understand Bell's preoccupation with the language of thought, it helps to know that he also showed the same enthusiasm for attempting to manipulate the most intimate thoughts and actions of Deaf adults that he showed for manipulating the thoughts of young Deaf children. And it is in his writings and statements about Deaf adults that his reasons for wanting to abolish signed language and for his peculiar emphasis on controlling the language of thought become most transparent.

Bell was a eugenicist. Like most of his generation, hearing and Deaf, Bell un-self-consciously described the condition of deafness as a calamity. But while the manualists, the term used to identify those who supported the use of signed language, sought an accommodation with deafness through the skillful use of a language created especially for the purpose, Bell sought to control the genetic inheritance of those not yet born in order to minimize the occurrence of the condition. His approach was to manipulate the lives of Deaf adults in the same sorts of ways that he sought to manipulate the lives of Deaf children. Success, in his view, depended on isolating the Deaf from one another.

By the late 1880s Bell had developed a theory centered about the belief that manualists had unwittingly created conditions favorable to the formation of a "deaf variety" of human being. He believed that this Deaf race was already in the process of formation. To be sure, he was more than a little uncertain of the mechanism of formation. For while Gregor Mendel had already published his theory of heredity, a theory that adequately accounted for the inheritance of many simple traits, Mendel's ideas had gone unnoticed by everyone including Bell. Furthermore, the genetic basis of deafness—when deafness has a genetic basis—can be more complex than the simple dominant/recessive relationships considered by Mendel. As a scientific phenomenon the heredity of deafness was completely beyond Bell (and every other scientist of the time), and Bell acknowledged as much.[17] His crude and un-self-conscious comparisons between the lives of the Deaf and the practice of animal husbandry serve only to emphasize the painfully narrow view that he sometimes expressed of the Deaf as a class of people.

The formation in the United States of what Bell believed to be a Deaf race had begun almost within his lifetime. Bell identified what he thought was the index case: the marriage on May 3, 1819 of Laurent Clerc, the best known Deaf individual in the United States, to Elizabeth Crocker Boardman, a former student of Clerc's at the Hartford School. According to Bell this was the first instance of Deaf intermarriage in U.S. history. In testimony before the Royal Commission, Bell stated, "As I look through the literature of the subject, I see evidences that the results of that marriage were watched with very great interest and eagerness by the deaf mutes of the country."[18] The interest arose, according to Bell, because Clerc had broken a social taboo against the Deaf marrying the Deaf, but in his testimony Bell presents no evidence of the existence of such a taboo. There is, in fact, another, more straightforward explanation for the fascination with Clerc among Deaf Americans: To them, Clerc was a celebrity.

Clerc had grown up in France and attended the school for the Deaf in Paris that had been founded by de l'Epée. (See Chapters 2 and 4 for more information about Clerc's life and accomplishments.) He had remained at the school to become a senior teacher under the abbé Sicard, de l'Epée's successor. During his 1816 trip to Europe to learn about European methods of Deaf education, Thomas Hopkins Gallaudet recruited Laurent Clerc to work at the proposed school in Hartford. Clerc worked as a teacher in Hartford for decades. His influence on the lives of Deaf Americans was enormous: Clerc taught Gallaudet and other faculty at the Hartford school signed language; a number of Clerc's students became some of the nation's first teachers of the Deaf; Clerc helped establish the Pennsylvania School for the Deaf, and perhaps most importantly, Clerc's language, the signed language that he introduced into the United States from France, formed the basis for the signed language used by Deaf Americans. His influence was recognized and his efforts were appreciated by many Deaf throughout the country. Interest in Clerc's marriage would have been high with or without Bell's so-called taboo.

Another reason that Clerc's influence was so great was that prior to his arrival in the United States, Deaf Americans were largely uneducated, unorganized, and without much language of any sort. The increase in Deaf intermarriage that occurred in the years following Clerc's marriage might more easily be attributed to the creation of a better educated community of people with common interests and a common (signed) language in which to express them. There was no need to appeal to the existence of a social taboo, but in the end either explanation worked for Bell: The existence of signed language increased the likelihood of Deaf intermarriage. Abolish signed language and, according to Bell, the rate of Deaf intermarriage would diminish and so would the rate at which Deaf children, the presumed products of those marriages, were born. (It is interesting to note that all of the Clercs' children were hearing.)

Without a theory of heredity that would enable Bell to predict the effect of Deaf intermarriage on the frequency with which deaf children are born, Bell set out to create his own theory. By 1888 he had created his own alphabetical registry using the returns of the 1880 United States Census. Though his list was not yet complete at the time of his testimony before the Royal Commission, it already consisted of the names of 23,969 Americans.[19] The purpose of the registry was to obtain information about every Deaf American. Bell was especially interested in identifying frequently occurring surnames in the hope of spotting patterns in the inheritance of deafness. Shared surnames might indicate families in which deafness was an inherited condition.

Bell also expended a great deal of effort studying the patterns of transmission of deafness in the town of Chilmark on Martha's Vineyard, where there was an unusually high incidence of congenital deafness. Bell undertook an extensive genealogical study of the town, tracing the transmission of the trait in island families back "10 or 12" generations. He produced complex charts for various families, and in an attempt to separate out the effects of environment from those of heredity, he even traced those who had moved off the island.

Bell also collected information from officials at schools for the Deaf located throughout the United States and Canada on the marriage patterns of their alumni. He wanted information about whether the students married their classmates, graduates of other Deaf institutions, or hearing individuals. He wanted to know how many children each couple had, whether the children were deaf or hearing, and whether the deafness was the result of disease or heredity.

In all cases these data were carefully collected and analyzed. The work involved was enormous, but Bell was indefatigable. He was not, however, content to search for patterns and develop a theory of heredity. He also sought cultural factors that might lead to an increase in the number of congenitally deaf. Bell believed that he was witnessing a calamity, the formation of a race of deaf humans—in fact, his most famous and controversial paper on the topic is entitled "On the Formation of Deaf Variety of the Human Race"—and although the total number of affected individuals was small and the issues involved were largely matters of personal choice, Bell's response was to propose ever more invasive and paternalistic measures.

Having identified his problem, the development of a "deaf variety" of human beings, Bell identified his main culprit: signed language. He often described signed language as a "special language," because it was rarely used in the wider, hearing community. The result was that the Deaf, fluent in this language created by them and for their own use, preferred the company of others who were similarly fluent. But if the Deaf associated preferentially with each other, they would be more likely to marry one another, Bell argued, and when both partners were congenitally deaf, they would be more likely to produce Deaf children. (Bell freely acknowledged that the chances that the congenitally deaf would have deaf children were not especially great. Most Deaf couples—congenitally deaf or not—still had hearing children. His own research indicated as much.)

Bell sought to abolish the use of signs as a means of isolating the Deaf *from each other*. Deaf adults would, of course, always experience substantial difficulties communicating with their hearing counterparts. At some level these difficulties could not conceivably be overcome, but absent signed language, Deaf adults would encounter the same sorts of difficulties when communicating with each other. For this reason nonsigning Deaf adults would not, according to Bell, have reason to associate preferentially with each other. Essentially, Bell wanted to apply the same isolating measures to adults that he wanted to apply to children. He saw it as the responsibility of hearing adults to do whatever was necessary—short of force—to manage the most personal decisions of their Deaf neighbors.

Nor was it only signed language to which Bell objected. Soon after the Hartford school began to produce graduates, there arose in the United States a Deaf press. These periodicals were generally produced by the Deaf for the Deaf. They contained news stories about associations of the Deaf, news concerning schools for the Deaf, editorials, letters, and other articles of special interest to their readerships. Bell found these periodicals objectionable, because they enabled the Deaf to stay informed about events and ideas *relating to the Deaf*.[20] In Bell's view this simply promoted "clannishness," and although nothing could be done about privately funded Deaf newspapers, those papers that depended upon public money should not, he asserted, be printed at all. And if, in the interest of teaching the trade of printing, the educational institutions that published some of these papers felt it necessary to produce a publication, Bell believed that it should contain only items "of what is going on [in] the great world outside, the items of news that interest hearing persons."[21] The Deaf needed to be directed away from information about Deafness as well as away from association with other Deaf for their own good. (Not surprisingly, the same strictures did not apply to Bell, who kept full sets of back issues of these same publications, because they often contained marriage and birth announcements, and Bell used the information in his study of the heredity of deafness.)

No Deaf activity was too insignificant to escape scrutiny. Bell advocated, for example, that schools for the Deaf ban class reunions or other activities for alumni, because these activities provided opportunities for the Deaf to meet each other and socialize separately from the larger hearing society, and this could lead to the formation of Deaf marriages.[22] The Clarke School for the Deaf adopted this proposal early on, and Bell considered it a great success: As of 1888 no pupils at Clarke had intermarried; all marriages had occurred between Clarke alumni and the alumni of other Deaf institutions or between Clarke's former students and hearing persons.

Even associations of the Deaf, formed for the benefit of the membership, were considered harmful by Bell. There were, of course, instances of such organizations doing work that clearly benefited the Deaf, but an organization *of* the Deaf indicated to Bell an opportunity for social interaction between Deaf adults and a concomitant increase in the possibility of intermarriage. Perhaps, Bell ventured in testimony to the Royal Commission about the value of such organizations, it might be possible "to bring together adults of only one sex at a time."[23] And in answer to the question of whether the association of the Deaf with each other was not an important element in their happiness—a word that is noticeably absent from much of what Bell says and writes about the Deaf—Bell answered, "Not necessarily...We want to make every effort to help them [the Deaf] make friends among hearing persons of their own age."[24]

Bell did not want legislation to ban associations of the Deaf. He always and explicitly rejected the use of force, preferring to emphasize the importance of what he called "persuasion," but his tactics of persuasion were often heavy-handed. Here is how he described his attitude toward organizations of the Deaf (notice how he uses the words "adult deaf" and "pupils" as if they were synonyms): "I do not think that we can do away with these adult associations entirely, for there will always remain a certain number of pupils who are not fitted to mingle with the world, and I do not know how else we are going to reach them and benefit them with out some such association, so that while theoretically I do consider them [the associations] harmful, I think that in certain respects they are necessary, but *we want to give great thought and great care to the subject of the association of the adult deaf.*"[25] (italics added)

Few of Bell's ideas on eugenics or education originated with him. He was simply their most influential expositor and most knowledgeable proponent. His willingness to intervene uninvited into all aspects of the lives of Deaf children and adults—their use of language, the associations that they formed, the newspapers that they published and read, and even the language in which they thought—was entirely characteristic of many of the oral educators of his and succeeding generations. These professionals viewed deafness as a pathology that could be partially cured, and the Deaf were perceived as a defective subpopulation that had to be managed for its own good. (In "Memoir on the Formation of a Deaf Variety of the Human Race," Bell refers to the condition of deafness as a "hereditary taint" and "their [the Deaf's] defect.") Bell's influence on subsequent generations was further magnified by his longevity—not only did he live a long time (75 years), he remained active in the field throughout his life. (He was, for example, on the board of the Clarke School for over two decades and was chairman of the board for the last five years of his life.) Moreover, his timing was right: He belonged to the first generation of Americans to forcefully argue for the adoption of oral methods in the education of the Deaf, and many of the ideas Bell advocated were soon institutionalized. Some of his ideas remain a part of educational practice.

The antipathy that Bell and other oral enthusiasts displayed toward signed language was a new phenomenon in the United States, and to achieve their goals they needed to supplant rather than modify the educational practices that had preceded them. They were not interested in reaching a compromise with their predecessors. In fact, Bell and others explicitly rejected attempts to combine the oral system with any system that used signs. For them there was no possibility of reconciling signed language with their educational goals. They were revolutionaries, and they were largely successful. In the narrow world of Deaf education, their ideas quickly became the new orthodoxy, and, in particular, Bell's attitudes, values, and goals were effectively passed from one generation to the next in part by the organization that today bears his name.

There are those—even today—who believe that Bell was essentially correct about signed language. There are still institutions, Clarke School and the Alexander Graham Bell Association are only the most prominent, where signed language is still regarded as foreign, the acquisition of which is perceived as disadvantageous for the Deaf. Today, the motivations for Bell's many attempts to suppress signed language and isolate the Deaf from one another are usually glossed over—they jar modern sensibilities—but the antipathy toward signed language that one continues to find at some institutions can be traced directly back to those ideas. Furthermore, without an understanding of those ideas it is not possible to appreciate the nature and depth of the hostility that was directed against American Sign Language by so many for so long.

As is also true of Thomas Hopkins Gallaudet's philosophy of the natural language of signs, Bell's arguments against the use of signed language represent something of an intellectual dead end. They were not substantially changed by any of his successors, although future generations of oralists had many opportunities to do so. (As the founders of the Hartford school had, the oralists also founded their own scholarly journal, *The Association Review,* and they published a great deal of writing that was sympathetic to oralist philosophy.) Bell's successors continue to believe that one must prevent the acquisition of signed language, integrate Deaf children into mainstream activities as soon as possible, isolate orally educated Deaf children from signing Deaf children and signing Deaf adults, and de-emphasize the importance of those activities, organizations, and people associated with what today is called Deaf culture.

At the present time, most educators have made an accommodation with the use of signed language in the classroom. Some have embraced American Sign Language as the language of instruction. Others continue to use a system of signs that emphasizes the grammatical conventions that one finds in spoken and written English, an English language version of de l'Epée's methodological signs. As with most past trends in Deaf education, these changes, too, were instituted first and justified second, if they were justified at all.

The distaste that many educators of the Deaf now express toward oral education is said to be founded on research that shows that oral education is not as effective a method of instruction as was once claimed. Interest in oral education, a methodology that played a very prominent role in the education of the Deaf for almost a century, began to drop precipitously at about the time that the National Theatre of the Deaf began their performances. Of course, educators do not cite theatrical performances when making decisions about educational methodologies, but in this case they probably should. Their emphasis on then-new research into the relative value of oral versus signed language education is certainly misleading. Oral education, introduced into the United States shortly after the American Civil War, was quickly adopted at many schools, so the data needed to objectively assess oral methods could have been acquired decades before signed language was first shown on national television. It could have been acquired before the invention of television, and, in fact, some of it was.

Job Williams, principal of the Hartford school during the latter half of the nineteenth century, wrote an early critique of oral education entitled "A System of Education Adapted to All Deaf Mutes, Not Excluding the Feebler-Minded,"[26] and in it he compares the philosophies underpinning the oralist's and the manualist's methods of instruction; he describes the student populations at institutions that use each method, and he compares the educational attainments of the students at institutions that used signed language with those that used oral methods. (The "Feebler-Minded" in the title of the paper refers to the fact that oralists often classified students who did not flourish under their method as "dull" or as "oral failures"—the two terms were often used synonymously—and sent them to institutions where the instruction was carried out in signs.)

In his paper Williams correctly asserts that manualist schools, that is, schools that employed signed language as the medium of instruction, accepted all students who, were they not Deaf, would have been admitted to a public school. Oralist institutions, he asserted, often did not. Early in the history of oral education this distinction was freely acknowledged. In the first annual report of the Clarke School this distinction is described in detail. The report enumerates three classes of students who cannot be taught articulation: (1) "Those whose mental powers are feeble by nature...," (2) "[t]hose whose organs of speech are imperfect...," and (3) "[t]hose with sufficient mental ability, but who can no more be taught articulation than many hearing persons can be taught singing." Similarly, those who can be taught speech fell into three categories: (1) "Those who lost their hearing at three years of age and upwards, after they had acquired some language...," (2) "[t]hose congenitally deaf who have good mental ability, and a capacity for learning to speak," and (3) "[t]hose who are semi-deaf and can distinguish articulate sounds, but not readily enough to attend the common schools with profit."[27] More formally and succinctly, other early annual reports of the Clarke School contain a section entitled Terms of Admission that begins with the statement, "This Institution is especially adapted for the education of semi-deaf and semi-mute pupils, but others may be admitted."[28] (The term "semi-deaf" meant hard-of-hearing and "semi-mute" meant that the student had some speech prior to instruction.) But as claims for the efficacy of oral methods became progressively more inflated such statements were often dropped in favor of the assertion that all but the "feebleminded" and those with damaged organs of speech would benefit from an oral education. Essentially, the claim was that the method worked for virtually everyone who was smart enough—where a smart student was defined as someone who profited from the method. The reasoning is evidently circular—the method works for the smart students and the smart students are the ones for whom the method works—and this was recognized by many, but to little effect, right from the start.

In his article Williams contrasts the writing samples of individuals educated with and without signs. This is a valuable approach since good written language was a goal that both methods strove to attain and so provided a common metric for success. (In fact, Bell also suggests the comparison of writing samples as the best way to compare various methods and institutions.) Williams included writing samples of two students who had transferred from an oral to a manual institution. One student had remained at the oral institution for 18 months; the second student for five years. The "before" samples were made when they arrived at the manual institution; the "after" samples were made after six months of instruction at the manual institution. In both cases the writing samples are much improved. (To be precise, Williams distinguished between a manualist method, instruction given in signed language alone, and a combined method, where sign and speech and speech reading were all used. Williams's institution was a combined school, but Bell dismissed such distinctions. He believed there was no real difference between the manualist and combined systems and that the combined system was a manualist system in disguise. There is some truth to Bell's criticism, and no distinction between the two methods will be made here.) By themselves, of course, case studies such as Williams's prove little. One can always find exceptions to any rule, and Williams is aware of this shortcoming in his argument. He produces the samples to demonstrate his method of evaluation. He then summarizes in a table his evaluations of all the students who transferred from oralist schools to his own institution. There were 32 students in all.

There are reasonable grounds to criticize this paper. Williams's analysis is hampered by small sample size, and he lacks precisely defined criteria for his evaluations, but small sample sizes are characteristic of all the papers in this field—it is a small field—and the analysis of writing styles does require subjective judgment on the part of the researcher. That was true then, and it is true now. His arguments are no more or less persuasive than many later, more influential studies. In 1969, for example, 85 years after Williams's article, Miriam Forster Fiedler published her long-term study of children at the Clarke School.[29] Fiedler concluded that one-fourth of the students in her study should not have been enrolled in a school for the Deaf, because they heard well enough to perform "in a school or class for the hard of hearing." In the vocabulary of another era they were semideaf. More tellingly, she also found that about half the children in the study group were "five or more years retarded in educational achievement." There were only 20 students in her group, and her methods were no more "analytic" than were those of Williams. Her conclusions are, in the end, not especially different from those of Job Williams, either. The difference is that her study, as well as studies similar to hers and carried out at roughly the same time, were published at a time when schools for the Deaf were *already* beginning to make the transition from oral to signed language education; Williams's paper was published at a time when educational policies were rapidly shifting in the other direction.

The changes in attitudes toward American Sign Language and toward the Deaf that occurred in the late 1960s and early 1970s profoundly impacted the lives of many Deaf. But Williams's paper demonstrates that many of the arguments made against oralism in the late 1960s and early 1970s would have been familiar to those American educators who opposed "pure" oralism in the late nineteenth century. It is even true that many of the arguments made against oral methods in the late 1960s would have been familiar to Pierre Desloges and the abbé de l'Epée centuries earlier. The increased interest in signed language and the move away from oral education could *not* have been driven by important new discoveries in the field of Deaf education, because there had not been any. The changes that occurred in educational policy were, instead, a reflection of changes in cultural attitudes toward deafness *as a condition* and toward American Sign Language *as a language*. The National Theatre of the Deaf—their performance on *Experiment in Television* was just the beginning—was more than a reflection of those changes; it was also a cause.

John Burton Hotchkiss in the film Memories of Old Hartford. National Association of the Deaf; courtesy of Gallaudet University Archives.

The Language of the Deaf

*A year ago there passed away a distinguished inventor well known to the deaf—
Dr. Alexander Graham Bell...In a sense he was interested in the deaf. His wife
was deaf. For an extended period he was the outstanding advocate of the teaching of
speech to the deaf and of laws compelling the use of speech methods in schools for the
deaf. He also did considerable publicity work in matters concerning the deaf. A lova-
ble man, a distinguished citizen, an eminent inventor, generous in his benefactions to
the causes he favored, Dr. Bell occupied a place too much in opposition to that favored
by the educated deaf generally for them to regard him as either a friend, teacher, ben-
efactor, or philanthropist.*

      —Dr. James H. Cloud, President, National Association of the Deaf.[1]

In 1848 in the first article of the first issue of the journal now called the *American
Annals of the Deaf,* Luzerne Rae, a teacher at the Hartford school, described the
Deaf in these words: "They [the Deaf] have a history peculiar to themselves,
extending back for many centuries into the past, and sustaining relations, of more
or less interest, to the general history of the human race." Rae goes on to describe
who might be interested in the Deaf:

> There is a class of persons in our country, and we are happy to believe that their
> number is constantly increasing...who hold nothing aloof from their hearts which
> pertains to the welfare of any portion of their fellow men. To such as these, the con-
> version of one born deaf, from his natural state of almost total ignorance, to a degree
> of knowledge and intellectual vigor which multitudes with all their senses in perfec-
> tion never reach, cannot be otherwise than deeply interesting; and it is not strange
> that they should seek to know something of the method, by which results so wonder-
> ful are, with so little apparent difficulty, accomplished.[2]

Rae's was the dominant view of the Deaf by American educators until the latter years of the nineteenth century.

Rae's view of the Deaf was challenged by the oralists, those who rejected signed language and advocated for the use of speech and speech reading in the education of Deaf children. They had little patience with the idea of the Deaf as a separate social class. They often spoke in the most disparaging terms of the signed language used by the Deaf, of the social organizations formed by the Deaf, and of social relations among the Deaf. They justified their oft-expressed contempt, in part, by appealing to the pseudoscience of eugenics. In 1908, Alexander Graham Bell, for example, described the marriage of two Deaf adults as a "marriage of inferiors."[3] His views were shared by many of his contemporaries. By eliminating signed language and the culture that the Deaf had created for themselves, the oralists sought not just to facilitate Deaf-hearing relations but also to create obstacles to Deaf-Deaf relations. The program that the oralists envisaged was a harsh one, but they were unapologetic because they valued their goals more than the suffering that often accompanied the implementation of those goals. They saw no reason to compromise. Unlike the manualists, the oralists did not find the Deaf at all "interesting"—not, at least, in the sense that they felt that they could learn something of importance from them. The oralist solution to what they perceived as the problem of deafness was as simple as it was brutal: eliminate the Deaf as a social class.

The disagreement engendered by these two competing views of deafness gave rise to a protracted and often bitter conflict that dragged on for more than a century. But this frequently uncivil debate took place in a larger context, and this broader societal context influenced the Deaf response. And there was, indeed, a Deaf response to the discussion of whether or not signed language, their language, should cease to exist. To understand the Deaf response, it is helpful to look at the wider cultural context in which it was formulated.

The late nineteenth and early twentieth century was a time of large-scale immigration into the United States. Many distinct linguistic and ethnic groups were finding new homes in America, and these groups often experienced the sometimes subtle and sometimes brutal pressures to Americanize, that is, to abandon those cultural practices that some perceived as un-American and, in the case of non-English speaking immigrants, to abandon their first languages. The pressures experienced by these immigrant groups were often similar to those experienced by American Deaf and so were the ensuing responses. In large measure, American Deaf behaved as other ethnic groups did. They perceived themselves as a people united by a common language and common cultural traditions. They did not, for the most part, perceive themselves as a group of individuals whose defining characteristic was a shared physical disability. In short, the Deaf responded to the oralists in a way that was strongly reminiscent of the way that immigrant groups responded to those who attempted to Americanize them.

Immigration, of course, has been an important aspect of North American culture since Columbus. The United States, in particular, has always been a linguistically and culturally diverse nation, and there have always been some who perceived diversity as a threat. Benjamin Franklin, for example, was suspicious of German immigrants in the Pennsylvania colony. In a 1753 letter,[4] he complains that they establish German-language book publishers and German-language newspapers; they issue bonds in their own language, they require interpreters in courts, and they display street signs and other public signage in their own language, and to all of this he objects. Worse, Franklin continues, if the French were to attack, it is not at all clear that the Germans would take up arms to defend the colony in which they reside—not, at least, until they had determined whether or not a French victory would unreasonably impinge upon their interests. His solution? Franklin proposes establishing English schools in areas where the Germans are "too thick settled," distribute the Germans more equally across the landscape, and "mix them with the English"—in short: assimilate them.

The debate over assimilation—at the time the word was used synonymously with the term "Americanization"—began to gain popular currency during the 1840s, and the topic loomed large in American political life for many years. While it has resurfaced in more recent times, it is difficult, even now, to appreciate how exercised many native-born nineteenth and early twentieth century Americans were over the effects of immigration. Despite the prominence of the issue in today's news reports, the current debate over immigration pales in comparison to its nineteenth century counterpart. Consider this: Between 1820 and 1860 the United States absorbed 6.8 million immigrants, but in 1820, there were only 9.6 million persons in the United States and its territories. The result was an almost frantic backlash against the new arrivals. Beginning in the 1840s, the Know-Nothing Party, a political party organized around the issue of immigration, reflected the fear that many native-born Americans felt toward the new arrivals. (The name Know-Nothing arose because early in the history of the organization, members were encouraged to deflect questions about the organization by saying that they knew nothing.) By the early 1850s, the Know-Nothings had become a major political party. Know-Nothing members held many local and state offices, and the 1852 Congress contained 43 representatives who identified themselves as Know-Nothings. Know-Nothings were staunchly anti-immigrant and anti-Catholic. They wanted to bar foreign-born citizens from voting or holding political office, and they supported a 21-year residency requirement for American citizenship. The Know-Nothing Party soon splintered over the issue of slavery, and it never recovered. Its anti-immigrant biases survived the destruction of the party, however, and formed an important part of the post-war discourse.

Many of the claims made during this time about the dangers of immigration are now easily recognized as simple prejudice against individuals who were often poor, uneducated, and initially powerless. Writers of the time looked toward the pseudoscience of eugenics and a crude and selective use of statistics to justify their assertions. Henry Cabot Lodge (1850–1924), for example, a long-time senator from Massachusetts, wrote an 1891 article in which, using an encyclopedia, he listed contributions that he considered important to American history and then grouped the contributors by "race." Not surprisingly, Lodge's own "English race" was the main contributor to U.S. history, far exceeding the contributions of, for example, the "Italian race" and the "Greek race." The post–Civil War discussion of problems associated with immigration continued to fester as the numbers of immigrants continued to grow: Between 1861 and 1890, 10.3 million immigrants arrived and between 1891 and 1930, 22.3 million settled in the United States. By 1900, New York officials were compiling information on the race of each immigrant with the goal of predicting the "influence [of the immigrants] upon the community of which they are to become members."[5]

As their racist contemporaries did, moderate voices of the time also viewed immigrants as a problem to be solved. Few writers saw immigration as an opportunity to grow and enrich U.S. culture. But in contrast to those who, as Lodge did, saw immigration as the importation of a permanent lower class to be managed as best one could, the moderates perceived the solution to the problem of immigration in terms of creating policies and institutions that facilitated assimilation. The sort of vocabulary that is common today—one that emphasizes multiculturalism and the advantages associated with a diverse population—is as absent from moderate writings as it is from the writings of their more extremist contemporaries. Unlike the extremists, however, the moderates did not express contempt for the languages and customs of immigrant groups, preferring, instead, to emphasize the acquisition of English language skills and what they perceived to be U.S. cultural norms through public education—including night classes for adults—the enfranchisement of community organizations and changes to the housing patterns of immigrant populations among other measures. All such measures were proposed with the view of entraining those individuals living in ethnic enclaves into what the moderates perceived to be the mainstream of American life.[6]

Not surprisingly, immigrants did not necessarily subscribe to either the moderate or extreme views described in the preceding paragraphs because they did not perceive themselves as problems to be solved. Nor, generally, did they see their complete assimilation into American society as either necessary or desirable. While each ethnic group's responses to the pressures of assimilation were somewhat unique—formed, as they were, by the group's native language (English versus non-English), their cultural practices, their absolute numbers, and geographic distribution—they were generally united by a desire to preserve their language and culture while simultaneously participating fully in U.S. society on their own terms. Immigrant groups often established schools, where their own language and culture were emphasized; they often established presses that published periodicals and books in their native language; clergy were recruited to perform religious services in the tradition and language of the community; benefit societies were formed to protect the financial and political interests of the membership and, often, to provide for the social needs of the group. In short, they organized to further their interests, keep informed about ideas of particular importance to their community, protect themselves from those who sought to eliminate their language and cultural traditions, and meet the many needs of the community in an often hostile environment.

The institutions established by the Deaf during the nineteenth and early twentieth centuries were often similar in structure or function to those created by certain groups of newly arrived immigrants. During the first half of the nineteenth century, Deaf Americans helped to create a system of residential schools for Deaf children, where their language, American Sign Language—then called the natural language of signs—was the language of instruction, and where Deaf teachers, staff, and administrators all played important roles. In 1880, Deaf individuals founded a national lobbying organization, the National Association of the Deaf, to protect and extend the civil rights of the membership. Deaf individuals founded numerous publications—the so-called Deaf press—that were run by the Deaf for a Deaf audience. In 1901, a group of Deaf men founded the National Fraternal Society of the Deaf (NFSD), a fraternal benefit society. (As of 2005 the NFSD operates solely as a fraternal society; the insurance component was dropped.) In short, the Deaf response to the pressures of the broader and sometimes hostile American society mirrored that of a number of newly arrived ethnic groups.

There are, of course, differences between American Deaf and immigrant groups. The Deaf view of themselves as an ethnic group, a viewpoint that is sometimes expressed explicitly and sometimes implicitly in the writings of Deaf intellectuals, was based on analogy. It was a perception that many Deaf shared, and to which many Deaf continue to subscribe, but as every analogy does, this one, too, has its limitations. The first difference between the Deaf and immigrant groups is that immigrant communities arose as their members moved to the United States. The Deaf, by contrast, created themselves.

As a social class the Deaf did not exist in the United States prior to the establishment of the first school for the Deaf in Hartford in 1817. There had, of course, been deaf individuals in the United States before 1817, but they were not united by a common language. Many had virtually no language whatsoever. But as they developed a common language and a common culture, they began to establish their own organizations. The delay between the opening of the Hartford school and the flowering of an American Deaf culture is remarkably brief.

Following the establishment of the American school, a number of other schools for the Deaf opened in quick succession: Laurent Clerc left Hartford temporarily to help found the Pennsylvania Institution, where he was headmaster from August 1821 until March 1822. Other schools established around this time include the New York School for the Deaf (est. 1818), the Kentucky School for the Deaf (est. 1823), the Ohio School for the Deaf (est. 1829), and the Virginia School for the Deaf (est. 1839). The natural language of signs was the common language of instruction at all of these institutions, and it was not an uncommon practice to hire Deaf teachers at these early schools. George Loring, a former student at the American school and a linguistically gifted native of Boston, who became fluent in English, American Sign Language (or the natural language of signs as it was then known), French, which he learned from Clerc, and later Italian, was one of the first. Many Deaf teachers, women as well as men, soon followed. By 1852, 38 percent of all teachers of the Deaf were themselves Deaf, and for the next 20 years the percentage of Deaf teachers in the profession remained at around 40 percent. Furthermore, many of the hearing instructors at these early institutions were also fluent in signed language. A number of schools, including the Indiana School for the Deaf (est. 1843), were even founded by Deaf individuals. This was an important educational accomplishment: The Deaf had successfully played a major role in founding a bilingual educational system in which instruction occurred in the language in which *they* were most fluent. The natural language of signs was, after all, a language in which they were at least as competent as (and often more competent than) the hearing members of the staff, faculty, and administration. It was *their* language, and it was the language in which they taught *their* students. These schools were the vehicles through which they assured the transmission of their language from one generation to the next.

Nor was Deaf participation in these schools limited to teaching and administrative positions. Deaf individuals were also hired as cooks, maintenance persons, and other support staff. (Oral institutions, by contrast, were very much opposed to having Deaf adults on campus in any capacity for fear that they would transmit signed language to the students or improperly model spoken language.) It was in these early manual schools that the first steps were taken toward the creation of the social class called the American Deaf community.

It is important to recognize that most African-American Deaf were not included in this early movement as they were located in the South, living as slaves, and hence deprived of an education as a matter of law (see Chapter 5). There were, however, a few African-American Deaf educated at some of these early schools. The school for the Deaf in Hartford, for example, may have become the first integrated school in Connecticut when it admitted an African-American student in 1825. (The American school has never restricted admission based on race. Thomas H. Gallaudet, a founder of the school, was sympathetic to the abolitionists, and Lewis Weld, an early principal, shared the sympathies of his brother, the prominent abolitionist, Theodore Dwight Weld.)

Out of this early educational system came a group of individuals with a shared language and a shared sense of identity. They were a new group on the American scene, linguistically distinct and united by a common and unique educational background. At the same time they also held many of the values of the broader society to which they belonged. So in 1849, when Thomas Brown, one of the earliest students at the American school, suggested a public ceremony to thank Thomas H. Gallaudet and Laurent Clerc for their foundational contributions to Deaf education in the United States, Deaf individuals from around the country enthusiastically agreed to support the effort. Six hundred dollars was raised, solely from the Deaf, and used to purchase two large silver pitchers and matching trays, one for Gallaudet and one for Clerc. The pitchers were elaborately engraved and publicly displayed prior to the presentation ceremony. They showed Clerc and Gallaudet, a series of images representing their passage across the ocean, the American school, the instruction of Deaf pupils, a picture of Roche Amboise Sicard, and other aspects of what was, for the Deaf, their creation story. Each also contained an engraved personalized message of appreciation to its intended recipient.

Hundreds of Deaf from New England and as far away as Virginia assembled at the Hartford institution on September 26, 1850, to present these gifts to Clerc and Gallaudet. The ceremony featured long presentations (in sign) by George Loring, Thomas Brown, Lewis Weld, Fisher Ames Spofford (1808-1877), a former student at the Hartford school and long-time teacher of the Deaf, and, of course, Gallaudet and Clerc. With the exception of Weld's brief speech, each of the presentations described some part of the story—described in this book in Chapter 2—of how Gallaudet and Clerc brought signed language to the United States and the process by which they founded what was then the only system of Deaf education in America. In his remarks, Clerc mentions that by the time of the ceremony, there were "nine or ten" schools for the Deaf, that most of the teachers at these schools had been qualified at Hartford, and that the Hartford school alone had taught 1,066 students. Clerc further observed that because all students at all the institutions then extant had been taught by the same method, they would "not be strangers to each other" should they meet one another.[7] He and his colleagues had by this time created a new American social class.

This ceremony was an extremely important event in the history of American Deaf. It was widely attended and reported. It put on public display not just the language, the values, some of the best orators, and the most important cultural figures of the Deaf, but also their economic empowerment. (The value of the gifts and the fact that the money had been raised entirely from contributions by the Deaf was an important part of the ceremony.) This was the first large public ceremony planned by and for Deaf Americans. Large regional and national meetings and ceremonies continue to the present day.

A nationwide set of schools was just the start of American Deaf culture. Former students began to write pieces of particular interest to a Deaf readership. In 1836, the book *The Deaf and Dumb: or, A Collection of Articles Relating to the Condition of Deaf Mutes; Their Education, and the Principal Asylums Devoted to Their Instruction* by Edwin John Mann appeared. Mann, formerly a student at the American school, created a wonderful work that remains interesting as a source of early ideas about the nature of signed language as well as for the information one finds on individuals who were important in the early history of the language. Only one year later, in 1837, Levi S. Backus (1803–1869), another student of the American school, became owner and editor of the *Canajoharie Radii*, a weekly newspaper based in Canajoharie, New York, the hometown, from 1823 to 1835, of the Central Asylum for the Instruction of the Deaf and Dumb. Backus had been an instructor at the school and bought the paper after the school closed. The *Radii* was a local newspaper, and it continued to operate in that capacity, but Backus also added a column of particular interest to Deaf readers and began using the manual alphabet to spell the newspaper's title. The newspaper was carefully produced and attracted some attention, which, in 1844, Backus parlayed into a subsidy from the state of New York to mail copies of his paper to "educated" Deaf throughout the state. In 1870, ownership of the *Radii* changed hands, and in 1875, the new owner, Henry C. Rider, began printing the *Deaf-Mutes'*

Journal, the first weekly newspaper aimed at a Deaf audience. In 1878, publication of the *Journal* was taken over by the New York School for the Deaf, White Plains, New York, which continued to publish it until 1951, when the *Journal* was discontinued.[8]

In 1860, the New England Gallaudet Association of the Deaf, an organization that grew out of the first large convocation of American Deaf in Hartford in 1850, began to publish *The Gallaudet Guide and Deaf Mutes' Companion,* the first periodical aimed at an exclusively Deaf readership. Two other periodicals of the time are especially worthy of note: the *Silent Worker* (1888–1929), which was one of the most popular and ambitious Deaf publications (the name was revived again in 1948), and *The National Exponent* (1894–1896), which is notable for having employed Robert P. McGregor, James H. Cloud, and George W. Veditz, all of whom later served terms as president of the National Association of the Deaf. The *Silent Worker* was printed at the New Jersey School for the Deaf, Trenton, New Jersey, by students at the school. Reporters, based around the country, wrote on a variety of topics, and the magazine also carried photography and art by many Deaf contributors. While the early issues were only a few pages long, some later issues contained 60 or more pages of high-quality text and art. The magazine was discontinued when George Porter, the print shop teacher responsible for starting the magazine, finally retired. In total, Jack R. Gannon estimates that there have been approximately 500 publications printed in the interests of American Deaf since the beginning of a Deaf press in the nineteenth century.[9] They served as one of the principal mechanisms by which news was exchanged and a sense of identity maintained among a dispersed Deaf population, most of the members of which had attended one or another of the residential institutions scattered around the nation.

Religion was an important unifying influence among many Deaf. Their religious beliefs and the desire to inculcate their students with certain religious values were two of the most important motivations for early teachers of the Deaf. Charles-Michel de l'Epée and Sicard were priests; Gallaudet was a minister, and Clerc's writings are replete with references to religion and the importance of signed language as a medium for conveying religious truth. Early schools for the Deaf had daily, nondenominational Christian religious services conducted in sign. Often, in fact, the school day began and ended in the chapel. Eventually, a number of Deaf men came to prominence as ministers, and the services were conducted in sign.

The existence of a Deaf ministry, and more generally signed religious services, was an important factor in the preservation of signed language throughout the period that the oralists were attempting to destroy signed language. As oral education began to supplant signed language in schools for the Deaf, one of the most insistent criticisms of oral education raised by the manualists was that speech could not be used effectively in religious services because most of the congregation must of necessity sit so far from the minister that speech reading was impossible. Oral educators asserted otherwise, insisting that their students could follow the sermons from the pews. Such claims proved to be too much even for some orally taught Deaf.[10] But while the protests did not diminish the enthusiasm of oral educators for making such claims, the Deaf knew otherwise. They continued to support a cadre of clergy, representing a variety of faiths, who were skilled in signed language. Certain Protestant sects, especially the Baptists, have a long and particularly distinguished record of providing accessible religious services and even of making the ministry accessible to Deaf applicants. The result is that religious services have provided (and continue to provide) a vehicle for the preservation and development of American Sign Language and Deaf culture.

Beginning in the latter part of the nineteenth century, American Deaf began to establish national organizations to further their economic, social, recreational, educational, and political activities. The NFSD furthered their economic and social interests. This organization was established as a benefit society; that is, it was organized on the principle of insurance wherein a condition of membership is that one had to purchase and maintain a NFSD insurance policy. (Benefit societies were common among a number of immigrant groups. Polish immigrants, in particular, formed almost all of their larger organizations as benefit societies.) In addition to its function as an insurance provider, the NFSD divided its service area, which included the United States and parts of Canada, into local "divisions," each of which provided members with opportunities to gather, socialize, and engage in community service. Although it portrayed itself as an organization founded to help "the" Deaf, the NFSD had a very narrow definition of its target population. In common with Gallaudet College and the National Association of the Deaf, the NFSD refused to accept African-American applicants until the latter half of the twentieth century; the NFSD also barred women from membership during this time.

The National Association of the Deaf

The organization whose policies best illustrate the perception of the Deaf as simply one more linguistic minority with its own distinct history and culture in a multilingual, multiethnic society is the National Association of the Deaf (NAD). The NAD was deeply committed to the analogy between the Deaf and those ethnic groups who sought to participate in American society while simultaneously maintaining their language and ethnic traditions. Just as importantly, they meticulously and self-consciously documented their ideas and policies because they believed, just as de l'Epée, Sicard, Gallaudet, and Clerc believed before them, that what they did had historical import. In fact, it was their perceived relation to these ethnic communities that provided a framework within which they developed their own history and sense of self. An eloquent description of the Deaf conception of themselves as a distinct cultural-historical entity in a wider American society was given by Alice T. Terry, a prominent Deaf writer and lecturer. In her address to the 1915 convention of the NAD she delivered these words:

> O, for a return of the good old days! We cannot have again on earth the immortal Abbé de l'Epée, the Gallaudets and others; but we can and we will keep alive their practical, imperishable ideals on deaf-mute education. The act of destroying these ideals produces upon the deaf world an unspeakable sadness. It means to us just what it would mean to this country if it substituted some one else for George Washington or Abraham Lincoln.[11]

In order to emphasize its view of the Deaf as a linguistic minority—and not as a group of individuals united by a common physical disability—the NAD carefully crafted its policies and proposals in such a way as to distance its members from individuals, organizations, or public policies that might make the Deaf appear weak or less capable. The NAD's actions sometimes resulted in additional financial costs to its members, but there seems to have been little in the way of protest from the membership. Most revealing in this respect are the NAD's policies toward peddlers, taxes, restrictions on driving rights of the Deaf, and eugenics. Understanding the ways that the NAD responded to these issues not only helps one appreciate how the Deaf perceived themselves and how they wanted others to perceive them, but also their responses to the oralist attacks on signed language.

A peddler is one who distributes cards showing the manual alphabet or other items of little intrinsic worth in return for a donation. The leaders of the NAD and at least some of the membership perceived peddling as a form of begging. They divided peddlers into two groups, those who were Deaf and those who were impostors; that is, those who were not Deaf but only pretended to be. Complaints about peddling appear late in the nineteenth century and continue into the post–World War II years. It was a phenomenon that was taken very seriously by many Deaf.[12] The NAD established a bureau, at least as early as 1913, called The Impostor Bureau, to try to suppress peddling. There were successes. Anti-peddling laws were passed in a number of states during the early years of the twentieth century, among them, Nevada, Indiana, Washington, Ohio, Tennessee,

Michigan, and Illinois. Members of the Bureau also worked with police to identify and punish those individuals, Deaf or hearing, involved in the activity. The 1920 convention of the NAD passed the following resolution which is found again in the Proceedings of the 1923 convention in John E. Purdam's Report of the Impostor Bureau:

> Resolved, That we express our strong condemnation of anyone using his or her deafness for soliciting financial aid in the way of peddling alphabet cards and other useless articles that do not give return for value received. They should be classed in the same category as Impostors, which the Association is combating, and referred to the Impostor Bureau.[13]

One year later Purdam wrote the following oft-quoted passage:

> [T]he genuine deaf-mute has no occasion to beg. Our people are self-sufficient and do not have to trade upon their misfortune in any way. Our local, state and national associations are united in an effort to stamp out the practice of these fakes [i.e., imposters] and appreciate it more than we can say when an intelligent officer of the law, or a private citizen, puts a stop to crime.[14]

The issue of peddlers, Deaf or impostor, caused many Deaf to search for ways of applying sanctions to those involved. In 1913, the NAD successfully lobbied the Minnesota legislature to amend a vagrancy law to explicitly include the crime of peddling by impostors, and in the Proceedings of the NAD's 1923 convention, the NFSD was applauded because they had "fined, suspended, and fired" several members of the Society who had been caught engaging in the practice of peddling.

The leaders of the NAD, the NFSD, and a significant fraction of their respective memberships felt that peddlers threatened the interests of the Deaf because they presented an image of the Deaf as people who were less capable than others and who depended on the charity of strangers. The NAD's response to the phenomenon of peddling was threefold. First, if the peddler was found to be an impostor, they advocated punishment. They also sought to advertise as widely as possible the fact that the individual was not Deaf but a hearing impostor. Their motto, "The Deaf Do Not Beg," was, for the 1913 NAD convention, emblazoned on 18,000 stickers, and a letter expressing this sentiment was mailed to over 400 of the nation's largest daily newspapers. Second, if the peddler was found to be Deaf, the individual was sanctioned away from the public eye. This double standard is illustrated in the Report of the Impostor Bureau given at the NAD's 1923 convention in which the chief of the Bureau, John E. Purdam, describes how he worked with the Chicago police to obtain convictions for three impostors and how he secured the release of two Deaf peddlers from jail under the condition that they leave town. The third response by the NAD to the issue of peddling was to take every opportunity to discourage the general public from giving to the peddlers. In his 1923 report Purdam suggests the possibility of paying for ads with this message to be placed on trolley cars.

All of the antipeddling activity was portrayed as being in the best interests of the Deaf, and it may have been in the best interests of some Deaf. The drive to criminalize the behavior would, of course, have had a negative effect on those Deaf engaged in the activity, and the act of peddling certainly had no direct effect on nonpeddling Deaf. Nor, in retrospect, is it immediately apparent that the latter had the right to control the economic activities of those with whom they disagreed. Rather, the considerable energy expended by the NAD to control peddling was undertaken because peddling violated the perception these Deaf had of themselves and the image that they sought to convey to society at large.

The desire to eliminate peddling and to conform to perceived norms that is exhibited by the actions of the NAD is also evident in the NAD policy on taxes. Since early in the twentieth century there have been several attempts on the state and federal levels to exempt the Deaf because they are Deaf from paying all or part of the taxes for which they would otherwise be responsible. Despite the economic advantage offered by such bills, the NAD and other Deaf organizations consistently opposed them, arguing that the Deaf not only should assume their full tax liability, but that they insisted on doing so. As early as 1915, for example, the *Silent Worker* reported that Deaf lobbyists had successfully turned back an attempt in the Connecticut State Legislature to exempt the Deaf from taxation:

> The protest of the deaf of Connecticut against the bill presented at the recent meeting of the legislature exempting them from taxation was exactly what might have been expected. The deaf do not ask for any such favors. They are self-respecting and self-supporting and in every way the peers of their speaking brethren. They are especially anxious not to be placed in the dependent class.[15]

The effort to turn back tax-relief legislation for the Deaf was vigorously and successfully pursued for several decades. As late as 1953 the NAD successfully opposed a piece of federal legislation, introduced by Senator Jacob Javits of New York, to grant the Deaf a modest $600 tax exemption. The importance of full and equal citizenship was worth the price of the taxes involved but having paid the price, they insisted on equality.

One area of civil rights where Deaf individuals and organizations—particularly the NAD—were able to leverage their status as a cohesive group of responsible taxpaying citizens was in the area of driving rights. Deaf driving rights became a central focus of the NAD in the 1920s and remained an important topic until the 1940s by which time the right of Deaf Americans to drive had been widely secured and firmly established. (It is not the purpose of the following paragraphs to give a complete account of this topic. The reader is referred to Burch[16] for a more complete overview.) Instead, the issue of licensing Deaf drivers, which was eventually resolved in a way that was entirely favorable to the Deaf, is here offered as an example of how the NAD successfully lobbied on behalf of its membership.

By the 1920s cars and car accidents had become fairly commonplace. Rising public expectations with respect to automobile safety led legislatures to begin to pass laws regulating who was entitled to drive an automobile and under what conditions. Although most states did not ban Deaf drivers, there were a few exceptions. Of special note are Maryland, New Jersey, and Pennsylvania, all of which had banned Deaf drivers by 1923. The NAD recognized these bans as threats to the interests of its membership, and in 1922 it organized a committee called the Traffic Bureau, the purpose of which was to protect the driving rights of the membership. In this effort the Deaf were supported by many education professionals as well as a number of public safety officials and other interested individuals.

In opposing each such ban, the NAD's mode of argument remained the same: (1) statistics were collected and cited, (2) reasoned arguments were offered together with the opinions of authorities, and (3) accident records were analyzed with the view toward demonstrating that the inability to hear did not of itself make the driver a threat to the public safety. By way of example, much was made of a June 1925 article in the *New York Times* quoting Charles A. Harnett, Motor Vehicle Commissioner of New Jersey, in which he said, "We have given operators' licenses to about 500 deaf mutes...and so far as I know, not one of them has been involved in an accident."[17] Similarly, much was made of a July 4, 1926, interview published in the Michigan *Mirror* with Kalamazoo police chief, Roy W. Carney, in which he asserted that the city records indicated that there had not been a single motor vehicle accident that could be ascribed to a Deaf driver.[18] Having established as best as they were able the assertion that the Deaf did not pose a danger, the Deaf argued for driving rights on the basis of their rights as taxpaying citizens. The following passage concerns the denial of driving licenses to the Deaf by the Pennsylvania Legislature. It is characteristic in linking the right to drive to the fulfillment by the Deaf of their responsibilities as citizens of the Commonwealth:

> It must not be forgotten that the deaf people of our Commonwealth are taxpayers and pay their share towards maintaining highways for the pleasure of all. Can they be legitimately prevented from using that which is as much theirs as their neighbors?[19]

In no state where a ban had been instituted did that ban remain in effect for long. The Pennsylvania ban, which lasted three years, was overturned by 1923, the year the Traffic Bureau made its first report to an NAD convention. The New Jersey ban was overturned by the time of the 1926 NAD convention. The Maryland ban was more problematic: It had been modified by 1926 to enable the Deaf to drive subject to several restrictions, chief among them was that the Deaf driver could not operate the car unaccompanied by a hearing person. The restrictions were, however, soon removed. These were not the last legal threats to the rights of the Deaf to obtain driving licenses, but in no case were the rights of the Deaf denied for long, and in most cases the threatened restrictions were never put in place. The NAD, together with other interested parties, had successfully defended a right of particular importance to its membership.

Another revealing parallel between the Deaf and immigrant groups is revealed in the Deaf response to the eugenics movement of the late nineteenth and early twentieth centuries. Eugenics, the pseudoscience that concerns itself with "improving" a population's store of hereditary traits by controlling reproduction, captured the public imagination in the United States throughout this time. Interest in the subject had been stimulated by the work of English eugenicist Sir Francis Galton (1822–1911), who wrote eloquently about the desirability of improving the physical and mental traits of humans through controlled reproduction. Broadly speaking, Galton and other eugenicists divided humanity into the desirables and the undesirables and sought to increase the percentage of the former at the expense of the latter. Not surprisingly, "desirables" generally included those ethnicities and social classes with which the eugenicists themselves identified; virtually everyone else was undesirable. (Although the term "eugenics" began to lose its popularity in the 1930s, when it became associated with the atrocities of the Nazis, the idea of selectively breeding better humans remains a fashionable one, and today some doctors and perspective parents remain ready to terminate a pregnancy for reasons related to the physical characteristics of the fetus but unrelated to its viability, and, subject to the availability of the necessary technology, many more are prepared to manipulate the genes of potential offspring to produce what they perceive to be more desirable children.)

During the late nineteenth and early twentieth centuries there was interest in the goals of eugenics across a broad spectrum of American society. Reactions to proposals that would result in restrictions on the reproductive rights of "undesirables" were generally positive—this is true even among many of the groups that were routinely classified as undesirable. Most Americans, it seems, agreed with the proposition that the undesirable element should, at the very least, voluntarily refrain from reproducing. Disputes did not generally arise until one tried to identify undesirables: No matter the segment of the population with which one identified, the undesirables always constituted a different group.

Although many writers describe the Deaf as opposing the eugenics arguments of Alexander Graham Bell—see Chapter 3 for a description of Bell's ideas—the truth is somewhat more complicated. Deaf organizations, and in particular the NAD, did not oppose eugenics in principle, something they shared with many ethnic minorities. The NAD was, in fact, often quite supportive of the idea of restricting the reproductive rights of criminals, the insane, alcoholics, the cognitively impaired, and others. Its objections to eugenics arose when it found the Deaf included with those same classes. The Deaf, it argued, were different. The report on eugenics given at the Fifteenth Triennial Convention of the NAD in 1926 begins with these words: "The Association has had, and probably always will have, the obligation and responsibility of safeguarding the deaf from inclusion in laws tending to classify them with the unfit and inferior, and putting restrictions on their marriage and the raising of families."[20] It accepted, then, the existence of "unfit and inferior" classes of people, it just did not happen to believe that the Deaf belonged among those classes. Alice T. Terry, a prominent Deaf writer and lecturer, in a long article in a 1918 issue of the *Silent Worker* went further: "Eugenics rightly treated is a noble subject far reaching in its possibilities for good."[21]

But even more telling was the distinction that many Deaf made among themselves. Among the Deaf, late-deafened individuals, those who lost their hearing after the acquisition of some speech, held a special place until the 1970s. The leadership of many Deaf organizations was generally comprised of late-deafened individuals. The first 21 presidents of the NAD, for example, were all late deafened. The first congenitally deaf president, Ralph White, was not elected until 1978, and the same sort of situation held for the leadership of the NFSD. Individuals who lose their hearing later in life generally have better speech. The relationship is a simple one: The later one loses one's hearing, the better one's speech. Although the Proceedings of NAD conventions often contained resolutions and reports critical of schools where oral education was the sole method of instructions, in retrospect they seemed to have internalized many of the values of those they criticized.

The existence of what was essentially a privileged class among Deaf Americans, the class of late-deafened individuals, also affected the response of the NAD to the eugenics movement, and specifically to the claim that the reproductive rights of Deaf Americans should be abridged. In fact, the leadership of the NAD was unwilling to forcefully defend the reproductive rights of a significant section of its own membership. Instead, at the 1920 NAD national convention, the NAD leadership urged those Deaf who were congenitally deaf to refrain from having children.[22] Their sentiments were introduced as a resolution—passed at the convention—that opposed marriages between the congenitally deaf. What was apparent to the membership, but not necessarily to outsiders, is that this resolution, which concerned the most personal and profound choices that an individual can make, affected the leadership not in the least.

The late-deafened leadership within the NAD were not alone in separating their interests from those of the congenitally deaf. In her 1918 article in the *Silent Worker* Alice T. Terry wrote in her article on eugenics (quoted previously),

> Should all the deaf who marry have children? No. No. Here it is necessary to discriminate. Deaf-mutes who in the light of their family history are liable to have deaf offspring should refrain from parenthood...There are different opinions as to whether normals should marry deaf who carry the defect in their germ plasm...Any law to prohibit the marriage of those deaf from hereditary causes would also have to be applied to normals in the same family.[23]

Not surprisingly, Terry was late deafened.

Out of this small, complex, fractured, and, in a very real sense, self-made cultural and linguistic subgroup arose a plea that Deaf children be permitted to learn signed language. By the early years of the twentieth century, oral education was the dominant form of Deaf education. Many Deaf individuals, including some who were orally educated, spoke out strongly against what they called "pure" oralism, that is, the educational philosophy that eschewed signed language entirely. They supported an educational philosophy called "the combined method," which embraced a certain amount of training in speech and speech reading but also involved the use of some signed language. The balance between speech and sign in various implementations of the combined method varied substantially from school to school and from grade to grade within the same school, but because Deaf children found sign much easier to learn and much more expressive than speech, exposing them to signed language, even in a very restricted setting, had profound implications for the manner in which the children henceforth expressed themselves. Given an opportunity to learn sign, the children inevitably adopted it as their first language.

Deaf arguments for the preservation of signed language—that is, the arguments made by adult Deaf on behalf of Deaf children asserting that the children be allowed to learn and use sign in school—were multifaceted and sometimes subtle. In what follows, it is important to keep in mind that this was not a disagreement about whether adult Deaf would sign. Deaf adults, as independent agents, were beyond the control of any teacher or educational institution. Adults signed (or not), and there was nothing that any school could do to change their linguistic behavior. The debate about the preservation of sign focused solely on whether Deaf children should be exposed to signed language. Oralists were determined that they should not. By preventing the transmission of sign from one generation to the next, it was the hope of the oralists to do away with sign altogether. By contrast, the manualists, and in particular the Deaf, believed it was wrong, even cruel, to deprive Deaf children of this mode of communication.

One argument advanced by some Deaf intellectuals, and documented in the Proceedings of a number of NAD conventions, was expressed in this way: They began by asserting that Deaf children were, in a figurative sense, the children of adult Deaf. In a biological sense this was usually false. Most Deaf children are and always have been the offspring of hearing parents. Instead, their claim rested on the shared condition of deafness. In her address to the 1915 NAD convention Alice T. Terry made her claim, "Let me speak now of our younger generation— our thousands of little deaf children throughout the United States...No one understands them better, no one loves them better than we do."[24]

Only the Deaf, Terry asserted, could know the Deaf. These sentiments were expressed in a less personal way in one of the resolutions of the 1923 NAD convention which reads as follows:

WHEREAS, We believe that our practical experience in life after leaving school, in actual contact with the affairs of the world as bread-winners, qualifies us to speak with authority and confidence as to which method or methods best fits the deaf to overcome their handicap, and as representing the thousands of deaf men and women in this country, we ask the earnest attention of all unbiased people to the following declaration of principles:[25]

This is central: The Deaf claim to standing in the debate over the use of signed language in schools was, in large measure, based on their own experiences and what their experiences meant to the debate over the use of signed language. It was their life experiences, their insights into the value of signed language, and the difficulties that they had experienced with oral methods that made their opinions invaluable in any discussion over the linguistic future of these children. Who, after all, could better understand the importance of signed language in the lives of the Deaf than Deaf adults?

One of the principles that comprised this same resolution reads as follows:

WE BELIEVE that the moral, social, and religious welfare of the deaf is best promoted by the system of instruction which recognizes and makes judicious use of the cultural value of the language of conventional signs; that to fully enjoy the benefits of social, intellectual, and communal gatherings the sign language is essential.[26]

This type of argument can be found repeatedly expressed at various conventions of the NAD and in the writings of individual Deaf authors,[27] but another, perhaps more modern-sounding assertion has always been made in parallel with this same argument, namely, for the Deaf, signed language is a human right. To deny a Deaf child signed language, this argument goes, is to deprive them of a right as basic as the right to free expression, the right to freedom of worship, and the right to free association, because according to many Deaf, signed language enabled all of these activities. A strict reliance on speech, according to this view, made such activities difficult or impossible.

Their ideas were not new. T. H. Gallaudet and many of his contemporaries could not have been surer of the right of the Deaf to learn signed language, but attitudes had changed following the Civil War. The increasingly paternalistic attitudes expressed toward the Deaf by hearing individuals on all sides of the signed language issue during the late nineteenth century meant that discussions about the use of signed language in the education of the Deaf often transpired without meaningful input from any Deaf organization or individual. This was as true of the manualists as it was the oralists. During a century of heated manualist versus oralist debate on how to serve the best interests of the Deaf, there were few manualists and fewer oralists who deigned to ask the Deaf themselves what their insights might be. Deaf writers, however, never stopped arguing that signed language for Deaf children was a human right and a necessary skill.

One of the most affecting articles, written by an anonymous "semideaf" author and entitled "The Sign Language and the Human Right to Expression,"[28] argues that the Deaf have a right to an expressive, pleasurable, and unrestrained form of communication and that only signed language suffices in this regard. Fingerspelling, while precise, is inexpressive, and speech reading is inexpressive, difficult to learn, and prone to error. Communication, she argues, is about more than the exchange of facts. "[T]he deaf-mute has a right to some kind of language whose chief power and charm for him shall be in expression," and she goes on to enumerate many ways that, with respect to the Deaf, signed language enriches the interior and exterior life of the user. In closing she asserts,

> Free, ardent, easily understood expression is a necessary form of speech for both speaker and audience... No other language but the sign language can ever so influence a deaf audience. It is their language; it appeals to them with force because they love it.[29]

In this view, there is no alternative to signed language, and Deaf children have an inalienable right to learn it and use it.

None of these arguments had any discernable effect on the situation in which Deaf children found themselves. For 100 years, many thousands of Deaf children were systematically denied the opportunity to learn to sign. They were punished if they tried to sign, and they found themselves linguistically isolated if they did not make the attempt. The situation was bleak. Opposition to the oralist methods among the Deaf was nearly universal.[30] Lack of enthusiasm for a strict oral education was expressed even by those who were educated according to an exclusively oralist philosophy. Oralist philosophy and methods, nevertheless, prevailed for generations.

The central facts regarding Deaf attempts to influence the education of Deaf children during this time are brutally simple: The Deaf constituted a linguistic group but not an ethnic group, and, in particular, most Deaf children were not the offspring of Deaf parents. Unlike the many immigrant groups that established schools where their children could be educated in the language and culture of the parents, the Deaf had, during the first half of the nineteenth century, established schools where the children of other parents could be educated in the language and culture of a group to which the parents did not usually belong. Alice Terry was right: Deaf children and Deaf adults shared a strong bond, but it was not a legal bond. Deaf adults had no legal standing in the debate over the education of Deaf children. The insights and experiences of Deaf adults were ignored by all parties directly employed in the education industry.

Neither was the NAD effective in communicating with the parents of Deaf children. Most hearing parents of a Deaf child were then, as they are today, completely unprepared for the discovery that their child could not hear. Although they could seek advice, they were unprepared to assess its value. Unfamiliar with signed language, they were, in particular, unable to make an informed decision on competing claims about the nature of sign and the efficiency of speech and speech reading as a mode of communication for the Deaf. Signed language is, moreover, difficult enough for most hearing parents to learn that most found neither the time nor the energy to learn the language prior to making a decision about its value to their children, and no hearing person can ever truly appreciate the difficulties involved in speech and speech reading for the Deaf. Nor were the absence of prior knowledge about signed language and the limitations of speech and speech reading the only impediments faced by these parents as they sought, in good conscience, to choose the best available method for educating their children.

Knowledge of the history of the Deaf as a social class was largely restricted to the Deaf and a small number of hearing persons, most of whom were engaged in the education of the Deaf. Articulate, creative Deaf individuals would have been unknown to most hearing parents of Deaf children during the time of the oral versus manual debate. Popular images of the Deaf, when they could be found, were often negative—until the 1967 performance by the National Theatre of the Deaf on network television, the portrayal of the Deaf and their language by the mass media was generally unrepresentative of the perceptions, values, and experiences of most American Deaf—and, as has often been noted,[31] oralists were poor sources of information about Deaf culture, in part, because they had no interest in the history of the Deaf. Indeed, many oralists hoped to eliminate the Deaf as a social class. Nor did the oralists evince any interest in individual Deaf adults. In particular, they showed little interest in their own graduates. They did not, for example, hire any Deaf to work at their schools. In the end, they treated deafness as if it were a childhood condition. Howsoever well intentioned, many parents made the most crucial decisions about their children's language and education based on fear, grossly incomplete information, and a general lack of familiarity with the ideas and opinions of successful (however one might define that term) Deaf adults.

Bereft of knowledge of the Deaf and their language, hearing parents were not only susceptible to disparaging descriptions of Deaf language and culture, but also to claims that their children could be taught to deduce the content of speech from the motions of the face and lips and that, deprived of knowledge of the sound of their own voices, their children could be taught to articulate anything more than the simplest of sounds. Parents' Associations, according to the resolutions on the education of the Deaf passed at the 1926 NAD Convention, exerted "a large influence in the choice of methods of instruction, often to the detriment of their own children." Moreover, some of the most prominent hearing individuals in the United States were strong supporters of an educational environment that prohibited the use—and, where possible, the knowledge—of signed language. In addition to Bell, Grace Anna Goodhue Coolidge, wife of President Calvin Coolidge, had been a teacher at Clarke School, the most prominent of the oral institutions, and she remained an advocate of oral education. Thomas Edison and Andrew Carnegie contributed money and lent their names to organizations that promoted the teaching of speech to the Deaf. It was in this environment that the hearing parents of Deaf children had to choose the best available school for their children.

In response, the Deaf sought an alternative mechanism by which decisions could be made about the education of Deaf children—and at the 1926 convention, the NAD even passed a resolution that read, in part, "while the wishes of parents should be given careful consideration, the choice of methods of instruction should be left to experienced educators"[32]—but there was nothing they could do to implement such an intrusive policy.

The Deaf knew from their own experience that signed language was expressive and empowering. They knew that signed language enabled them to take part in conventions, religious services, and informal multiparty conversations, and they knew, too, that speech and speech reading techniques, even if they could have worked with the effectiveness that their practitioners claimed, could never enable one so trained to take part in these larger communal activities, and they knew from their own experience that oral techniques were often impossible for the pre-lingually Deaf to master. Far from enabling the Deaf to participate fully in the larger society, oralist techniques isolated those who relied on them. None of these insights affected the educational environment of Deaf children.

By the early years of the twentieth century, adult Deaf had been disenfranchised from most of the country's Deaf education institutions, and, in particular, from some of the very institutions where they had obtained their educations. Deaf teachers had been barred from working at oral schools since the inception of those schools, and most of the schools that continued to permit signed language had, during this time, changed to a policy that largely limited Deaf instructors to vocational courses. Not surprisingly the percentage of Deaf instructors at schools for the Deaf also decreased: In the years immediately following the Civil War, Deaf instructors constituted about 40 percent of the faculty. By 1920, they constituted only about 15 percent.[33] Furthermore, hearing educators—even those who were skilled in signed language—had come to accept many of the assertions of the oralists. Edward Miner Gallaudet, president of Gallaudet College and son of T.H. Gallaudet, expressed the belief that signed language should be used "as little as possible" in the education of the Deaf.[34] He was also involved in instituting a policy that banned the Deaf from Gallaudet College's own teacher training program, a ban that lasted 50 years. Deprived of a mechanism through which they could express their strongly felt beliefs, the Deaf failed to affect the decisions of the majority of parents of Deaf children, nor did they affect the policies of the institutions involved in the education of those children.

Bereft of influence, the Deaf could only watch what happened to the language in which they took such pride. At oral schools, signed language was sometimes furtively transmitted between students. At many combined schools, sign was often relegated to industrial classes or the playground. The attitude once found at Hartford, where Clerc would regularly meet with faculty to instruct them in "correct" and expressive signing, when all teachers were expected to become experts in a "noble" language, was largely a thing of the past. Instead, knowledge of sign was often conveyed surreptitiously between students or between students on the one hand and faculty and staff on the other. The Deaf children of Deaf parents could, not surprisingly, contribute more to the preservation of the language than their peers, but the linguistic sensibilities of children, irrespective of their background, are a thin reed upon which to rest one's hopes for the transmission of the subtleties and eloquence that one finds in any language, including a language of signs.

For decades, conditions in most schools for the Deaf for the transmission of this highly evolved language were poor. From the point of view of adult Deaf, then, the future of their language seemed bleak. They worried that the language of conventional signs, as it was then called, would soon become extinct. Out of this perception came a remarkable and creative plan to preserve signed language as they knew it for future generations.

In the early years of the twentieth century, the NAD began a project to record on film a number of individuals that it identified as exceptional signers. These performances, it hoped, would preserve for future generations what it believed was best about signed language. Film technology had advanced just enough to make the project practicable, and the possible demise of the articulate classical signed language that it so valued gave the project urgency. The collection of these performances, now called the Veditz Collection after George W. Veditz, president of the NAD from 1904 until 1910, is a remarkable historical record.

The first film, made in 1910, entitled *The Lorna Doone Country of Devonshire, England,* shows Edward Miner Gallaudet, son of T. H. Gallaudet and president of Gallaudet College, describing a visit to England. The last films were made in 1920. The entire collection consists of 16 brief performances. No film exceeds ten minutes in length, and the varied subjects include humorous performances, a signed rendition of the Gettysburg Address, and a recounting of the discovery of chloroform.

Of particular interest is the 1913 film by John Burton Hotchkiss, a professor of English, rhetoric, and history at Gallaudet College, and a renowned signed language orator. Hotchkiss was 68 years old when he made his brief film. A small wiry man with an opulent, carefully trimmed beard and an effulgent moustache, he dressed formally for the occasion: an elegant double-breasted jacket and a stiff white shirt coupled with a white tie. Hotchkiss clearly understood the importance of his task, but it does not appear to have weighed on him. He looks relaxed and confident. His presentation is both beautiful and un-self-consciously theatrical.

Hotchkiss was a graduate of the Hartford institution. He was also one of the first graduates of the National Deaf-Mute College—now Gallaudet University. During Hotchkiss's time at the Hartford school, the faculty consisted largely of scholars who kept themselves and their pupils busy mastering a signed language that they often described as "beautiful" and "elegant," and from an early age Hotchkiss absorbed both the lessons and the aspirations of his teachers. As a young man he joined a debating society where the topics of the day—"Resolved: It would be better to colonize the freed slaves in Mexico than to return them to their native country"—were presented in signed language. The debating society was just the beginning. Throughout his life his contemporaries recognized Hotchkiss as a skilled signed language orator, and he was repeatedly called upon to make important public presentations. In the making of this film Hotchkiss was passing the torch—not to the next generation—but to those who lived at some undetermined later time, when attitudes toward signed language would be less hostile, a time when there would be renewed curiosity about what constitutes "good" signed language.

Hotchkiss's *Memories of Old Hartford* is a beautiful work. He stands alone against a dark, plain background. He begins with a bow to an off-camera audience, who, he establishes right at the outset, are Deaf. He signs in a manner that has since largely fallen out of favor: He produces his signs with expansive, fluid, often openhanded movements; his gestures begin at his shoulders and move in great sweeping arcs; he does not depend on any lip movements to convey his ideas. In fact, his mouth is completely hidden behind his moustache and beard. It is a style that is largely foreign to younger Deaf Americans of any race and to virtually all white Deaf Americans alive today. They have since adopted a smaller, more angular version of American Sign Language, in which signs tend to begin at the elbows rather than the shoulders and are marked by shorter, quicker movements, and today, simultaneously with the production of manual signs, the signer sometimes also voicelessly pronounces an English language word. This newer version of American Sign Language provides a sharp contrast to the style of Hotchkiss and his contemporaries.

Remarkably, Hotchkiss's manner of signing has not disappeared entirely. It is still practiced, for example, by many of the now-aging African-American graduates of the former Texas Blind, Deaf and Orphan School (BDO), originally known as The Texas Institute for the Deaf and Dumb and Blind Colored Youth, a school that existed from 1887 until it was merged with the previously all-white Texas School for the Deaf in 1966. (See Chapter 5.) BDO alumni also tend to sign expansively, using larger, more sweeping gestures that begin at the shoulders and flow through open hands. Unlike most of their white contemporaries, but in a manner strongly reminiscent of Hotchkiss and other signers in the Veditz Collection, these former BDO students mouth no words when they sign, preferring to use facial expressions that are completely decoupled from the spoken word.

The resemblance between Hotchkiss and this group of signers is particularly striking when they are observed in more formal situations at which time the former BDO students often stand to sign, and their signs flow with a rhythm and in a manner that is remarkably similar to that of Hotchkiss.

(It is worth noting that The Texas Institute for the Deaf and Dumb and Blind Colored Youth was established in Austin, Texas, in 1887 and that the first teachers were Deaf. Furthermore, oralists, although they claimed to be interested in all Deaf, evinced little interest in African-American youth, and so the students at this Austin school were largely spared the oralists' attempts to eliminate sign. Consequently, signed language flourished continuously at the Institute, largely through a policy of benign neglect, until it was closed in the 1960s. The author knows of no formal research into the similarities described here—nor is this the place to undertake such a study—but he has spent thousands of hours signing with former students of the BDO and would be remiss if he did not at least mention the remarkable resemblance. Former BDO students also evince the same pride in their formal signed language that Hotchkiss shows in his.)

Hotchkiss's brief presentation is the closest that the modern viewer can get to seeing Clerc himself sign. The movie is essentially Hotchkiss's memories of Laurent Clerc. Hotchkiss was one of the very few Deaf to have known Clerc and to have lived long enough to have made a movie about the experience. He was not, however, a student of Clerc's. By the time Hotchkiss arrived in Hartford, Clerc had retired from teaching. Gone but not forgotten, Clerc lived in what Hotchkiss describes in the film as a beautiful house not far from campus. Despite Clerc's retirement, Hotchkiss describes how groups of students often made the trek from the campus to the old man's house to "see, meet, and talk." Clerc apparently greeted them warmly.

Memories of Old Hartford is largely a tale of childhood memories. Hotchkiss does not describe Clerc as a fellow educator and a scholar with a peculiar gift for learning languages. Instead, he emphasizes his visual impressions of a dapper elderly man who still showed traces of youthful vigor. We learn little of Clerc the intellectual. Instead, Hotchkiss describes Clerc's coat (double-breasted), his cane (fancy), and his hat (stovepipe). More than half a century after their last meeting Hotchkiss is still describing his hero.

The quality of the films in the Veditz Collection is not especially good. They were victims of their own success. Hotchkiss's movie and those of several others in the series proved to be very popular with Deaf audiences. The films were loaned out to Deaf organizations and shown at social gatherings around the country for many decades before fading in popularity. (The author saw a few at social gatherings as late as the early 1980s.) Despite the intent of the makers, these films were long perceived primarily as entertainment. In recent years, however, the Hotchkiss film and others have been transferred to more modern media and *Memories of Old Hartford* has undergone something of a revival. Times have changed. American Sign Language has again become an accepted part of American and Canadian culture. Hotchkiss's movie is studied in schools and universities for its content and as an example of classical nineteenth century signed language. Hotchkiss has finally found his audience.

Race, Deafness, and American Sign Language

We secured the services of Prof. Julius Garrett, a deaf mute, who had been recommended by the principal of the North Carolina institute, and placed him in charge of the deaf mutes.
—Report of the Superintendent, Institute for the Deaf and Dumb and Blind
Colored Youth, for the school year 1887–1888

"The Deaf community" is a phrase used by the Deaf, by hearing members of Deaf households, by interpreters, social workers, politicians, librarians, students of signed languages, and others who, for one reason or another, have regular contact with Deaf individuals. It is a phrase that rolls off the hands as easily as it rolls off the tongue. For some, it is a highly emotive term. Some of these individuals fiercely declare their allegiance to the Deaf community, and their self-image is tightly bound to their ideas about the existence and composition of this community. The Deaf community prospers if and only if they prosper. For others, the Deaf community represents something to which they stand in opposition, even disdain. Included in this group are some hearing-impaired adults who, as Alexander Graham Bell did, regard the Deaf community as a linguistic ghetto, shut off from the larger world and populated by inward-looking individuals united by a common disability; a "deaf variety of the human race" is a descriptive phrase used by Helen Keller as well as by Alexander Graham Bell.

The Deaf community is, however, a fiction. There has never been one Deaf community. Since American Deaf were first established as a social class during the early years of the nineteenth century in Hartford, Connecticut, there have

Students from what was then called the Texas Deaf, Dumb, and Blind Institute for Colored Youths, ca. 1935. Thousands of students attended the Institute and its successor, the Texas Blind, Deaf, and Orphan School. They created a unique linguistic community. Courtesy Betty Henderson and Archie L. Henderson.

always been at least two groups of Deaf, one African-American and the other "community" consisting of everyone else.

While race-based public policies long affected all African-Americans—more or less, depending on where one lived—for Deaf African-Americans, the effects were particularly profound because these Americans were also excluded, systematically and mercilessly, from those educational, economic, and social institutions that were established by white hearing and white Deaf Americans. The National Association of the Deaf (NAD), the National Fraternal Society of the Deaf, and Gallaudet College all excluded African-Americans until the latter half of the twentieth century. These organizations showed no interest in the struggles of African-American Deaf even when those struggles were identical with their own. In fact, they spurned African-Americans who expressed interest in joining their institutions. The NAD, an organization of particular interest to this history, originally required only that members be Deaf American citizens, but that changed in 1926 when the organization's bylaws were amended to restrict membership based on race.

(Because there is a great deal of uncertainty about the year, the place, and the circumstances under which the NAD changed its bylaws and expelled nonwhite members,[1] we digress slightly to detail what the NAD's records reveal: On the first day of business of the 1926 convention, an NAD organizer from Virginia, R. A. Bass, asserted that it would have been much easier to increase the number of NAD life members from his home state in the years since the 1923 convention if "colored people had been barred from membership in the N. A. D."[2] On the last day of business Mr. W. H. Schaub of Missouri moved that the bylaws be amended to read that membership be restricted to white Deaf only. His motion passed without a dissenting vote. It was followed by a motion by a member from Illinois to refund all past dues and fees to "those members who are not 'white,'" and this motion passed as well.[3] While there is a great deal of text in the convention proceedings about proxy voting and the oral versus manual debate, there is virtually no discussion on this change to the bylaws—nothing to indicate why these motions were introduced at this particular convention nor why they were passed without a single dissent from the membership.)

The results of racial discrimination among the Deaf have been as long lasting as they have been pernicious. Even after race-based policies were changed to allow for the admission of African-Americans to historically whites-only institutions, African-Americans remained underrepresented in the leadership as well as in the membership. (Today these institutions still claim—as they have always un-self-consciously claimed—to represent the Deaf community.) The effects of segregation also remain visible in the signed language used by many Deaf

African-Americans and in the institutions that they have founded to meet their needs.

In what follows, it is important to keep in mind that the signed language used by African-American Deaf is American Sign Language. It shares many of the same grammatical conventions and many of the same signs that one finds in American Sign Language as it is used outside the community of African-American Deaf. This is to be expected. The signed language of African-American Deaf can also be traced back to that introduced by Laurent Clerc in Hartford in 1817. Nor can one point to a particular linguistic idiosyncrasy that is unique to the signed language of African-Americans—at least not in the sense that there exists a phrase or grammatical convention that is shared by all African-American Deaf and no others. In fact, the American Sign Language used by African-Americans is probably more heterogeneous than what one finds among most groups of American Sign Language users. Three factors, in particular, have served to increase the variability of American Sign Language among African-American Deaf.

First, many older African-American Deaf were educated in the South at segregated residential schools for the Deaf. The students at these schools were linguistically as well as physically isolated from their white contemporaries. Each group was subject to its own unique linguistic pressures, and for many decades the signed languages of the two groups developed and diverged accordingly. When federal law finally brought the era of racially segregated residential schools for the Deaf to an end—and both school systems were heavily utilized at the time—the differences in the signed languages of the two groups was quite striking.

Second, variation can also be correlated with geography. The particular American Sign Language variant that one uses depends very much on the location of the school one attended. The American Sign Language used by African-American Deaf who attended the segregated school that was located in Austin, Texas, is, for example, different from that used by African-American students who, during the same time period, attended Hartford's American School for the Deaf.

Third, substantial temporal variation also exists in American Sign Language as it is used by African-Americans. The signs of young African-Americans are quite different from those used by older African-American Deaf. The existence of some temporal variation in any language, signed or spoken, is hardly surprising, but the variation among African-Americans is particularly pronounced. Keep in mind that most Deaf children learn their first language, American Sign Language, not at home but in the schools they attend. When the racially separate residential schools were merged, the teachers of each school were not generally treated equally. In Texas, for example, where the faculty at the Texas School for the Deaf (TSD) was white and the faculty of the Blind, Deaf, and Orphan School was entirely African-American, the African-American teachers were not retained at an equal rate when the schools merged. Moreover, most of the African-American faculty who were retained in the new, merged school left within a year or two. According to one white teacher employed at the school at the time, the African-American teachers left in the face of harassment by the white students. As a result, the signed language used at the merged school was more similar to that used at the white school than at the African-American school, a fact that was reflected in the American Sign Language variant acquired by succeeding classes of students, white and African-American.

It is not the purpose of this chapter to provide a broad historical description of American educational policies as they have affected the signed language of African-American Deaf. The topic is too broad; there is too much variation, and the amount of space that can be devoted to this topic is here far too limited. Furthermore, some of the required information about the topic is difficult, perhaps impossible, to acquire. With the end of enforced segregation, what records on African-American schools for the Deaf that had been kept were often lost or destroyed. Until recently, few outside the alumni of these schools recognized the importance of these institutions to the lives and culture of a significant segment of American Deaf. Fewer still were willing to research the education of African-American Deaf during the era of American apartheid. While this is changing, important information is by now probably irretrievably lost. Rather than a broad picture of the education of African-American Deaf, we confine our attention to the state of Texas, which, in 1887, opened the Texas Institute for the Deaf and Dumb and Blind Colored Youth.

William H. Holland and His School

From its beginning, the Institute was different from the American schools for the Deaf described in previous chapters of this book. The initial motivation for founding the Hartford school and the Clarke school, for example, was to address the educational needs of the founders' children. In the case of the Hartford school, Mason Cogswell sought to establish a school where his daughter Alice could be educated. In the case of the Clarke School, the Hubbards decided to found the first oral school in North America for their daughter, Mabel. Gardiner Greene Hubbard, Mabel's father, even served as the first principal. By contrast, the Institute for the Deaf and Dumb and Blind Colored Youth grew out of the work of William H. Holland (1841–1907), a humanitarian whose motivations seem to have arisen out of a general concern for the welfare of the children of Texas.

Holland was born a slave in Marshall, Texas. He and his two brothers, James and Milton, may have been the sons of Captain Bird Holland, who bought their freedom in the late 1850s and brought them to Ohio. Once in Ohio, William and Milton attended the Albany Enterprise Academy, a school that was owned and operated by African-Americans. William Holland later attended Oberlin College's Preparatory Department from 1867–1868 and again from 1869–1870. He followed a general course of study called "English Studies," which was designed to prepare students for college or to work as teachers in "common schools." Latin, Greek, and arithmetic were among the offerings. Between his time at the Albany Academy and his time at Oberlin, Holland fought in the Civil War, as did his brother Milton.

When Holland left Oberlin, he returned to his native Texas. Initially, he earned a living as a teacher in the Austin schools and in various county schools. Later he worked in the Austin post office for several years. In 1876 he was elected to the House of the Texas State Legislature. He was very active in politics and attended the Republican National Convention in 1876 and again in 1880. As a representative, he introduced legislation that led to the founding of the Institute as well as Prairie View Normal College, now Prairie View A&M University—Prairie View, which is still thriving, was originally an institution of higher learning for African-American citizens of Texas—and Holland also founded a charitable institution called Friend in Need that gave money to African-Americans who were unable to meet educational expenses.

Despite his accomplishments and his long tenure as principal of the Institute, little is known of Holland's views on signed language and the education of the Deaf. He seems to have left little behind. Unlike Gallaudet and his colleagues, who loved to write about educational philosophy and the nature of signed language—indeed, they established their own journal to facilitate publication—Holland's thoughts on these subjects must be deduced from the superintendent's reports that he filed yearly during his tenure at the Institute. (For the first few decades of its existence, an annual report on the condition of the Institute was submitted to the governor by the board of trustees and the superintendent. The report consisted of separate statements, one by the trustees, one by the superintendent, and, depending on the year, statements by the school's physician and oculist. Usually, the longest report was the superintendent's.)

Holland served as superintendent for two periods, 1887–1897 and 1904–1907. The reports filed during his ten-year term yield a picture of a man ferociously devoted to the success of the school and its students, but hampered by lack of support from the state. Prior to opening the school, Holland had no data on the size of the population he wished to serve. Consequently, he began his search for students by advertising in what he described in his first report as "the leading colored papers." Next, at his own expense, he visited "eight or nine" Texas counties with large African-American populations "and by different methods succeeded in advertising the existence of this institution, and making known to the people the great benefits which could result from it."[4] In this way, Holland found a "sufficient" number of students to open the school. By April 1888 the school had an enrollment of 31, of which 23 were Deaf and 8 blind. Enrollment rapidly increased. By 1890, for example, the roster included 68 students, of whom 38 were Deaf and the remainder blind.[5]

Holland began the first year at the Institute with one teacher for the blind and one teacher for the Deaf. The teacher for the Deaf students, Julius Garrett, was himself Deaf. Before the end of the year Holland had hired a second teacher, Amanda A. Johnson. Both Johnson and Garrett were hired out of the North Carolina Institute for African American Deaf. This, in fact, set a racial pattern that persisted throughout the history of the school: Almost all employees, from the superintendent down, were African-American—the only exceptions were medical staff.

In the beginning, Holland and his staff were concerned with the most basic instruction. Foremost among these lessons were discipline and "mental and moral culture." By the end of the first year, and in addition to whatever lessons in mental and moral culture Holland and the teachers managed to inculcate, the Deaf students had, apparently, also become fluent in signed language, which must have been the signed language of their North Carolina teachers. They had made, according to Holland, good progress in reading and writing, and they continued to evince enthusiasm for their studies. Holland clearly expected his students to do well academically, and, in so far as he was able, he provided them with the opportunities to do so. Over the course of his first ten-year term at the Institute, Holland worked hard to ensure that his students received the benefits of a liberal education.

Holland also recognized that a liberal education was not enough. He wanted all students to receive what was then called "industrial training," by which he meant a skilled trade. Keep in mind that the Institute provided a terminal degree. Academically, there was nowhere else to go. Many colleges did not accept African-American applicants, and the remainder made no accommodations for the Deaf. (Helen Keller's experience at Radcliff College in the early years of the twentieth century was possible, in part, because she was able to furnish her own full-time interpreter/tutor. Most students, howsoever deserving, did not have sufficient resources to do this, and, in any case, many colleges would not have considered making the necessary accommodations.) As for Gallaudet College, it did not accept an African-American applicant until well after World War II. Howard University, which did not make accommodations for the Deaf, was sometimes suggested by the Gallaudet administration to aspiring African-American applicants as an alternative.

For these reasons, Holland saw vocational education as his students' best hope for productive and prosperous lives. In his first report, he estimates that there were about 450,000 African-Americans in Texas, but only about 25 professional tailors or dressmakers among them. The situation, he asserts, was similar for skilled carpenters, blacksmiths, shoemakers, and other trades. While this presented a serious problem in terms of hiring skilled vocational teachers, it could also be viewed as an opportunity: If he could procure equipment, hire teachers, and establish classes, his Deaf male students would be well positioned to earn their wages as *skilled* craftsmen. While his goals for the Deaf girls were more modest in the sense that he did not seek to create a large variety of vocational courses for the girls, he originally envisioned hiring a seamstress and establishing a sewing program.

Holland encountered a great deal of difficulty in implementing his plans. By the 1889–1890 school year, he had found a seamstress to teach the girls sewing as well as "crochet, and fancy needlework" and a shoemaker and a mechanic to teach the boys their respective trades. Faculty turnover was high, however—it is not clear why—and the mechanic stayed only a year or two. He was not replaced. Meanwhile enrollment increased to 86. The state allocated funds to construct new facilities to house and educate the ever-increasing number of students, but enrollment always remained far ahead of the accommodations. By 1892, it was so crowded that there was no place on campus large enough to house an assembly of either the entire Deaf or the entire blind class. The school had managed to retain a seamstress and shoemaker, but there were no other vocational teachers and no space for additional vocational classes. For years, therefore, boys learned the trade of shoemaking or they learned no trade at all; the girls were similarly restricted to sewing.

Julius Garrett, the original instructor for the Deaf, left after the first year, but Amanda Johnson remained. By 1892 the advanced Deaf class was being taught by H.L. Johns, a "semimute," a not uncommon term at the time meaning someone who is hard-of-hearing. Holland established a kindergarten class. In the 1893 report, the school had approximately 100 students, double its capacity, and Holland suspended all efforts to increase enrollment. Students were housed in the chapel and in other areas that were less safe, and Holland describes how some of the older blind boys were sleeping in an unventilated room next to a coal furnace.

In 1894, blocked from expanding the vocational program due to lack of space and a scarcity of instructors, Holland instituted philosophical societies that met on Friday nights. One society, the Silentia Society, was open to Deaf students, the other, the Philosophian Society, was open to the blind. Silentia Society meetings included signed song performances, debates, and storytelling. Philosophian Society meetings consisted of musical performances, both instrumental and vocal, original essays, orations, and debates. The meetings were open to the public.

With respect to the instructional methods used to teach the Deaf, Holland remarks briefly in the 1894 report that the Deaf students were educated using the combined method (see Chapter 4), a popular educational philosophy at the time that relied on signed language and on oral methods. In this report, he mentions that he was having difficulty finding a qualified instructor to teach speech reading. At the time the Deaf education department had an enrollment of 52, and in addition to studying "the manual alphabet and sign language" the course of study for the Deaf included reading, writing, language, history, composition, number, arithmetic, geography, and physiology.

One of the characteristics that distinguishes Holland from so many of his Texas contemporaries was his attitudes about deafness and blindness and race. He saw his charges as students with a future. In more than one place in the 1894 report, Holland argued that he was the superintendent of a school, an educational institution, *not* an asylum. In fact, many of his reports closed with a section called "General Information," which included a numbered list of facts about the Institute. Number 1 was the following statement: "This is a state school, and not an asylum." It was an important distinction since the latter term conveyed the impression that the students (or inmates as they would be called almost as soon as Holland left his position at the Institute) were helpless wards of the state. By contrast, the word "students" conveyed the idea that they attended the Institute to obtain an education, that graduation rather than custodial care was the goal, and that upon graduation they would be ready to earn their livelihoods as educated people.

During his ten-year term, in report after report, Holland repeatedly and strenuously made the case that the school needed a large expansion to accommodate not just the physical but the educational needs of the students. The state was slow to respond—not surprising since his pleas to the Texas State Legislature occurred near the end of Reconstruction—but at least during this period it is clear that he had the respect and tacit support of the white school trustees. Trustee reports were invariably brief and complementary of the superintendent. While they did not strenuously defend Holland's proposals, they did not oppose them. Instead, they generally had a supportive sentence or two or else they commended the governor's attention to particular proposals in the superintendent's report. But times were changing. After two decades of African-American representation in the Texas State Legislature, the state was returning to a period of all-white rule.

Holland was replaced in 1897—the 1897 report, if it was filed at all, is not in the archives—and there is no additional information about the circumstances under which he left. All that is known for certain is that Holland was replaced by Samuel J. Jenkins. The 1898 report is also of little help because it contains no information on the school. Instead, it consists of a simple tribute to a trustee who had recently died. By 1899, however, everything had changed, as is apparent from the 1899 trustees' report. It is much longer than any previous report and repeatedly emphasizes how harmonious the Institute is under Jenkins, how free from extravagance his administration is, and how carefully Jenkins watches over the moral purity of his students. They write, "Possessed as he is of a keen insight into the characteristics of his people, and impressed with their needs and a great desire to better their condition, we believe Superintendent Jenkins can do much to aid his State in its work of educating the heads and hands of its unfortunate charges." From this point forward, the reports of the trustees are longer and filled with explicit and condescending references to race.

For his part, Jenkins also wasted little time in implementing a very new agenda. He repeatedly describes his charges as "inmates" and as "almost helpless wards of the State," terms Holland never used. Jenkins writes glowingly of a new mess hall and dormitory, facilities necessary to house the inmates, and he asks for a new laundry, but he does not raise Holland's annual plea for more instructional space. In fact, one would not even know from Jenkins's report that there was a shortage of instructional space although no new classrooms had been added. In his 1899 report Jenkins wrote, "That the general work of the institution for the year has been satisfactory, in a marked degree, is a source of much gratification. All features of the work have been so operated as to lend to the fulfillment of the purposes of the institution." Contrast this with the last report that Holland wrote before he was replaced:

[A]mong the many questions asked by visitors, the one most frequently asked is: "What do you teach the pupils that will enable them to earn their own livelihood when they leave school?" For all answer we point to the shoeshop, and show how the deaf are taught to make a living. This is the only trade taught; the blind receive no industrial training whatever. I do not think the State designs to deprive any of its unfortunate youth of the chance to earn a living; but the failure to teach the trades results from a lack of room and conveniences for that purpose. The additional building asked for, and for which I ask an appropriation of $35,000, could be made to furnish all the room required.

Jenkins instituted a permanent change in institutional goals. In his 1901 report, he begins to refer to the Institute by a name of his own choosing, the Deaf, Dumb, and Blind Asylum for Colored Youths of Texas. As previously mentioned, Holland never used the term asylum and in one report he even criticizes legislators who use the term in their debates. All that changed with his departure, and lest there be any doubt about the Institute's new direction, at the 1902 graduation ceremony, the main speech, delivered by J. W. McKinney, an African-American and Grand Master of the Masonic Lodge of Texas, is reprinted in the 1902 report in its entirety. It is even described as an "intellectual treat." In his speech McKinney vigorously defends the post-Reconstruction status quo. For example, all-white juries are, for him, not a source of concern: "I have yet to see a single civil case in court where a black man has received injustice at the hands of a white jury," he says, and he goes on to defend the "loving treatment" of slaves by the white slaveholders of the South. "In the old days of slavery," he allows, "there were many individual cases of cruelty and oppression. But it was the exception and not the rule...And today, my friends, the same blood and the same white people live in the South as in the old days when they won the love and devotion of our race." It makes for fairly uncomfortable reading today, but it fit nicely into the institutional environment that Jenkins and the trustees were creating at the Institute.

Jenkins died in April 1904, and Holland was rehired. He remained superintendent until his death in 1907, but the battle to create a school as opposed to an asylum was already lost, something the trustees were anxious to make clear. In their 1904 report, written a few months after Holland was rehired, they published what was by far their longest report in the 17-year history of the Institute. They patronize Holland in a way that he had never been patronized in his earlier term as superintendent. The trustees describe him as having "an intelligence and character far above the average of his race" and in describing his abilities as the head of the Institute staff they write, "And this is his strong point, the work [Holland directs] is done by negroes with the thoroughness characteristic of the white man." Academic courses have, by this time, been largely abandoned. In fact, the trustees complain in their report that in previous years, by which they evidently mean Holland's first period of service as superintendent, the students had been taught Latin, algebra, and geometry, all of which they label a waste of time and money. Henceforth, the trustees assert, "only the elements of an education, such as reading, writing, arithmetic, English composition, geography and music, will be taught…and the other time will be given to industrial training." It is clear that for the first time in the history of the Institute, the trustees used their report to establish the parameters under which Holland must operate, and they are very specific. "We hope," they write, "to make the school strictly industrial, and in this undertaking the State is fortunate in having the service of Superintendent Holland, who has a keen appreciation of this character of education for these charges of the State *as well as for the entire colored race.*" (italics added)

In particular, the trustees describe a new industrial course for the Deaf girls, "cooking and housework." They describe the course in extremely positive terms. "This is a splendid move, for the Board has for some time realized the need of teaching this class of pupils domestic science in connection with the other industrial features. Heretofore the girls have only been taught needlework. This, we believe, will prove to them a much more certain livelihood; and there is nothing to hinder them, when properly taught the art of cooking and housekeeping, to serve in any family." Holland had believed that the sewing would make it possible for the women graduates to earn an independent living. The new class was simply to prepare the girls to work for white families.

And if the times had changed so, apparently, had Holland. His reports during his brief second term as superintendent are noticeably shorter and lacking in the advocacy and vision that he once displayed. There is no mention of philosophical societies or academic achievements. His 1906 report, devoid of information on academic activities, mentions instead that the students' brooms were being sold by stores in town. Compared to the reports he filed in his first term as superintendent, the later reports are disheartening to read. They would also set the standard for future superintendent's reports. As best as can be determined—available records are not quite complete—there is no further discussion of philosophical societies or literary departments, another topic of Holland's early reports, in any succeeding superintendent's report. In his 1908 report, superintendent H.S. Thompson, successor to V.S. Lane, who, for only a few months, served as Holland's immediate successor, devotes exactly one sentence of his two-page report to academics: "The teachers of the deaf department, besides teaching the deaf to hear and the dumb to talk both in good English and by means of the manual signs, taught a class (sic) the art of basketry and hammock making."

Henceforth, these were the central facts in the lives of the students of the Institute for the Deaf and Dumb and Blind Colored Youth: First, the Institute would offer only the most basic academic classes. It had, in fact, become a nonacademic institution. Second, even if the students acquired more academic skills on their own, there would be no college for graduates of the Institute, no matter how well they performed, and no matter how promising they were in ability. It is remarkable that by 1904 the trustees had created an institution where even the most modest of academic qualifications were not a necessary requirement for graduation. In the 1904 report they write, "Hereafter, the readiness of the pupils of the institution to graduate must be determined by whether or not they have learned a trade, or art, sufficiently well to earn their daily bread at it, and not whether or not they have completed so much Latin, algebra or geometry." Blind pupils, for example, were expected to train in the mattress and broom-making trades. In their 1904 report, the trustees expressed their support for the mattress and broom-making classes in these words, "An outfit of tools and tables for mattress-making can be obtained for about fifteen dollars. Tools and machinery for broom-making can be had for about one hundred and twenty-five dollars. So any enterprising colored boy can go back to his home county and raise at least enough money to begin a mattress business; and if he keeps to the industry he is taught at the institution, he can soon make enough out of this business to get his tools and machinery for broom-making." Holland, a former teacher, postal worker, legislator, a man who worked hard until the day he died, a man who made permanent and lasting contributions to the state of Texas and who fought to establish a state school—not an asylum—for the Deaf and blind, returned to the Institute to find his students' education cut short and his own educational vision thwarted.

Superintendents' reports eventually gave way to biannual reports on the Institute by the State Board of Control. Each of these reports consisted of a few paragraphs, one of which was usually a brief history and description of the school. Sometime between 1932 and 1934 a $5.00 per week support and maintenance fee was imposed on financially able parents, but it was never collected as all families were routinely classified as unable to pay. In 1934 the statement released by the State Board of Control contains an interesting one-sentence addition to the usual descriptions of mandatory industrial training at the school: "The instruction [at the Institute] is patterned after that at the State Schools for the Blind and the Deaf," by which was meant the state schools for the white blind and white Deaf children. The Board of Control statements and the occasional Catalogue and Announcements of the Texas Deaf and Dumb and Blind Institute for Colored Youths, as it was sometimes called, contain frustratingly little information about the school.

It is known that some distinguished African-Americans were drawn to work at the school. Maud Cuney-Hare (1874–1936), a musician and writer, taught music at the Institute for two years beginning in 1897. (Much of her work would, of course, have been with the blind, but some of her work would probably have been with the Deaf. Music classes for the Deaf were a staple at schools across the country for many years.) Cuney-Hare later settled in Boston and performed and lectured throughout the East. She also wrote for a number of music journals and for the *Christian Science Monitor*. Mattie B. Haywood White (1867–1951), an award-winning artist, taught art as well as knitting, embroidery, and rug making at the Institute for 40 years beginning in 1900. And perhaps most importantly from the Deaf students' point of view, Otis Massey, one of the first African-American students to graduate from Gallaudet College—he graduated in the early 1950s—was hired to teach at the Institute as well. In interviews with the author, former students say that Massey was a favorite, the only Deaf instructor on the faculty, a role model for the students, and the only faculty member during the time that he taught at the Institute who signed fluently.

Enrollment continued to increase at the Institute throughout its life, but a major change in its mission occurred in 1943 when the State Colored Orphans Home was closed, and the children were moved to the Institute. Originally founded as a private religious orphanage, the state took control in 1929. Under the State Board of Control, it was managed in a way that was similar to the Institute: All staff, from the superintendent down, except the part-time dentist and the physician, were African-American; the boys received training in a variety of industrial classes, and the girls received training in home economics. Because of the merger, a new institution was created, the Texas Blind, Deaf, and Orphan School, or as it is known among its alumni, the BDO.

As a general rule, the three groups that comprised the BDO, the blind, the Deaf, and the orphans, attended separate classes. Nevertheless, it is apparent from conversations with Deaf alumni that some believed that the presence of the orphans at the BDO was an important component of their education—that is to say, an important component of the culture of the BDO—something that distinguished their education from that of their white contemporaries in a way that was positive and permanent. What was significant to many of the Deaf alumni was that some of the orphans became skilled in signed language. As a consequence, Deaf students at the BDO were accustomed to signing with hearing children. This was an experience, some said, that widened their view of the world.[6]

The Deaf world, it is sometimes said, is a small world, and in so far as this statement is true, it could have been especially true of African-American Deaf, denied as they were of many of the opportunities that were available to their white Deaf contemporaries. But, because of the presence of the orphans, Deaf students had a number of hearing friends, skilled at communicating in signed language, who could serve as intermediaries between what are sometimes called the Deaf world and the hearing world. The orphans could serve as interpreters, of course, but more generally they served as bridges between the Deaf culture that flourished at the BDO and the surrounding non-Deaf culture. Depending on the year in question, very few if any teachers employed at the BDO knew American Sign Language. Consequently, the Deaf students were not just isolated from the outside world; they were, in many ways, isolated from most of what occurred in their classrooms at the BDO. After class, however, they had a broader circle of friends than many white Deaf students. Even today some of the Deaf alumni and some of the orphans of the BDO maintain the old social contacts. By contrast, the white students at the Texas School for the Deaf had few if any opportunities to form close, long-term friendships with hearing contemporaries skilled in signed language while they were growing up—something which has been pointed out to the author by more than one BDO alumnus.

It is, paradoxically, easier to learn about the BDO early in its history than it is to learn about the institution in its later years. Records are sparse. Much of what is described here was learned from Betty Henderson, a student at the BDO during the last years of the institution, and a member of a family with strong ties to the BDO—Henderson's sisters and father also attended the BDO—and the late Oliver Blaylock, a friend of the author's. Henderson has taken it upon herself to collect photographs and stories about the BDO and to maintain contacts among the alumni. Through her extensive network of friends she has collected numerous photographs of life at the BDO and many affecting black and white portraits of neatly dressed boys in suits and girls in immaculate dresses and white gloves preparing for graduation ceremonies in front of proud families at a school that no longer exists. She is also active in social functions involving BDO alumni. Today she works as a supervisor in the U.S. Postal Service, one of only a few Deaf individuals to be so employed. She has also served as national vice president of the National Black Deaf Advocates (NBDA) and as president of the Philadelphia chapter of this organization. (The NBDA is described at the end of this chapter.)

Whatever educational shortcomings the BDO had—and there were several, and they were significant—life in the years immediately preceding the closure of the BDO were not unpleasant for the Deaf students who lived there. There were a few on-campus clubs that the Deaf students enjoyed—the girl scouts and a theatrical club, for example—and two basketball teams, one for the boys and one for the girls. Even today, the boy's basketball team remains a source of pride among alumni for its winning record. For the most part, however, the students were responsible for their own entertainment. For younger students entertainment was relatively straightforward: When classes ended at 2:30 P.M., students filtered outside and resumed an apparently endless and unsupervised game of kickball. Older students, too, were responsible for their own entertainment, and, because students were generally confined to campus, the activities that they created for themselves were simple. In particular, there were no organized football or baseball teams. Nevertheless, most alumni look back with affection on their time at school.

BDO students were part of a linguistic community, a place where language became invisible and the members of the community could devote their attention to the content rather than the form of a conversation. For those students whose parents or siblings were also Deaf, this was one linguistic community of several. Henderson, for example, warmly recalls picnics and parties with the Ebony Club, a Houston, Texas-area club, founded by African-American Deaf during the days of enforced segregation. Both her parents belonged. Most students, however, had fewer options. Oliver Blaylock often recounted to the author how he spent his summers in Decatur, Texas, the only Deaf African-American child in the area. No one in his family signed. It would have been a lonely environment, but within walking distance of his home lived an elderly Native American couple, both of whom knew a little of the signed language used by tribes that once roamed the Great Plains. Visiting that couple as often as possible, he learned as much of their signed language as he could. It was a very important experience for him. Even as a middle-aged man, he was quite proud of his facility in the language, and he frequently encouraged the author to learn it so that one of his languages, the signed language of the tribes of the Great Plains, would not become extinct. While Blaylock's story is not entirely typical, it does demonstrate how isolated many BDO students were when they were away from school.

Finally, BDO students had little contact with the white Deaf students at the Texas School for the Deaf located several miles away. But time spent away from everyone else meant more time spent with each other, a situation fostered by the accommodations. The Deaf students at the BDO were housed according to sex and age. There were three different age groups, and the members of each group slept in bunk beds situated in large open common rooms. The dorm was four stories tall. The youngest students were assigned beds on the first floor; the middle students, the second floor, and the oldest students were assigned beds on the third floor. Staff slept on the fourth floor. There were no strangers at the BDO.

No serious linguistic analysis of the signed language used at the BDO or its predecessor, the Institute has, to the author's knowledge, ever been undertaken, and no such analysis will be undertaken here. Furthermore, there are few alumni of the Institute still living, and few, if any, movies were made of these individuals signing. Much of the necessary linguistic data is probably permanently lost. It is reasonable to suppose, however, that one can gain insight into the signed language used at the Institute by learning about the sign of the graduates of the BDO. Some characteristics are evident.

First, compared to their white contemporaries in Texas, signs produced by students who attended the BDO are broader in the sense that BDO alumni tend to produce signs where the pivot point is the shoulder. By contrast, their white contemporaries generally produce signs from the elbow, by which is meant that the upper arm remains more or less fixed. As a result, the signs produced by students who grew up at the BDO tend to be somewhat less angular than those produced by their contemporaries at the TSD. A further consequence of "signing from the shoulder" as opposed to "signing from the elbow" is that the signs produced by BDO students tend to be somewhat larger; that is, they use a larger signing space than their white contemporaries.

Second, many graduates of TSD tend to voicelessly pronounce certain important words simultaneously with the production of the signs that they associate with those words. This is much less common among BDO graduates, who, free from any perceived relations between signs and the spoken word, use their facial expressions in ways that depend not at all on lip reading.

Third, there are, naturally enough, some differences in vocabulary between the two groups.

The first two differences, the rounder, broader, less-angular nature of the signs of BDO graduates and the almost complete dissociation of signed movements from speech movements were not considered especially remarkable by the author until he watched the films in the Veditz Collection described in Chapter 4. The signed language used by these white, "master signers," chosen by the National Association of the Deaf to represent to future generations what they believed to be best about American Sign Language at the beginning of the twentieth century, is much more similar to that used by the graduates of the BDO than it is to the signed language used by today's white Deaf Americans. Signed language, as practiced by the graduates of the BDO, is, by the standards of the men and women in George W. Veditz's series of films, classical. And that, of course, is the irony: Deaf African-American students of the South were largely ignored by the white educators and educational theorists who tried to destroy American Sign Language. The oral versus signed language debate that affected so many white Deaf students for a century had little effect on the students of the Institute and the BDO. (Holland, aware of the debate, chose the combined method. Little awareness of the controversy is evident in later reports.)

Ignored by the white oralists, the students of the BDO largely escaped the consequences of the antisigned language policies that are visible in the signed language used by graduates of many other institutions. (BDO students, according to Henderson, could take speech lessons or, with a note from the parents, be permanently excused. Training in speech was not emphasized at the BDO the way that it was at so many white institutions.) American Sign Language flourished at the BDO for more than seven decades: Each new class of students learned their signed language from the older students. They had to learn from the older students because, as previously mentioned, most teachers were poor signers. Further isolated by the racist laws of the state of Texas, BDO students had little opportunity to see the effects of the antisign debate on the signed language of their white contemporaries. Freed from attempts to destroy their language, they passed it along unimpeded from generation to generation from the time it was introduced at the Institute by its first teachers of the Deaf, Julius Garrett and Amanda Johnson, both graduates of North Carolina's school for African-American Deaf. And while the details of how their sign might differ from their white contemporaries might be of little interest to most BDO alumni, the author has repeatedly noticed the great pleasure that former students of the BDO take in eloquent self-expression. At parties and in formal occasions, they will sometimes stand (rather than sit) and sign to each other in a self-conscious, almost theatrical way, each seeking to express himself or herself in a way that is graceful, transparent, and memorable. This, perhaps, is Holland's most lasting legacy among the Deaf.

As is by now apparent, the educational model originally envisioned by William Holland was never brought to fruition. Rather, the model imposed by Samuel Jenkins and later Boards of Trustees, a model based on vocational training and one that de-emphasized academic achievement, was retained throughout the life of the BDO just as it had been maintained throughout the life of the Institute for the Deaf and Dumb and Blind Colored Youth. Even art classes, normally a popular offering at schools for the Deaf, were not offered during the later years of the BDO. Instead, right to the end of the life of the institution, students' choices were limited to a small number of trades. In the last years of the BDO, for example, girls were taught typing, home economics, and cosmetology. Boys learned, among other trades, carpentry and how to press clothes using the industrial equipment found in the dry cleaning establishments of the time. Courses in upholstery were open to both sexes.

In 1965 the BDO closed and the process of integrating the previously all-white Texas School for the Deaf began. Desegregation occurred in stages, and by all accounts it was a difficult process for the faculty and students at the BDO. Because of a lack of emphasis on academic course work, most BDO students were ill prepared to attend the same academic classes as their white counterparts.

While academic work at TSD was not particularly rigorous when compared with most other white schools of its type, the amount of homework was, according to Henderson, much greater than what was given at the BDO, and the BDO students were not prepared. In addition, the reception students at the BDO received from the white faculty at TSD was sometimes hostile, and the reception given to the African-American teachers by the white students was also sometimes hostile. Within a few years of integration most of the former BDO teachers and many of the former students had left. Many of those students left without graduating.

In retrospect, the BDO and its predecessor, the Institute for the Deaf and Dumb and Blind Colored Youth, provided an environment where Deaf culture—or more precisely, *a* Deaf culture—could flourish. And it did flourish. Friendships formed and interests developed, and some former students, Betty Henderson is only one, went on to distinguish themselves in a variety of ways. The isolation imposed on African-American Deaf by the state and, more generally, by the white citizenry of Texas, fostered a unique and uniquely beautiful form of American Sign Language, more similar to the classical signed language of the previous century than that of the whites who regularly enjoyed Veditz's films, designed as they were to celebrate just this type of American Sign Language.

As mentioned previously, African-Americans were underrepresented in the NAD long after the NAD changed its bylaw restricting membership based on race. To address this situation, a new organization, the National Black Deaf Advocates (NBDA), was formed in Cleveland, Ohio, in 1982.[7] It performs a variety of functions for its membership, some practical, and some cultural. As the NAD did, the NBDA also has worked to document the history of important Deaf Americans, but in the case of the NBDA these Deaf individuals are also African-Americans. By way of example, the NBDA has installed a sculpture of Andrew Foster at Gallaudet University. Foster was born in Ensley, Alabama, and attended the Alabama School for Negro Deaf in Talladega, and the Detroit Institute of Commerce before enrolling at Gallaudet College. In 1954 he was one of the first African-American students to graduate from Gallaudet. In 1956 he established the Christian Mission for Deaf Africans and eventually founded numerous schools in 13 African countries, where students received their education in American Sign Language.

The NBDA has continued to grow and as of this writing has 30 chapters. It has proven itself an active and effective voice in advocating for African-American Deaf. The projects undertaken depend on the leadership and resources of individual chapters. Some of the projects undertaken in the Philadelphia chapter, where Betty Henderson has served as president, include voter registration, establishing referral systems for professional services, literacy programs, HIV/AIDS education, and technology education. This last item is important because technology is having an increasingly important effect on the lives of American Deaf. The videophone, for example, which is the true analogue of the telephone for the Deaf, can be extremely useful because it enables the Deaf to gain access to the telecommunications system using natural (signed) language, something that just cannot be done with its still widely used predecessor the text telephone or TTY. At present, videophone technology is hardly user-friendly. One must have a sufficiently fast computer, a router with a compatible video phone, an Internet connection that is suitably fast, and it requires regular technical support. Because their constituency has access to this technology, the NBDA also ensures that they have a high level of access to a wide variety of services. In a culture where race continues to affect access and opportunity, the NBDA serves a vital and irreplaceable function.

A Language Like Any Other

We could not have done without a good dictionary, ascertaining the exact purport of every word, to teach us to use them in a sense strictly consonant to the subject we were treating.

—Charles-Michel de l'Epée

Early in the 1960s, for the first time in almost 100 years, scholars again began to investigate signed languages. William C. Stokoe, an English professor at Gallaudet College, is generally credited with being the first researcher to apply modern linguistic insights to the study of American Sign Language, but this is not quite true. Stokoe's insights were not modern. Modern linguistic thought during the 1960s was informed by the work of Noam Chomsky, who sought to create a highly formal, quasimathematical theory of language.[1] This was not the theory that Stokoe attempted to apply to the signed language of American Deaf.

Chomsky had absorbed the work of previous generations of linguists and found it wanting. He asserted that earlier theories of language could not hope to account for the complexities present in every language, and one of his goals was the creation of grammars that could do just that. The result was the theory of generative grammar, a theory of language where the idea of transformation plays a central role. Chomsky asserted the existence of a set of what are essentially primitive sentences or sentencelike phrases—these he called the kernel of the language—and a set of transformations to act on the kernel. The transformations had to be sufficiently powerful to transform the elements of the kernel so as to yield the entire set of grammatical utterances associated with the language—what he called the corpus of the language—but in addition the transformations had to

Chapter Six

Art meets science: the same two-word phrase in English and in Stokoe's American Sign Language notation. Calligraphy by Linda Everett.

be sufficiently sensitive so as not to transform any element of the kernel into a nongrammatical utterance. Chomsky's theory of transformational grammar influenced many linguists of the time, but it had little discernible effect on Stokoe's efforts. Stokoe's goals were always far more modest than those of Chomsky; they were also more conservative. In fact, they would have been familiar to most linguists of the 1930s and 1940s, and in this sense Stokoe was not modern at all. It was his choice of subject (American Sign Language) that was new, not the linguistic concepts he used to study it.

Signed language was not Stokoe's first interest. Born in 1919 William Stokoe arrived at Gallaudet College in 1955 to teach English. He was not fluent in American Sign Language nor was he trained as a linguist. (His degrees were in English, and he never became particularly fluent in sign.[2]) Nevertheless, within a few years of his arrival at Gallaudet, Stokoe formulated the hypothesis for which he is best remembered: American Sign Language is a language that in its most essential aspects is the same as any spoken language, and this assertion was new.

During the first half of the twentieth century most professional linguists paid no attention to signed language, because they did not believe it to be a language at all. Leonard Bloomfield's book *Language*,[3] one of the most important and widely quoted linguistics texts of the twentieth century, devotes almost no attention to what is now called American Sign Language. This 500+ page tome on the nature and structure of language contains numerous references to Tagalog, Turkish, Algonquin, Menomini, Latin, German, French, Russian, English, and other languages besides, but on signed languages Bloomfield is practically silent. The signed language of American Deaf, Bloomfield believed, was simply a visual representation of English—essentially, English on one's finger's—and consequently there was nothing new to be learned from the study of it. Stokoe believed otherwise. American Sign Language, he asserted, has little in common with English and a great deal could be learned from its study. It is Stokoe's beliefs more than anything he discovered about the nature of signed language that have had such an important impact on the way signed language is understood today.

Stokoe's first paper, published in 1960,[4] contains most of the ideas for which he would eventually become known, but this first paper had little apparent impact—perhaps because it is such a hodgepodge. There is a brief review of the history of signed language, observations on the social relations among the Deaf, observations on deaf education, an overly meticulous description of the manual alphabet, and other topics besides. It is not until page 39 (out of a total of 78 pages) that Stokoe even mentions his central premise: Standard linguistic concepts and methods of analysis could be brought to bear on the study of the signed language used by American Deaf.

To appreciate Stokoe's ideas, it is helpful to recall two basic linguistic concepts. First is the definition of a morpheme. In linguistics a morpheme is defined as the smallest unit of language to which one can ascribe meaning. Morphemes are often "smaller" than words in the sense that one word may be comprised of two or more morphemes. For example, the sound represented by the letter *s,* when used to signify plural, as in the case of the word *cars,* represents a morpheme, as does *car.* Stokoe asserted that it is a characteristic of the signed language used by American Deaf—the term American Sign Language had not yet been coined—that signs are the smallest units of the language to which meaning can be ascribed; therefore, signs are morphemes.

Second, a phoneme is usually described as a set of minimal speech sounds all of which are perceived as somehow "the same" by native speakers of the language. For example, the sound represented by the letter *p* represents a phoneme as does the pair of letters *th.* Of course, the actual pronunciation of phonemes may vary somewhat from region to region and even individual to individual in the same region, and this explains why the phoneme is generally defined as a *set* of functionally equivalent sounds. Native speakers generally overlook these variations, because they are able to identify the variants as representatives of the same class of sounds. (Variants belonging to the same functional class are called allophones.) Phonemes are generally meaningless of themselves. They constitute, instead, the fundamental units of sound out of which spoken language is constructed.

Stokoe asserted that there was a signed language analogue to the phoneme that he called the *chereme,* a term of his own invention. He called the various functionally equivalent forms of each chereme *allochers,* another term he coined himself. An allocher is the signed language analogue of the allophone. In place of phonology, the study of the phonetic structure of a spoken language, Stokoe proposed the study of cherology, the signed language analogue of phonology.

Part of the goal of phonology is to identify the relatively small collection of fundamental sounds associated with each language, which, when combined in various ways, produce all of the (spoken) words and phrases of that language. English, for example, has about 45 phonemes. Exploiting his analogy between cherology and phonology, Stokoe sought to identify the minimal set of gestures, most of which are meaningless in themselves, out of which all signs and signed utterances are constructed.

There are, however, differences between phonology and cherology; Stokoe's analogy is not exact. A fundamental difference between phonology and cherology is the concept of simultaneity. A speaker pronounces one phoneme at a time. It is often said that spoken language consists, in its most elemental sense, of the sequential production of phonemes. By contrast, Stokoe identified three aspects of a sign that are generally produced simultaneously by the fluent signer. These aspects are (1) the position or location of production of the sign with respect to the signer's body, (2) the manual configuration of the sign, that is, the hand shape used in the production of the sign, and (3) the motion required to produce the sign.

Each of the three aspects of a sign was given a name. The tabula, or tab for short, identified the sign's location with respect to the signer's body. Stokoe identified 12 different tabs or "cheremes of position," e.g., the brow, the midface, the lower face, the side of the face, the trunk of the body, etc. The designator—abbreviated dez—identified the configuration of the hand and or hands necessary to produce the sign. Here, Stokoe identified 15 distinct dezs or cheremes of configuration, e.g., the fist, the flat hand, the *h* hand shape (the "*h* hand shape" refers to the manual alphabet version of the letter *h*), etc. Finally, Stokoe identified 27 cheremes of motion, which he called sigs, an abbreviation of the term signation. Some typical sigs are an upward vertical motion of the hands, a downward vertical motion, a right (lateral) motion, etc. He also created several diacritical marks to better delineate the motion involved in producing the sign. Each tab, dez, and sig was assigned its own unique symbol.

With Stokoe's system of notation, writing a sign became, in principle, a simple matter: First, identify the dez, tab, and sig of the sign in question, and then write the corresponding characters. Because the dez, tab, and sig generally occurred simultaneously, Stokoe adopted the convention of always writing the tab first, the dez second, and the sig last for each sign. He believed that writing a signed sentence was only a matter of writing the signs in the order in which they were produced.

Stokoe was not the first person to attempt to devise a system for writing signed language. As mentioned in Chapter 2, Roch-Amboise-Auguste Bébian had proposed a system for writing French Sign Language in the first half of the nineteenth century, and Stoke makes a brief reference to Bébian's work in his first article—but Stokoe went much further in the process than any of his predecessors. At the time, however, no one cared.

Stokoe was not deterred by the lack of interest shown in his first paper. He continued to study the nature of signed language, and his next major publication had a much larger impact on the field of linguistics and on the way that many perceive American Sign Language. Stokoe decided to create a dictionary of signs.[5] The dictionary was important for two reasons: First, it would provide a practical demonstration of his system of sign notation. Second, in contrast to the efforts of his predecessors, Stokoe's dictionary would document signs *as they were used by the Deaf*. Such a dictionary was different in concept from that created de l'Epée. He not only created a dictionary of signs, but also created many of the signs included therein. De l'Epée's dictionary was not (nor was it intended to be) a record of the signed vocabulary of the Deaf of eighteenth century Paris, but rather a teaching tool created for those interested in learning his method of deaf education. This is what de l'Epée wrote about his dictionary:

> But having had subsequently to form masters that were to return to their own country, in a short time, it was not practicable to make of them as ready at signs as my pupils, who, supplying my place, served them as living dictionaries: (I appeal to the gentleman themselves for the truth of this.)—with a view of qualifying these persons the more effectually for instructors, I was induced to think of compiling a Dictionary for the use of the Deaf and Dumb.[6]

The value of Stokoe's contribution and the difficulties inherent in the creation of his dictionary are rooted in his determination to record signs in a way that is analogous to the way that other dictionaries record words in spoken languages. To create his dictionary of signs, Stokoe had to create a system of notation powerful enough to represent any sign in American Sign Language. To accomplish this goal, he applied the same linguistic concepts and system of notation—albeit somewhat modified—that he had used in his 1960 paper on the nature of signed language.

It is important to understand that Stokoe was, except for his choice of subject, very conservative. He believed that the standard linguistic concepts of his day were as adequate for analyzing signed language as they were for analyzing spoken language. All that was needed was to make allowance for American Sign Language's visual (rather than aural) modality. But to William Stokoe, in the early 1960s, modality was a surface feature. He believed that the key to understanding American Sign Language was to *perceive* it in such a way that one could apply classical linguistic concepts to its study. His dictionary depended heavily on the analogies he believed he had found between signed language (specifically American Sign Language) and spoken languages: Cheremes are the analogues of phonemes; allochers are the analogues of allophones, and the hands are the analogue of the voice. But as with all analogies, these, too, have their limitations.

To better appreciate the unique nature of Stokoe's dictionary, it helps to compare his signed language dictionary with other dictionaries of signed and spoken languages. Even today many readers of this book, a population in which signed language enthusiasts are certainly overrepresented, have not seen a dictionary *of* signs. Most of today's popular signed language dictionaries are actually dictionaries of words rather than signs. The words are listed alphabetically and each word is usually accompanied by a line drawing that illustrates the corresponding sign. It is the word, not the sign, that predominates because it is the word, not the sign, according to which the dictionary entries are organized.

The dominance of the word over the sign in these so-called sign language dictionaries is a profound limitation on the way that the dictionaries can be used. By way of comparison, notice that an English language dictionary is intrinsic to the English language. If one wants to learn the meaning of the word *ameliorate,* for example, one "looks under the *a*'s" until one locates the word of interest, where one finds a brief explanation (in English) of its meaning and, perhaps, a synonym or two. By contrast, one cannot locate an unfamiliar sign in the same way in any popular signed language dictionary—not in Stokoe's time and not today. In popular signed language dictionaries—the types generally favored by most signers (the ones found in bookstores, for example)—signs are *unordered.* To be sure, one may be able to find a drawing or a photograph of an unknown gesture by examining the illustrations sequentially, but this is inefficient. One cannot locate an unfamiliar sign in any of these dictionaries on the basis of its cheremes alone. Practically speaking, to find an unfamiliar gesture, a putative sign, one must already know a spoken word corresponding to the sign or one must be willing to sift through numerous pictures in the dictionary in the hope of stumbling across an illustration corresponding to the sought-after gesture. From the point of view of the user, the signs in popular signed language dictionaries are listed randomly; only the words are ordered. Popular signed language dictionaries establish a correspondence between the words of one language and the signs of another, but the relationship between words and signs is asymmetric.

Notice that a signed language dictionary is not similar to the standard foreign language dictionaries created for English speakers of European languages. Any such dictionary contains two alphabetical lists. In a German/English, English/German dictionary, for example, there is one alphabetical list of German words —and next to each German word is one or more English words corresponding to it—and a second alphabetical list of English words together with a corresponding list of German equivalents. There is a symmetry to the treatment of the two languages. Each popular signed language dictionary was and is, in effect, half of a standard foreign language dictionary. They enable the user to go from words to signs, but they offer no rational procedure for going from signs to words.

The *Dictionary of American Sign Language on Linguistic Principles* is ordered by sign, and next to each sign are one or more English equivalents and perhaps a written expression—expressed in Stokoe's system of sign notation—by way of illustration. In effect, Stokoe and his collaborators, Dorothy Casterline and Carl Croneberg, attempted to provide the other half of an American Sign Language/ English, English/American Sign Language dictionary.

To create the dictionary, they had to make explicit the manner in which information is conveyed via signs. This involves more than simply identifying tabs, dezs, and sigs. They had to examine how meaning is conveyed via sequences of gestures. Not every gesture, not every motion of one's hands over the course of a conversation is *significant* in the sense that it conveys meaning. A similar (but not identical) difficulty is encountered in creating a written form of a spoken language, but because we are taught from an early age to identify written symbols with spoken words, the difficulties involved in creating a written form of a spoken language are masked by our overfamiliarity with the solution. We might better appreciate some of the challenges faced by Stokoe, Croneberg, and Casterline if we briefly examine the problem of creating a correspondence between spoken words and written symbols.

Part of the problem in creating a written form of a spoken language centers on the identification of those aspects of speech that convey meaning. Consider the utterance, "My car is in the shop. Its transmission is broken." The spoken form of the same utterance might more accurately be represented as two "words": "mycarisintheshop itstransmissionisbroken," because this is how the sentences tend to sound when pronounced by a native speaker. In the spoken version, there are no breaks between the individual words; the only definite pause occurs between the two sentences. Furthermore, as the two sentences are spoken the speaker's voice rises and falls in pitch; some syllables are stressed more than others, and the tempo at which the syllables that comprise the words are pronounced—and, consequently, the rate at which the words themselves are pronounced—varies.

Variations in tempo, stress, and pitch are all part of the English language, but not every variation is significant in the sense that introducing a change in the tempo, stress, or pitch changes the meaning of the utterance. In addition, it is obvious to every native speaker of English that pronunciation varies from speaker to speaker. There are, in fact, as many ways of saying "My car is in the shop. Its transmission is broken" as there are speakers to say it, and it is neither practical nor desirable for a system of writing to capture all such variation. Creating a written language from a spoken one requires the researcher to distinguish between significant variation and what is, essentially, noise and to create a system of symbols that corresponds to those parts of speech that are significant. For English, of course, the problem was substantially solved long ago, but Stokoe, Casterline, and Croneberg were the first to claim to have solved the problem for American Sign Language.

One need only observe native signers in conversation to see some of the difficulties inherent in separating signed "signal" from signed "noise." Conversation between individuals fluent in American Sign Language can be fascinating to watch even when one does not understand the language. The tempo of the language is rapid, often more rapid than is the tempo of English. (This is one reason why signed language interpreters are generally able to keep up with a speaker for long periods of time without the assistance of the speaker.) Facial expressions of native signers tend to be very animated. Some signers even prefer to stand when they converse so that they can shift their weight from one foot to the other as a way of visually conveying changes in location or speaker over the course of a narrative, but no two individuals sign exactly "the same."

And there is the motion of the hands themselves. While they generally move rapidly, the speed varies from phrase to phrase. The position in space about which the gestures are centered frequently shifts. Signs may be made closer to the face or closer to the navel, or to the left, right, or center of the signer's axis of symmetry. Variation between individuals is easy to notice—even for a nonsigner. The variation manifests itself in the creation of the specific hand shapes that make up the individual signs as well as in the motions, the rhythm, and the tempo with which the signs are made—but despite the many differences, communication occurs.[7] The problem, as Stokoe, Casterline, and Croneberg saw it, was to recognize which parts of gestures are significant—that is, which gesture components convey specific linguistic meaning recognized by all fluent signers—and which gestures are, in effect, visual noise. They wanted a written version of American Sign Language that would convey all of the former and as little as possible of the latter.

In their analysis of American Sign Language, Stokoe, Casterline, and Croneberg relied heavily on the ideas in Stokoe's 1960 work, but those results had to be extended before they could be used. In the dictionary they again emphasize the existence of three aspects or characteristics of every signed gesture. The first characteristic was the position (in relation to the signer's body) where the sign is made, the so-called tab, and they identified 12 distinct tabs. (These are identical with the tabs in the 1960 paper.) Among these, for example, are the face, which they represented with the symbol $\cap$, the forehead ($\cap$), chin ($\cup$), neck (π), and "zero" ($\emptyset$), or neutral place, by which they meant the position in front of the speaker where "the hands move easily."

The second characteristic was, again, the designator or dez for short. The dez identified the hand shape—that is, the configuration of the fingers—taken by the dominant hand during signing. (While signing, the so-called dominant hand usually does most of the work.) When both hands adopted a specific shape, Stokoe's notation employed two dez indicators, something that he called the double dez. There are 19 dez symbols—as opposed to 15 in Stokoe's previous work—most of which are simply upper case letters representing letters in the manual alphabet of American Sign Language.

The third and final characteristic of a gesture is, according to this system of notation, the action involved in creating the sign. Recall that this is termed the signation or sig of the sign. They identified 24 different sigs—as opposed to 27 in the 1960 work—including an upward movement ($^\wedge$), a downward movement ($^\vee$), a rightward movement (>), and a leftward movement (<). Other sig symbols represented the rotation of the wrist, contact between hands, and so on.

Additional "conventions" needed to be employed as well in order to represent various characteristics of gestures such as the repetition of a motion or the position of the hands relative to each other. While these characteristics were also represented with various symbols, the conventions played a role more analogous to diacritics than spelling. Taken together, the tab, dez, and sig symbols yielded an alphabet of 55 different characters that Stokoe asserted could be used to uniquely represent any gesture occurring in American Sign Language.

By fixing the order in which the 55 symbols were listed, Stokoe, Croneberg, and Casterline established an "alphabetical" order. The tabs occupied positions 1–12, the dezs occupied positions 13–31, and the sigs occupied positions 32–55. Finally, the authors also created a spelling convention: To write a gesture, one first writes the tab symbol associated with the sign, then the dez, and last the sig. To locate an unknown gesture in the dictionary one must first identify the three characteristics of the sign—its tab, dez, and sig—and use the alphabetical order established by the authors to find the sign, which was described in English rather than the written sign notation.

A Dictionary of American Sign Language on Linguistic Principles succeeded in capturing the attention of researchers and others interested in signed language in a way that Stokoe's original monograph did not. Signed language became a topic for serious research for the first time in over a century. The dictionary itself, however, was more praised than used. It was clever but not practical—more interesting than informative. Some of the problems with the dictionary were of a technical nature, and others were conceptual.

On the technical side, Stokoe chose to create his own character set. Many of the 55 symbols in this "American Sign Language alphabet" were not part of any standard font, and this continues to be true. As a consequence Stokoe, Casterline, and Croneberg may have succeeded in creating a written form of signed language, but they failed to create a typable one. In Stokoe's 1960 article many of the letter-like symbols were simply hand drawn. The symbols in the dictionary are neater, but many are impossible to type, and some are difficult to draw. Such an awkward choice of symbols greatly increased the cost and difficulty of printing the original work, and they remain a barrier to its use.

Furthermore, Stokoe's system is not complete. In the dictionary he claims to have created a one-to-one correspondence between signs and written symbols, so that each sign could be represented with a unique set of symbols and each set of symbols—if it represented a sign at all—represented exactly one sign. Experience has proved otherwise. Later researchers quickly identified common, distinct signs that have the same written forms. The 55-symbol alphabet had to be expanded to identify, for example, the orientation of the palm, which proved to be an important aspect of American Sign Language not recognized by the authors of the dictionary. Absent a symbol for the orientation of the palm, very different looking signs are represented by the same set of Stokoe characters.

Conceptually, the great drawback of Stokoe's system stems from a misunderstanding about the nature of signed language. Specifically and paradoxically, his system fails to accomplish what he envisioned for it because of its overemphasis on the role of (manual) gesture. American Sign Language is a visual language, but it is not exclusively a gestural one. Stokoe, as previously mentioned, knew this. He had read the works of Bébian and Thomas Hopkins Gallaudet, both of whom wrote about the importance of nonmanual aspects of signed language, but he made no provision for notating any component of a sign that was not manual. Essentially, the authors of the dictionary passed all visual communication through a filter that retained certain purely manual cues and discarded the rest.

Of course, nonvocal cues—a raised eyebrow, for example—are often used to convey information when used in conjunction with spoken English, but they are not essential components of English. The prevalence of talk radio—a medium that filters out everything except the voice—as a form of light entertainment indicates that visual cues are not integral parts of spoken language. By contrast, in American Sign Language some common signs and signed sequences are difficult or impossible to interpret correctly when produced without their nonmanual components. In fact, there are even signs that may be successfully conveyed while suppressing the manual component of the sign and producing *only* the requisite facial expression. The sign that is sometimes translated as *late* or *not yet* is an example of this type of sign. In addition to its manual component, the signer simultaneously tilts the head slightly and places the tongue on the lower lip at the corner of the mouth. During informal conversation one can sometimes observe instances of native signers making the nonmanual component of the sign without the manual component and communicating with no loss of clarity. Note one more example: A common way to negate a sign is simply to produce the sign or sign sequence manually while simultaneously shaking one's head. In this construction the meaning is changed completely if the nonmanual component is suppressed. Many other such examples exist.

In the end, Stokoe's analogies between signed and spoken languages were not as strong as he had thought. The hands are not the analogue of the voice. But even if Stokoe's notation were to be augmented by a set of signs that conveyed facial expressions, the expanded alphabet would still not be a satisfactory method for notating signs. The manual components of signs exist in three-dimensional space, and a fluent signer makes thorough use of the three-dimensional nature of the language. The manner in which one places a sign and the position in space in which it is placed—for example, to the left or to the right of the signer's axis of symmetry, whether one makes it higher or lower, closer or farther from one's body —may fundamentally change the meaning of the sign. An example of this type of phenomenon is the use of pronouns in signed language. When signing one can refer to another person in the room simply by pointing, but when that person is absent a similar construction exists. The signer produces the sign representing the person in a particular location about the signer's body and thereafter points to that location when referring to that person. Different persons are "placed" at distinct locations. In signed language this type of pointing behavior is used in a way that is analogous to the way that pronouns are used in English.

There is no adequate notation in Stokoe's system for these spatially complex types of three-dimensional constructions—and other three-dimensional constructions exist—nor does he show any apparent awareness of the problems created by the absence of such notation. Stokoe had hoped to create a written version of signed language, and at one point in the introduction to the dictionary he asserts that he could have written the entire dictionary—definitions, and, apparently, every other remark—using only his notation. In retrospect, it is doubtful that had he done so, anyone, including the authors, would have been able to read it.

In 1972 Stokoe published a self-critical work in which he acknowledges the limitations of his system for writing signs and the problems inherent in his signed language/spoken language analogy.[8] In *Semiotics and Human Sign Languages* he (again) describes his system of sign notation, but this time he also describes the shortcomings of the method. Two of his objections are especially interesting. First, with respect to the nonmanual nature of signed language, he now uses the symbols $S \rightarrow F/M$ to convey the idea that signed language is a "dual channel activity"[9] in the sense that an American Sign Language sentence contains a facial component and a manual component and both are expressed simultaneously.[10] (S = sentence, F = facial component, and M = manual component).

This concept of signed language as a dual channel activity is entirely missing from his earlier work and its absence, as previously mentioned, is one reason that neither Stokoe nor anyone else has found his system for notating signs adequate. Stokoe's dissatisfaction with his previous work is expressed honestly and repeatedly. He describes, for example, Gallaudet's experiment, described in Chapter 2, in which Gallaudet demonstrates the importance of nonmanual communication by successfully conveying a story from antiquity to students at the Hartford school without using any manual gestures at all, relying instead on "body language" and facial expressions. It is clear from his account that now Stokoe recognizes what Gallaudet's experiment implies about the nature of visual communication. It is also clear that he understands what it implies about his own system of American Sign Language notation, which would not have captured a single "chereme" of Gallaudet's story.

Second, he acknowledges in his 1972 work that his system for notating the motions of the hands—his so-called "sigs"—is also problematic. Decomposing the fluid, complex motions of the signer into a limited number of component gestures, each of which is to be represented by its own symbol, proved to be more difficult than he had anticipated. He had sought a method for mapping three-dimensional signing space onto two-dimensional paper with no loss of information, but, upon reflection, he decided that he had not found it. In particular, he explicitly expressed dissatisfaction with his 1960 paper and his 1965 dictionary.[11] Unlike Gallaudet,[12] Stokoe did not dismiss even the possibility of writing signs, but he did not suggest a way to ameliorate the shortcomings that he identified in his own work.

Throughout the 1970s Stokoe's work and his decision to apply standard linguistic techniques and concepts to the analysis of American Sign Language garnered ever-increasing amounts of attention. Stokoe had successfully demonstrated to his contemporaries that with respect to American Sign Language there was something to study. But while Stokoe had recognized by 1972 that modality mattered in the analysis of language, many of his contemporaries were less quick to adapt. They continued to assert that American Sign Language was, in most important aspects, "like" other (spoken) languages. They downplayed the effect of modality on language to the extent that they abandoned even the few special-ized vocabulary words that Stokoe had coined to describe the special nature of visual language. In their place signed language researchers used the corresponding terms that had already been developed for spoken languages: Stokoe's cherology was replaced by phonology, his chereme was replaced by phoneme, and his allocher was replaced by allophone. For a while, at least, American Sign Language was made ordinary.

Modern Ideas about Modality

*And if some reader had not yet accepted A and B as true, he might still accept the
Sequence as a valid one, I suppose?*

   *No doubt such a reader might exist. He might say "I accept as true the Hypothetical
Proposition that, if A and B be true, Z must be true; but I don't accept A and B as
true." Such a reader would do wisely in abandoning Euclid, and taking to football.*
                    —Lewis Carroll, taken from "What the Tortoise Said to Achilles"

Linguistics is an ancient science. Two thousand five hundred years ago Indian
scholars created a grammar for Sanskrit that is to modern linguistic thought what
the mathematical works of the Greeks are to modern mathematics. These ancient
Indian scholars identified rules that transformed simpler underlying grammatical
structures into more complex utterances, and they developed a sophisticated phonetic description of their language that influenced the development of phonetics
in Europe more than two millennia later. But unlike mathematics—or physics,
or medicine—linguistics has had less success in making the transition from an
ancient to a modern science. Mathematicians have continued to develop concepts
and techniques that facilitate deductive reasoning. Proofs are the currency of
mathematics and standards of rigor continue to increase. Physicists have learned
to express their deepest insights via differential equations and to seek validation
for the resulting predictions in the outcome of sophisticated experiments. The
methods and standards by which knowledge in the science of physics is increased
are generally agreed upon. Physicians have a less certain hold of causal relationships and are less dependent on mathematics in general—in part, because, unlike
physicists, who create sweeping theories about the nature of the cosmos but are

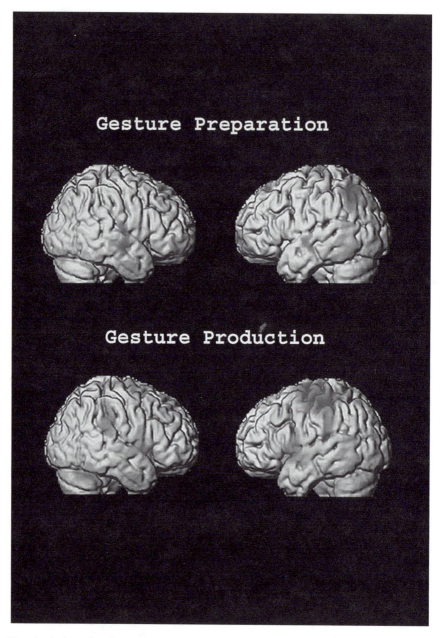

Gesture Preparation

Gesture Production

Neurological studies have shown that signed languages and spoken languages are processed in the same regions of the brain. Nonlinguistic gestures are processed elsewhere. Copyright Dr. Scott T. Grafton/Visuals Unlimited.

unable to predict tomorrow's weather, physicians must temper their "theories of everything" with the outcomes of particular (human) cases—but in medicine there is, at least, general agreement that the validity of various medical assertions can be evaluated statistically provided there is enough relevant data. Linguists have none of these advantages. They continue to debate the value of various methodologies, the nature of linguistic proof, and their most fundamental assumptions about the nature of language. Specialized terminologies vary from researcher to researcher. Radically different concepts about the nature of language are proposed and inconclusively debated, and how could it be otherwise? What one researcher accepts as proof is dismissed by others as meaningless. Consequently, linguistics remains a highly personal and peculiarly philosophical—as opposed to scientific—field of inquiry. As a consequence, before one can appreciate the work of any particular linguist one must first acclimate oneself to the often highly personal terminology and concepts that the individual in question has developed to express his or her insights. Modern linguistics is fragmented in a way that many sciences are not.

What is true of linguistics in general is true of the linguistics of signed languages in particular. Scott K. Liddell, for example, a widely published researcher in this field, wrote in the preface to one of his many works on the linguistics of American Sign Language that he had originally planned to begin his book with a review of current, competing ideas about a particular aspect of signed language linguistics, but was talked out of the approach by his editor when he reached the 150-page mark without beginning a description of his own ideas or even completing his review of the works of others.[1] Today, there are almost as many theories of signed language as there are signed language linguists, and this has been the situation since the 1970s. But today there are many more signed language linguists.

Conceptually, William C. Stokoe's assertion that American Sign Language is, in its most essential aspects, the same as any spoken language continues to be reevaluated. Originally, it was a statement meant to minimize the importance of modality in communication. This was a radical statement that many of Stokoe's colleagues at Gallaudet College initially found difficult to accept—not because they believed that modality mattered, but because they failed to see the signed language of American Deaf as a language at all. But many other researchers accepted Stokoe's assertion and interpreted it to mean that modality was almost incidental. To the extent that standard linguistic concepts and techniques sufficed in the study of spoken language, these researchers believed, the same concepts and techniques sufficed for the study of American Sign Language. Increasingly, however, Stokoe's assertion has come to be viewed as an invitation to reexamine what properties *all* human languages share, that is, to identify those properties that are exhibited by all languages independent of the modality in which each language is expressed.

As a practical matter there is an important difference between conducting linguistic research into American Sign Language and conducting such research into English: American Sign Language remains an unwritten language. The existence of a written form of a spoken language facilitates references to the corpus of the language, that is, the set of all grammatical utterances. For any written language it is certainly true that the set of all written utterances is not identical with the set of all spoken utterances, but one would never know that from the work of most linguists. Instead, the distinctions that exist between written and spoken forms of the same language are often ignored because fudging the differences facilitates the exposition of theory. Such a convenient expository technique is, unfortunately, impossible in the study of American Sign Language, because no proposed system of sign notation has yet proved expressive enough to capture the language as it is actually used. Instead, describing a signed utterance often involves producing a written English description of each sign in the utterance in a manner that is often awkward and laborious. A one word "gloss" or definition is rarely sufficient because it does not identify the sign uniquely. Instead, several words or sometimes several sentences, often accompanied by photos or line drawings, are used to describe each sign. Furthermore, an author's words and pictures are often supplemented by additional notational formalisms that vary from author to author. With such awkward techniques for describing individual signs and signed utterances, it is easy to see that frequent references to the American Sign Language corpus, the set of all grammatically correct signed utterances, is difficult, and a complete transcription of a signed story is as rare as it is challenging to produce.

Signed languages, and American Sign Language in particular, are important, in part, because modality does matter. It is not an incidental aspect of language. The modality of a language does affect the expression of linguistic content. Identifying those aspects of language that are independent of modality and those aspects that are inseparable from it has proved to be both challenging and illuminating.

Iconicity in American Sign Language

To T. H. Gallaudet, iconicity, the correspondence between the form of a gesture and the concept that it represents, was at the very core of the natural language of signs. Today, his concept of signed language iconicity is often misrepresented by saying that Gallaudet posited a universal correspondence between signs and the concepts used to represent them or that he believed that signs, even iconic ones, would be transparent to the casual observer. As shown in Chapter 2, he held neither of these beliefs. Instead, he believed that given a concept and an array of putative signs from which to choose, the best choice of sign was the most iconic. He did not believe that everyone would choose the same sign; rather, he believed that those most familiar with the natural language of signs were in the best position to make the best choice. Signs to Gallaudet were pictures in the air, and signed language was a pictorial language, a language of pantomime.

By contrast, Stokoe gave very little attention to the topic of iconicity of signs. When he wrote his *Dictionary* he was operating under the assumption that the set of manual signs was the analogue of the set of spoken words, and except for a few instances of onomatopoeia, there is little in spoken English that corresponds to the concept of an iconic sign. For Stokoe, therefore, iconicity was not a topic worthy of his attention.

But many signs *are* iconic—though many are not—and the iconic nature of these signs is frequently exploited for humorous or dramatic effect by fluent signers in the course of daily conversation. Furthermore, even today many new signs are created with an eye toward iconicity: The sign for *video conferencing,* for example, the technology that for visual language is the true analogue of the telephone, is iconic. It is modeled on a sign that was previously used for film projection. The principal difference is that the new sign is made with both hands symmetrically—the hands being oriented in opposite directions. (One iconic sign for film projection used the dominant hand for the projection sign and the nondominant hand for a base so that "projection" occurred in one direction only.) For someone fluent in signed language the meaning of the video conferencing sign is usually clear at first glance and without further explanation, but it is doubtful that it would suggest much to a person not familiar with signed language. This raises the question of what it means to say that a sign is iconic when it is evident that it is not universally iconic. To offer a nonsigned illustration, consider computer icons. The meaning of a newly created computer icon is often immediately clear to the experienced computer user, but it is doubtful that it suggests anything at all to someone who has never seen a computer. Even some experienced computer users find the meaning of some computer icons opaque. Is the computer icon iconic? The question of iconicity in American Sign Language has been studied in some detail, and the results are worth describing briefly.

Iconicity of signs is always a matter of degree. Fluent signers who use the same signed language—U.S. citizens using American Sign Language or Danish citizens using the very different Danish Sign Language, for example—are far more likely to be sensitive to the iconic aspects of a particular sign when the sign is produced in the signed language with which they are most familiar. For example, the sign for tree in American Sign Language—which is produced by spreading the fingers of the dominant hand into a 5 hand shape, holding the forearm vertically, placing the elbow on the back of the nondominant hand, and then twisting the dominant hand back and forth slightly along the axis of the forearm—has a certain treelike structure to it. This is recognized and exploited by those who use American Sign Language. The idea of a falling tree, for example, is often communicated by producing the sign for tree and then allowing the upright forearm to fall over into a horizontal position.[2]

On an artistic level, during the late 1970s the actor Bernard Bragg performed a two- or three-minute work as part of his one-man performance that described a pilot of a military aircraft dropping bombs on a village. He used relatively few formal signs, but among them were the iconic signs representing *tree, house,* and *explosion.* The iconic nature of these signs was fully exploited by Mr. Bragg to produce what the author found to be a profoundly moving performance piece. It is doubtful, however, that the work would have had the same emotional impact on someone who was not already very familiar with the iconic nature of these particular signs.

In contrast with American Sign Language, the sign for tree in Danish Sign Language is produced with both hands moving symmetrically: First, the crown of the tree is produced by beginning at the top of the imagined tree and outlining a spherical shape with a symmetric curving motion of both hands; the trunk of the tree is produced by bringing the hands closer together—palms facing each other—and lowering them simultaneously to produce the tree trunk. This sign is evidently iconic as well, but the icon has little in common with the one used by American Deaf. Someone fluent in Danish Sign Language but unfamiliar with American Sign Language might understand little by observing two individuals fluent in American Sign Language conversing about trees and vice versa. The mutual unintelligibility of differing signed languages has been well documented by contemporary researchers. But what contemporary researchers often fail to mention—and what Gallaudet and his contemporaries believed to be central to their understanding of the nature of the natural language of signs—is how much faster the Deaf are able to learn each other's signed languages than hearing individuals of different language backgrounds are able to learn each other's spoken languages. Deaf who are fluent in one signed language quickly become proficient in another. Indeed, the learning curve for a Deaf individual fluent in one signed language who then attempts to learn another is generally much steeper than that of a hearing person attempting to learn an unfamiliar spoken language. The iconic nature of the new and unfamiliar signs makes them easier to learn and use effectively. (Once one appreciates the iconic nature of the American Sign Language symbol for tree, for example, one picks up the expression "The tree fell over" with little additional effort. Compare this with the more difficult problem of passing from the word "tree" to the phrase "The tree fell over." in any spoken language.)

As a general rule, the greater the linguistic or cultural gap between two individuals, the harder it is for the two of them to simultaneously identify the iconic aspect of any given sign. An interesting set of experiments dealing with iconicity is described by Edward S. Klima and Ursula Bellugi.[3] They began with a list of 90 signs commonly used in American Sign Language. A fluent signer was videotaped producing each sign and then the tape was shown to a group of ten hearing individuals, none of whom had knowledge of signed language. None of the test subjects was able to guess 81 of the 90 signs. Responses on the remaining 10 percent of questions included an occasional individual correct answer, but even for these questions accuracy was poor on average.

Another, easier version of the test was then administered to a new group of nonsigning test subjects. In the second test, the same 90-sign videotape was shown together with a set of multiple choice questions. For each sign the subjects were to choose which one of the given five answers best represented what the sign appeared to symbolize. (Most of the wrong alternatives were obtained from the incorrect answers given by the first group of test subjects.) The accuracy rate was no better than what one would obtain by choosing answers at random—about 1 in 5. These two tests offer no support to the idea of iconicity, but there was one additional test to administer.

A still easier version of the test was administered to a third nonsigning group of test subjects. This time each of the 90 signs on the videotape was shown together with a correct, spoken translation of the sign. The subjects were then asked to identify in writing the relationship between the spoken word and the corresponding sign. In other words, as part of the test the subjects were asked to assume that there was an element of iconicity in each sign; their job was to discover and expound the relationship. In contrast to the results of the two earlier tests, there was good agreement between the explanation and the sign in the third test, a result that validates—but only weakly—the oft-made assertion that there exists a meaningful connection between some concepts and the signs used in American Sign Language to represent them.

It is doubtful that Klima and Bellugi's results would have surprised Gallaudet and his colleagues at the Hartford school. These nineteenth century scholars knew from their own experience that signs varied according to the educational and linguistic background of the signer. They knew that a sign that was perceived as iconic by one group may not be perceived as iconic by another. Much depended on the education and the background of the signer. In fact, Gallaudet believed that the scholars at Hartford had actually *improved* upon the collection of natural signs as "originally employed by the deaf and dumb" through a program of careful study and experimentation.[4]

But comparing the works of early nineteenth century signed language researchers with research performed more than a century later must be done with care. Gallaudet's experiments, some of which are described in Chapter 2, were richer and more open-ended than those of Klima and Bellugi. Because of the open-ended nature of Gallaudet's experiments, they were not then—and are not now —easily amenable to statistical analysis. (Most of the field of statistics had, in any case, yet to be invented.) Nor was it just the experimental design that differed. The terser, more tightly controlled prose preferred by most contemporary researchers also makes comparisons with Gallaudet's elegant, often ebullient language problematic. Still, a careful reading of both indicates substantial overlap in their conclusions about the relationship between some signs and the concepts they represent.

Finally, it is important to note that even as iconic signs regularly enter the lexicon of American Sign Language—the sign for video conferencing is but one example—there is a simultaneous tendency for older signs to lose their iconicity. Loss of iconicity is not a new phenomenon, nor is it restricted to signed languages. A great deal of the Christian religious imagery so evident in medieval painting, e.g., halos, sheep, certain manual gestures, and crosses, was iconic in nature at the time of its creation, but some of the meaning and most of the emotional impact of these icons are now lost on many contemporary viewers. Similarly, signs lose their iconic nature over time. The author has, for example, observed some older signers using a sign for *computer* that is clearly modeled on the revolving reels of magnetic tape that were once used for data storage in early computers. Not surprisingly, the nature of this sign is completely opaque to many younger signers who are unfamiliar with a technology that was obsolete before they were born. And as late as 1980, the author regularly conversed with an older signer who used a two-fisted sign for *telephone:* One fist held the receiver in front of the mouth and the second fist held the speaker next to the ear. While computers and telephones are more ubiquitous than ever, these old signs and the physical appearance of the devices they represent have diverged beyond recognition. (These old signs are, not surprisingly, only rarely used today.)

More generally, it may be inevitable that over time the iconicity of any particular sign must diminish. The argument in support of this statement has nothing to do with changes in technology. It is, instead, a statement about the desire for error-free communication on the part of the user when communicating in a language with an ever-growing vocabulary and in which the new signs (or words) are chosen with a view toward iconicity. In an iconic language, as concepts evolve and multiply, different signs (or words) are introduced to convey different shades of meaning, to distinguish between old concepts and new, and to distinguish between different contemporaneous ideas. *Because* the signs are iconic and the concepts are similar, the signs will also tend to be similar in form—they were, after all, chosen to represent similar concepts. Retaining iconic representations eventually results in a situation in which distinguishing between similar-looking concept/sign pairs becomes problematic, especially because the presentation of every sign varies somewhat from speaker to speaker and even when produced by the same speaker in different contexts. This loss of clarity can be reversed by employing signs whose relationship to their corresponding concepts is more abstract and so freer of the constraints imposed by iconicity. That, at least, is how the argument goes.

To use a nonsigned language example, suppose that a bank issues account numbers sequentially. The first person to apply for an account has account number 1; the second person has account number 2, and so on. Suppose, to simplify the exposition, that 999 accounts are issued. If the customer or bank misreads or misprints any digit, money is deposited in or withdrawn from the wrong account. The reason that two existing accounts are so easily confused is that the account numbers are, numerically speaking, too close together. The solution is to use a great many digits to identify each account and to be sure that each account differs from all other actual accounts by several digits. This method of assigning account numbers increases the numerical "distance" between accounts in the sense that misreading or misprinting one or even a few digits will result only in a "read error"; that is, the computer or bank employee will notice that the faulty number fails to correspond to any account at all. (Recall that when the accounts were assumed to be numerically close together, an error of a single digit identified someone else's account, which is a more serious mistake because it both misdirects funds and makes immediate identification of the mistake impossible.) The extra digits that are used to increase the numerical distance between accounts are not required to identify a particular account; their role, instead, is to prevent the misidentification of an account.

Here is the linguistic analogue to the numerical example of the previous paragraph: Imagine a coordinate system where the horizontal axis is the "concept axis" and the vertical axis is labeled the "symbol axis." The first "coordinate" of a point in this coordinate system is its concept, and the second coordinate is the corresponding symbol. If two concepts are similar, they will be positioned close to one another on the concept axis, and, in an iconic language, if two points have similar concepts, they will also have similar symbols. As a consequence, similar concepts will yield concept/symbol pairs that will be located near each other in the concept/symbol coordinate system. Assigning similar symbols for similar concepts means that confusion between the concept/symbol pairs eventually increases as the number of similar concepts increases.

The solution to the problem of indistinguishable symbol/concept pairs is to "decouple" the symbol from the concept in the same way that the number assigned to each bank account should, for security reasons, be decoupled from the sequence in which the account was assigned. In the concept/symbol coordinate system, when arbitrary, unrelated symbols are assigned to closely related concepts, the distance between concept/symbol pairs can be made as large as desired. When one decouples the concept from the symbol, the result is an abstract language. This quasimathematical argument predicts that over time the distance between particular concept/symbol pairs (either concept/sign or concept/word) in an appropriately defined concept/symbol space must increase in order to accommodate additions to the vocabulary while simultaneously avoiding confusion between closely related concepts. In other words, in order to keep an increasing number of similar concepts distinct, it becomes *necessary* to use increasingly abstract signs. An informal examination of lists of older signs seems, at least to the author, to support the assertion that over time signs become less iconic, but pseudomathematical arguments about a "concept/symbol space" are difficult to make precise in the absence of real mathematical reasoning. (Michael Gasser describes some interesting computer simulations to test these ideas about loss of iconicity.)[5]

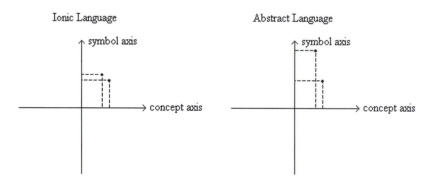

According to one school of thought, as concepts and their associated signs proliferate in an iconic language, confusion eventually results. The solution is to decouple the sign from the concept; the result is an "abstract" language.

Modern Ideas About Grammar

Today, most agree that there is some truth to Gallaudet's ideas about the existence of a weak form of iconicity in American Sign Language, but no researcher accepts his ideas about the *role* of iconicity in American Sign Language. To Gallaudet the iconicity of signs was an important organizing principle. He believed that ionic signs are expressive, and noniconic signs are needlessly inexpressive. Good signed language, according to Gallaudet, consisted of expressive pictures created with the hands, face, and body, "the language of the countenance and gestures" is how he described it, and better signed language consisted of more iconic gestures and more expressive facial and body language. There is now ample evidence to demonstrate that the situation is, and has always been, considerably more complex than Gallaudet imagined.

First, Stokoe's concepts about the linguistic structure of individual signs, if not his precise conclusions, still resonate with contemporary researchers. His sign alphabet, consisting of hand configurations (dezs), places of articulation (tabs), and movements (sigs), was, by his own admission, incomplete, but his assertion that there is a finite set of signed phonemes—abstract, essentially meaningless, fundamental units out of which all signs are composed—has stood the test of time. Comparative analysis of various signed languages shows that just as each spoken language is comprised of a relatively small set of characteristic, vocally produced phonemes, every signed language is comprised of a characteristic set of signed phonemes. All formal manually produced signs of each signed language—*even the iconic signs*—are combinations of the relatively small set of signed phonemes that are characteristic of that particular signed language.

For a native signer, mastering the set of phonemes characteristic of his or her language is a remarkably durable behavior. Consider the phenomenon of "slips of the hand" a behavior that is analogous to a "slip of the tongue" in a spoken language. When a slip occurs—irrespective of whether the language is spoken or signed—the phonetic structure of the language persists even when nonsense words or signs are produced. For example, in attempting to say the sentence, "The book is on the table," an English speaker might say, "The took is on the bable" and in the process produce one word, *took,* which makes no sense in the given context, and a sound, *bable*—rhymes with *table*—which is not part of the English vocabulary but which *is* comprised of phonemes characteristic of the English language; that is, although it is not an English word, it sounds like an English word. This is what is important: The accidentally produced word *bable* is composed of phonemes that belong to the set of phonemes of which English is composed. It is extremely unusual for a native English speaker, when accidentally mispronouncing an English word, or accidentally producing a non-sensical word, to utter a non-English phoneme. Similarly, research has shown that in American Sign Language, when fluent signers experience a slip of the hand—a situation analogous to pronouncing *bable* in the example above—the nonsensical sign is still composed of sign phonemes that are characteristic of American Sign Language.[6] The existence of a set of fundamental units, what linguists call a "sub-lexical structure," to American Sign Language is now well established and accepted by all current researchers even if there continues to be disagreement about the details.

But the phonetic structure of American Sign Language is, in some sense, the easiest part of the subject, because it is somewhat similar in concept to the phonetic structure of spoken language. Stokoe asserted that an important effect of modality on American Sign Language is that in American Sign Language sets of phonemes are produced simultaneously. In contrast, it is often asserted that in spoken languages phonemes are produced sequentially. There is some truth to both claims, but the situation is more complex than it might first appear. Even in Stokoe's Dictionary, there are representations for signs that consist of two or more motions (sigs) that must be made in a particular sequence in order that the sign be well formed. And while spoken English, for example, might be fairly characterized as the sequential production of phonemes, tonal languages—Chinese is but one example—where the meaning of the word is, in part, determined by the pitch at which it is produced as well as its simultaneously produced, nontonal phonetic structure, cannot be so characterized. The effect of modality on the formal phonetic structure of language is subtle.

The real divergence of spoken and signed languages becomes apparent when one attempts to account for the rich three-dimensional nature of signed languages. Consider, first, the problem of producing a single isolated gesture. Not surprisingly, it generally takes longer to produce a single sign than it does a single word. The "articulators" for spoken language that is, the lips, tongue, throat, etc.—are much smaller; they make smaller movements, and are less massive than the articulators for signed language, which include but are not limited to the fingers, hands, and arms. As a consequence, vocal articulators move faster. Furthermore, signers sometimes fingerspell words—e.g., proper nouns for which no common sign exists, unfamiliar words, and words that are fingerspelled for effect—and this would seem to further slow the rate at which information is conveyed because it is parsed out one letter at a time. Nevertheless, conversations among fluent signers generally proceed at a rate that is comparable to that found among those using spoken language. It might, in fact, be somewhat faster: Skilled signed language interpreters, for example, are generally able to "keep up" when translating from spoken to signed language without too much difficulty and are often able to maintain their pace without the cooperation of the speaker. They are even able to slow down somewhat in order to occasionally fingerspell words —during which time the speaker moves ahead of the interpreter—and then revert to signs and quickly catch up. This indicates that there is more to signing than the production of isolated signs.

A great deal of the meaning conveyed by a fluent signer depends on the *way* that the signs are produced. As has been noted previously, both Gallaudet and (eventually) Stokoe recognized that signing is a dual-channel activity, both manual and nonmanual movements are involved in the production of many signs. This is not to downplay the importance of the sort of manual gestures that students learn in introductory signing courses. Of course some information about the meaning of a gesture is gleaned from the elementary "presentation form" of the sign, but in practice additional, indispensable, semantic information is often conveyed simultaneously via the facial expression, the tilt of the head, or the direction of the gaze that accompanies the gesture.

Nor can the meaning of a sign necessarily be summarized by describing its manual component, a corresponding facial expression, and, perhaps, the tilt of the signer's head. As signs are actually used in the course of conversation, a great deal of information can also be conveyed by the way a sign is oriented in three-dimensional space. A sign that begins near the center of the signer's torso and ends away from and to the left of the signer's body may, depending on the context, have a very different meaning from the same sign beginning near the center and ending on the right. There are still other ways that the three-dimensional space around the signer is sometimes utilized to convey information. Signs are, therefore, highly inflected semantic objects, and it is by exploiting the dual-channel, highly inflected nature of their language that signers compress additional meaning into each gesture. By exploiting these grammatical conventions, one correctly produced sign can often convey the same amount of information as would be conveyed by several spoken words. Put another way, correctly produced signs tend to be semantically dense, or full of information, a characteristic that explains why the relatively slow rate of production of individual signs is a poor indicator of the rate at which information is actually conveyed. It also explains why intermediate students of American Sign Language, those who have usually learned a number of signs in an isolated presentation form, can sometimes identify all the signs used during the course of (signed) conversation, but still have only the vaguest idea of what was discussed. They are able to identify the root signs, but may not have recognized the way that the signs were inflected to convey additional meaning.

Part of describing a grammar for American Sign Language, therefore, involves determining how signers use the space around them—the so-called signing space —to convey linguistic meaning. In contrast to all spoken languages, the corpus of American Sign Language—the set of all possible grammatical utterances—is a set of *three-dimensional,* dual-channel, visual utterances. The difference should not be overemphasized. American Sign Language is first and foremost a human language, and it has much in common with other languages, spoken and signed, but because its modality is different, there is much that distinguishes it from spoken languages. Some of the unique characteristics of American Sign Language— and some of the ways that modality affects grammar—become evident when one examines signed pronouns.

At their simplest level of description, pronouns in American Sign Language are pointing gestures. The sign corresponding to the pronoun *I,* for example, is usually expressed by merely pointing to oneself—usually with the index finger. The pronouns *you, he, she,* and *it* generally involve pointing away from the signer— again, usually with the index finger. Correctly translating among the words *you, he, she,* and *it,* given a particular pronominal pointing gesture, is often easy. If the signer looks and points directly at the person being addressed, it is usually clear that this gesture can be correctly translated as *you,* and if a third party, a woman, for example, is in the room and the signer points toward her in an unambiguous way, this gesture can often be correctly translated as *she.* The correspondence between each of these pronominal gestures and the referent is often so obvious that the linguistic nature of these gestures went unexamined for a long time. This was unfortunate because identifying these signs as simple pointing gestures fails to account for how they are most often used in practice, and this failure masks some very interesting properties of signed language.

The singular pronouns become more interesting when one realizes that the same pointing gesture is used without ambiguity to refer to individuals who are not present. In this case, the signer parses out the space around him or her and establishes a one-to-one correspondence between regions in signing space and the individuals to whom the signer wishes to refer. For example, if the signer wants to describe a story involving two characters, Gertrude and Harvey, he or she might begin by pointing to the left and labeling a region to the left as *Gertrude* and then pointing to the right and labeling a region on the right as *Harvey.* Henceforth there is no ambiguity in dropping the names entirely and simply referring to each of the characters by pointing to the region of space that has been placed in correspondence with the character. The identification of nouns of all sorts with locations in signing space is deeply ingrained in American Sign Language: To return to the Gertrude/Harvey example, suppose that during the course of the story the narrator quoted one of the characters, but it was not clear to the person to whom the story was addressed, the addressee, which character had said the lines in question. The addressee might ask, "Who said that?" and the signer might well respond by simply pointing to his left if the quotation was meant to be ascribed to Gertrude—which might be translated as "She (did)"—or to the right if the quotation was meant to be attributed to Harvey, in which case the sign might be translated as "He (did)." These aspects of American Sign Language grammar are used and understood by all those fluent in the language.

Plural pronouns are handled in essentially the same way. The signer produces the sign corresponding to the pronoun *we* by first pointing toward, and often making contact with, his or her own shoulder—usually with the index finger—and then moving the finger along a horizontal arc that ends with the index finger near or in contact with the other shoulder. The nonfirst person, plural pronoun—the pronoun that, depending on context, might correctly be translated as *you* (plural) or *they*—is, as the nonfirst person singular pronoun previously described, a pointing gesture, but for the plural nonfirst person pronoun, the finger moves along an outward pointing arc. When the group to which the sign for *they* refers is actually present, the arc of the sign is generally directed toward the referents. But, as in the case of singular nonfirst person pronouns, the sign corresponding to the words *you* (plural) and *they* can also be employed even when the group to which the pronoun refers is absent. First, the signer identifies a region in signing space that is to be placed in one-to-one correspondence with the group in question, and thereafter, the nonfirst person, plural pronoun is directed toward that region.

Possessives are produced in essentially the same way that pronouns are produced. The difference is that an open palm is employed rather than the index finger. The sign corresponding to the possessive *my* is made by placing the palm of the dominant signing hand on the chest. The sign corresponding to the words *his, hers,* and *its* is made by holding the hand up, palm directed out (as if one were directing traffic to stop), and then, in a short pushing motion, moving the palm toward the region in space that represents the referent. If the individual to whom the possessive refers is present, then it is generally directed toward that individual, but the hand motion and the meaning of the sign is the same whether or not the referent is physically present.

To use the singular, nonfirst person possessive to refer to someone who is not present, one need establish a correspondence between a region of signing space and the referent and henceforth to direct the possessive toward that region. In a way that is similar to the first person plural pronoun, *we,* the possessive that is usually translated as *our* is produced by beginning at the shoulder on the same side of the body as the signing hand—the hand should be in a B shape, fingers slightly bent, with the palm vertical, and in a plane perpendicular to the signer's front—the hand is then moved in an arc, palm directed toward the center line of the torso, ending at the opposite shoulder with the palm facing in the opposite direction. Finally, the possessive that might be correctly translated as *your, yours* (plural) or *their, theirs* is made by moving the hand configuration for *his, hers,* or *its* in an arc directed toward the group in question if they are present, and when the group is absent the motion is directed toward the region in space that was previously defined as representing the group.

Notice how the motion of the hand—what Stokoe called the sig—is the same for each pronoun and its corresponding possessive. The elements of each pair are distinguished by the hand configuration alone. (The pronominal gesture corresponding to the word *I,* for example, and the corresponding possessive, i.e., the gesture translated as *my,* are directed toward the same location—they have what Stokoe would have called the same "tab"—and for nonfirst person pronouns and their corresponding possessives the motions and principles regarding placement of the signs are identical.) What is most remarkable, however, about the pronouns and possessives in American Sign Language (and apparently every other signed language of the Deaf) is how they appear to differ from pronouns and possessives in every spoken language. It is often observed that every spoken language studied so far has at least two "numbers," that is, plural and singular, and at least three persons. (In English the "three persons" are first, second, and third person singular and first, second, and third person plural.) American Sign Language likewise has two numbers, but it has only two persons, first person, and nonfirst person, a characteristic that it shares with all other known signed languages.[7]

[This "geometrical grammar" pervades American Sign Language. Consider, for example, the transitive verb that might be translated *give*. In presentation form, it is produced by forming both hands in the shape (Stokoe's dez) of the manual alphabet letter "*x*" with the palms facing each other. The motion necessary to produce the sign in presentation form begins near the torso of the signer. Both hands move forward in a slight arc as if one were presenting a gift. The motion ends abruptly slightly ahead of where it began. In conversation, however, information about the subject (the giver) and the object (the recipient) of this sign is often inflected in the production of the sign itself. To return to the fictional characters Harvey and Gertrude mentioned previously—remember that the character Harvey is represented by a region to the right of the signer and the character Gertrude has been placed in correspondence with a region to the signer's left—the sentence, "He (Harvey) gave her (Gertrude) a gift" might be expressed by using the single sign usually translated as *give* in the following manner: The sign will begin at the location representing Harvey and, by moving the *x* hand shapes in parallel arcs across the line of symmetry of the signer's body, terminating the sign in the region representing the character Gertrude. This description assumes, of course, that all correspondences have already been established. The verb *give,* then, derives much of its meaning from the way that it is oriented in signing space, a characteristic of verbs that is more the rule than the exception in American Sign Language.]

This discussion has, so far, been confined to the *way* that pronouns are produced. Explanations for what is occurring linguistically when signers employ pronouns are varied. Some linguists, influenced by more classical ideas, have described the pronominal signs as consisting of two morphemes, or meaningful parts. The first morpheme consists of the pointing gesture in presentation form, that is, the gesture made without reference to a particular region of signing space, and the second morpheme consists of the region toward which the sign is directed. Another explanation consists of what are essentially quasigeometric rules that describe how concepts are "mapped" from the signer's imagination into the three-dimensional space about the signer. These researchers posit the existence of a "mental space," which is, at its most basic level, observable as electrical activity in the brain, and a set of grammatical transformations that enable the signer to construct in signing space a visible representation of his or her mental space activity. This is, essentially, a geometrical grammar. Other explanations exist as well.

Absent a generally accepted notion of proof, researchers often claim to have presented convincing proof of the correctness of their perceptions without convincing those researchers whose perceptions differ. Explanations are important because they affect how the language is understood as a whole. If one accepts a particular explanation as true, this opens up additional avenues of inquiry into how information is represented in other types of signs—avenues that are logical extensions of the previously accepted explanation—and if an explanation is rejected as false, then the act of rejecting the explanation also closes off avenues of inquiry that are logically consistent with the rejected explanation.

Another aspect of the natural language of signs that Gallaudet and his contemporaries devoted a great deal of time to discussing, an aspect that is largely absent from the work of Stokoe and his immediate successors, is what Gallaudet called pantomime. The word pantomime is not used anymore, but part of what Gallaudet seems to have meant by the term *pantomime,* some contemporary researchers call *blending.*[8] The difference is not, however, simply a matter of nomenclature. There are sound linguistic and even neurological reasons for making the distinction. (The neurological evidence is described later in this chapter.) Briefly, during blending the signer incorporates (or blends) some of the characteristics of the person(s) or object(s) being described into the production of the signs used in the description. When this occurs, the meaning of the signs used during the blend changes. This is easily illustrated by considering how the signed first person singular pronoun, I, is often used in practice. Suppose that the signer is relating a story about the two characters, Gertrude and Harvey, described earlier. Recall that the character Gertrude was placed on the signer's left, and the character Harvey was placed on the signer's right. Consider the following putative translation of a three-line "excerpt" of a signed story involving the two characters:

(1) "I worked hard," said Gertrude.
(2) "I work harder," said Harvey.
(3) I knew that they were about to argue.

(The third line is the narrator.) Notice that the pronoun *I* appears in each line of text.

In signing the first line the signer would first look toward the signer's right in the direction of Harvey. Rightward is, in fact, the direction that the character Gertrude would have to look if she were addressing Harvey and if she were, in fact, situated to the left of the signer, as her position in signing space indicates. Furthermore, if Harvey were much taller than Gertrude, for example, the signer would probably also gaze upward toward Harvey's face. Before producing the first utterance, the signer would pause for a fraction of a second. The pause would be followed by "I work hard" while the signer simultaneously employed the facial expression and body language characteristic of the character named Gertrude. Notice that under these circumstances the pronoun *I* refers to the character Gertrude, not the narrator.

As a general rule the words *said Gertrude* are implied rather than explicitly stated provided that it is clear from the narrative—and it usually is—who in the story is talking or signing. Similarly, reciting the second line would generally entail the signer shifting body and gaze toward the left, in the direction of the character Gertrude (which *demonstrates* the perspective of Harvey), pausing for an instant, and then signing "I worked harder" where the signs are uttered with the demeanor of the character Harvey. Again, the words *said Harvey* are generally suppressed because they are, given the body language of the signer, redundant. In fact, most aspects of the character and the character's behavior are demonstrated in the signer's motions and demeanor rather than described with a string of manually produced adverbs and adjectives. Notice, too, that the meaning of the first person singular sign for *I* has also changed in the second utterance. It refers to Harvey, not Gertrude.

The third line would be preceded by a very brief pause as the signer shifts gaze in order to sign directly to the addressee. In reciting the third line with a demeanor characteristic of the narrator, the pronoun *I* would refer to the narrator and not to either Harvey or Gertrude. The technique of blending enables the signer to economically describe many aspects of a human or nonhuman character in a way that is immediate and compelling and brief. Most words that might be used in a spoken version of the same narrative to identify the speaker, the actions of the speaker, the demeanor of the speaker, the relative positions of the characters in the story, their relative heights, and so forth, are suppressed during a blend in favor of the more immediate technique of inflecting the signs so as to *demonstrate* the information the signer wishes to convey. This technique generally requires much less time than a third-party description of the same scene. The formal signs, gestures, facial expressions, etc., that occur during a blend may be produced with great intensity. In theory, of course, much of what is characteristic of a (signed language) blend could be produced in English and sometimes blends are used in conjunction with spoken English, but English language blends are employed at a very low frequency compared with American Sign Language, where they are used routinely in a wide variety of situations.[9]

From a theoretical viewpoint, what occurs during a blend? Are the "rules" that govern how blends are used in American Sign Language linguistic in nature, or are the rules that govern blends more similar to the rules that govern charades? How can one be sure that blends are not, as Gallaudet suspected, an especially sophisticated form of pantomime? Surprisingly, evidence about the effect of modality on language and specifically the relationship between pantomime and signing can be obtained directly from neurological studies.

Modality, Another View

Interest in the signed languages of the Deaf is out of all proportion to the total number of individuals actually fluent in a signed language. Part of the reason that studies of signed languages are important is that they provide insight into languages in general. Linguists have long been fond of asserting the existence of properties universal to all languages when what they meant was "universal to all spoken languages." Signed language studies enable researchers to evaluate statements about the nature of all languages from another viewpoint entirely. If one accepts that the signed languages of the Deaf are, in fact, languages—and there is little dispute on this point anymore—then a property shared by spoken languages and signed languages may well be a universal property. That a universal property does not depend on modality is, at least, a necessary condition for it to be classified as universal. Consequently, researchers continue to attempt to determine in what ways modality affects language. One fascinating area of inquiry has been to look directly at neurological studies and their relationship to the field of linguistics.

Neurological information is important for yet another reason: Because theories about the nature of signed languages—in particular, the effects of modality on grammar and phonetics—are numerous and often conflicting, it is important to have some objective means of comparing and testing competing claims. Linguists are fond of asserting the existence of various "structures." The more they look for structures, the more they find them—so-called deep structures, surface structures, grammatical structures, and a host of others. They have a similar propensity for asserting the existence of "spaces"—so-called signing space, mental space, and semantic space to name a few—and it is not always clear, even to other linguists, that these putative structures and spaces have any basis in reality. Neurological studies are another way of examining the effect of modality on language, and they have the advantage that the measurements on which they are based are unambiguous even if their meaning may still be open to interpretation.

Until relatively recently the brain was a "black box." Researchers could introduce input and observe output from the brain but the actual workings of the brain were unobservable. Absent machines that enable researchers to observe certain brain functions directly, knowledge was gleaned largely from so-called *lesion studies,* which involve identifying correlations between specific brain injuries and language or other behavioral impairments. Despite advances in medical technology, lesion studies continue to provide some of the most thought-provoking insights into the biological basis of language.

It has long been known that spoken language is produced in certain specific areas of the left hemisphere of the brain. Individuals who suffered injuries to these areas have demonstrated (spoken) language impairments of various types, and different types of impairments can be associated with different regions of the left hemisphere. Difficulties in speech production have been correlated with injuries to a region of the left hemisphere called Broca's area. These are the so-called nonfluent aphasias. Specifically, the injured person may exhibit halting speech and find it difficult or impossible to produce grammatically correct utterances. Despite these difficulties in language production, individuals with injuries to Broca's area may, nevertheless, retain good language comprehension. The existence of individuals with injuries to Broca's area who exhibit good language comprehension and simultaneously exhibit nonfluent aphasias provides information about how the brain has compartmentalized various aspects of language production and comprehension. In contrast to those with injuries to Broca's area, injuries to Wernicke's area, another region of the left hemisphere, tend to result in so-called fluent aphasias. Speakers with fluent aphasias may speak without difficulty, but the sentences that they produce often make little sense. Their ability to comprehend speech is also often impaired.

Lesion studies have also produced interesting results with respect to how the brain processes American Sign Language. The studies are limited in number, in part, because the Deaf population is so small, but some of the results are intriguing. What follows are two lesion case studies that demonstrate how neurological information has been used to gain insight into the nature of American Sign Language.

Case 1. Is American Sign Language a Form of Pantomime?

Gallaudet and his colleagues believed that pantomime is a vital component of the natural language of signs. He made no distinction between mime and signed language. Contemporary researchers, by contrast, have asserted that much of what Gallaudet called pantomime is linguistic in nature. At first glance, the phenomenon of blending, described in the preceding section, might be interpreted as an alternative description—an unnecessary relabeling—of the phenomenon of pantomime because in some ways blending resembles pantomime. It is, therefore, reasonable to ask whether the distinction between the (linguistic) concept of blending and the practice of pantomime has any basis in reality. Is the signed language of American Deaf simply pantomime done by experts?

An intriguing lesion study was published in 1992 of an individual identified as W. L., a study that demonstrates that Gallaudet got it wrong: mime and sign are, neurologically speaking, quite different.[10] The region of the brain that enables one to perform pantomime is not identical with the region that enables one to sign. A brain injury can destroy one ability and leave the other intact.

At the time the study was undertaken W. L. was 76 years old and recovering from a stroke. He was Deaf and prior to the stroke had been fluent in American Sign Language. He had used the language all of his life: He had two Deaf brothers; he had been married twice—both wives were Deaf—and had been an active member of the Deaf community throughout his life. Only 10 months prior to his stroke, W. L. had made a two-hour videotaped interview—the taped interview enabled researchers to directly observe W. L.'s facility in signed language just before the stroke—and the tape revealed an articulate signer.

Seven months prior to the study, W. L. had been admitted to the hospital with weakness on his right side. While he was being treated at the hospital his wife and the hospital's American Sign Language interpreter reported that he evinced considerable difficulty understanding signs. Moreover, his signing was riddled with errors, ambiguities, and nonsense signs. Careful observation revealed that he produced almost no pronouns and relatively few nouns. His signing consisted largely of uninflected verbs, that is, verbs made in presentation form. A CAT scan showed brain damage to a region of the left hemisphere. The link between left hemisphere damage and language impairment was not surprising. The correlation between left hemisphere lesions and language impairment—spoken or signed—had already been established by the time of the study. What was unique about W. L.'s disability is what it showed about the relationship between pantomime and signed language and the way that signs are represented in the brain.

First, although the injury to his left hemisphere severely impaired his ability to express himself in sign and to comprehend the signs of others, his ability to express himself via pantomime and to understand the pantomime of others was unaffected. He freely and fluently mimed various concepts and often substituted pantomime for sign, a trait that he did not display prior to his stroke. As a consequence, even when a simple sign would have sufficed, W. L. sometimes communicated an idea via an elaborate sign-free pantomime. This was true even for supposedly iconic signs. One time, in place of the sign that would be correctly translated as *flower*—an iconic sign made at the nose—W. L. substituted an elaborate set of gestures outlining the stem, petals, and blossom of a flower. Another time, in place of the *flower* sign, he mimed the action of holding a flower to his nose and smelling it. As with most of his pantomimes, these are substitutions for nouns. Note one more example: The sign usually used to represent *airplane* is, as the sign for flower is, also iconic. It is produced with a single, short, one-handed motion; the shape of the hand suggests the wings and fuselage of an airplane. W. L., however, communicated the concept of an airplane differently: He thrust his arms out from his sides and tipped his head and torso from side to side to mime the action of a plane. He did not produce the much simpler sign for the same concept. It is important to keep in mind that prior to his stroke this type of miming would have been highly atypical for W. L., but after his stroke mime was an essential part of his attempts to communicate with those around him—even with those who were fluent in sign. That one can lose the ability to sign without suffering any noticeable impairment to one's ability to mime is remarkable because it demonstrates that, neurologically, signing and miming are distinct behaviors, and in particular, signing is not pantomime.

Second, when W. L. unsuccessfully attempted to produce a sign, there were regularities involved in his difficulties. The most interesting one involved hand configuration. It is well-known that a stroke may leave one with some paralysis, but W. L.'s ability to produce gestures was unimpaired. The proof of this statement was not only in his ability to mime fluently, but also in his ability to copy abstract, or meaningless, gestures. The authors of the study employed tests to determine whether W. L. could produce sequences of hand and arm gestures. The tests involved imitating abstract (nonlinguistic) sequences of motions, and W. L.'s ability to copy these motions was unimpaired. Nevertheless, in unstructured conversation W. L. demonstrated difficulties producing the hand configurations—what Stokoe called the dez—associated with particular signs. There were 17 errors elicited by the researchers wherein W. L. produced signs that were recognizable but incorrect. In each case he demonstrated hand configuration errors. In only three cases were these hand configuration errors accompanied by movement errors. By the time the study of W. L. was undertaken, Stokoe's three aspects, movement (sig), place (tab), and hand configuration (dez), had been augmented by a fourth major parameter, the orientation of the palm. Of these four characteristics, the stroke had preferentially affected his ability to produce the correct hand shape showing that there is some neurological basis for Stokoe's identification of the hand shape as a primary part of the sublexical structure of signed language.

In summary, W. L.'s poststroke behavior pointed toward the existence of a neurological basis for the assertions that signed language is not pantomime and that signs are composed of distinct elements, often meaningless in themselves, that act much as phonemes do for spoken language. (For hearing individuals, left hemisphere injuries may also affect the production of phonemes.)

Case 2. Signed Language and the Organization of the Brain (Part 1)

Geometrically the brain is a bilaterally symmetric structure: the right half is the mirror image of the left and a deep groove, called the longitudinal cerebral fissure, separates the two. Functionally, however, the brain is highly asymmetric. Different tasks are controlled by different parts of the brain. Most language tasks, whether signed or spoken, are generally controlled by certain regions of the left hemisphere. Spatial perception, by contrast, is generally handled by certain regions on the right side. These simple facts were established long before the existence of technologies that enabled researchers to monitor brain activity. Lesion studies, for example, have shown that injuries to specific sites on the brain— either to the left or right hemisphere—can be correlated with specific impairments, and, in particular, injuries to the left hemisphere impair the production and/or comprehension of language, both signed and spoken. Taken together, however, the assertion that language is controlled by the left hemisphere and the assertion that spatial perception is controlled by the right hemisphere caused researchers to investigate the possibility that the right hemisphere may play a special role in the production and perception of signed language.

Each sign occupies a specific region of (three-dimensional) signing space, that region around the signer's body where signs are actually produced. Furthermore, as previously described, there is usually specific linguistic import associated with where and how a sign is produced in signing space. The ability to understand signed language depends, in part, on the ability of the signer to perceive how signs are oriented in three-dimensional space. The ability to express oneself in signed language requires one to parse and utilize signing space in a way that is linguistically productive. Failure to perceive the three-dimensional context in which signs are produced or failure to use signing space effectively leads to ambiguity and confusion in communication. It is not readily apparent that the same visual/spatial abilities are required to produce or comprehend spoken language.

Lesion studies have been used in an attempt to gain insight into the role of the right hemisphere in American Sign Language. One individual, identified as D. N., was studied and tested repeatedly over the course of several years by different groups of researchers. Her right hemisphere was injured, and the injury affected her signing. One group of researchers devised the following test:[11] D.N. was asked to watch and immediately repeat two types of signed stories. The stories were "matched" for information as closely as possible by constructing them so that they contained roughly the same number of propositions. One set of stories emphasized topographic information—the layout of an office, for example. The other set of stories contained little or no topographic information—favorite foods, for example. After each story D.N. was asked to retell the story. She repeated the stories that de-emphasized topographic information easily. In fact, her recall was somewhat better than the control group of signers. The stories that emphasized topographic information, however, were harder for her to repeat. She could, for example, remember the contents of a dentist's office, but she was unable to correctly describe the layout of the office even though the storyteller was quite explicit about its spatial organization.

Other researchers report that although she could use spatial indexing within a sentence—that is, she could place objects in correspondence with regions of signing space—she could not maintain her use of signing space from sentence to sentence.[12] In other words, the region of space that she would assign to represent a given object would shift from sentence to sentence. Because the ability to establish and maintain these spatial correspondences is an important part of using American Sign Language, her signing tended to be difficult to understand. D. N., however, was aware of her difficulties and compensated by repeating each noun phrase in each sentence where it appeared and hence avoiding the use of pronominal constructions. This style of signing is awkward but clear. Is this evidence that D.N.—and so other users of signed language—used the right side of her brain in processing signed language in a way that users of spoken language do not? The answer is not readily apparent, but one way of addressing this question is to attempt to look directly at the brains of individuals involved in signing and speaking.

Functional Magnetic Resonance Imaging   An important source of information about how the brain processes language comes from functional magnetic resonance imaging (fMRI) studies. To appreciate what fMRI scans reveal it helps to know a little about how they are created. One common technique for making an fMRI scan depends on the fact that oxygen-rich blood is more easily visible in fMRI images than oxygen-depleted blood. (And although other methods exist, the basic approach is the same.) When neurons become active, blood flow to the region of the brain in which the active neurons are located increases. As the amount of oxygen-rich blood increases in a particular region so does the visibility of that region. One scan, of course, cannot detect the change. Consequently, the fMRI technique involves making multiple scans of the brain. These are analyzed statistically with the goal of isolating significant differences between successive images. It is the *differences* in flow that are illuminated by the pictures generated via this technique. But while fMRI scans reveal changes in blood flow to various regions of the brain, signed language researchers are almost never interested in blood flow changes. They want to know what those changes reveal about how the brain processes language, and this is the difficulty: Data from fMRI machines may be unambiguous, but interpretations of those data usually are not.

One of the most famous of all fMRI studies of how signed language is represented in the brain was undertaken in 1998.[13] The goal was to determine whether the modality of a language affected the functional organization of the brain. To this end the researchers recruited three groups of individuals to participate in the study. The first group consisted of hearing, monolingual English speakers. The second group consisted of Deaf signers, and the third group consisted of hearing individuals who were bilingual in English and American Sign Language. Each individual in the study was then scanned using fMRI technology while each was presented with four types of stimuli: (1) simple, written declarative sentences in English, (2) written strings of nonsensical consonants, (3) a film of a Deaf signer signing American Sign Language sentences, and (4) a film of a Deaf signer producing nonsense signs that were "physically similar" to American Sign Language. As the participants processed these images, scans were made of their brains, and when the data were collected and the results compared, the researchers noticed something remarkable: While the study showed that there was significant overlap between the hearing monolingual, the Deaf, and the hearing bilingual participants in terms of activity in the left hemisphere, it also showed that the Deaf and bilingual subjects used more of the right hemisphere in processing American Sign Language sentences than their monolingual, English-speaking counterparts did in processing the written word. The researchers wondered whether this result was due to auditory deprivation or the visual/spatial nature of the language.

The study was criticized right from the start for comparing reading with signing. It seemed obvious to many that a much better comparison would have been between spoken sentences and signed ones. The first group of participants was, after all, described as composed of "monolingual, native speakers of English" rather than, say, "monolingual, native readers of English." Nevertheless, the possibility that American Sign Language—and perhaps signed languages in general—would require additional, right hemisphere regions of the brain to process sign—and that processing speech did not require these same areas—was too interesting a possibility to ignore. A great deal of research followed. After speculating on the effects of modality on language for so many years, researchers at last claimed to have found evidence that the modality in which a language is expressed left its trace in the functional organization of the brain. This paper continues to be cited in scientific journals, but perceptions about its value have changed.

Today it is generally acknowledged that the brain processes language in ways that are largely independent of modality. Early assertions that fluent signers signed from the right, or nondominant, hemisphere were based on the false comparison between signed utterances and the written word. Better-designed studies have looked for the effect and failed to find it.[14] Comparing the written word with the signed utterance was a false comparison. To be sure, there are differences in how Deaf and hearing populations use their brains to process or produce language—hearing individuals, not surprisingly, tend to use more of their auditory cortices, and the Deaf tend to use more of that part of the brain responsible for controlling movement. Overall, however, the brain seems remarkably plastic: Broca's area, Wernicke's area, and other regions used to process speech also seem well adapted for processing sign. Researchers now accept that the functional organization of the brain is not changed by the modality of the language in which one expresses oneself.[15]

Case 2. Signed Language and the Organization of the Brain (Part 2)

And what of D. N.? First, notice that it is relatively easy to discuss topographic information in English and remain ambiguous. Anyone who has ever stopped the car and asked for directions knows this is true. In fact, it can be difficult to give precise topographic information in English, and the process of doing so generally involves a fair amount of verbiage. By contrast, it is difficult not to give precise topographic information in American Sign Language. One learns early on how to exploit the three-dimensional nature of the language to describe groups of real-world objects via signing space in a way that preserves their relative real-world positions. Spatial orientation is simply more important in American Sign Language than it is in English. (Take a simple example: One can use the English words *right* and *left* correctly without knowing one's directions, but in American Sign Language the directions that are described by the signs *right* and *left* are also revealed by the directions in which one moves one's hands when signing these concepts. One cannot *sign* the concepts *right* and *left* repeatedly and correctly without knowing which direction is right and which is left, but one can repeatedly *say* the words for the concepts *right* and *left* in English without having a clear idea of what they mean, and, moreover, the speaker's confusion may not be immediately obvious to the listener.) A brain injury that diminished a speaker's ability to visualize spatial relationships would, therefore, not necessarily be obvious to a listener; nor is it clear that such an impairment would be called linguistic in a hearing person. By contrast, the same visual/spatial confusion would be much more apparent in a signer because so much topographic information is revealed in the production of the sign—that is to say, it is often the case that topographic information must be conveyed in American Sign Language in order to convey anything at all. Can a brain injury be a linguistic impairment in one language and a nonlinguistic, visual/spatial impairment in another? These questions are subtle, and the answers are not always clear.

What are the effects of modality on language? The simplicity of the question belies the complexity of the answer. Three-dimensional grammars and the existence of "two person" pronominal forms seem to be aspects of signed languages that distinguish them from spoken languages. But the existence of sublexical structures, the flexibility and expressiveness of all languages, and even the parts of the brain that process signed and spoken languages are characteristics shared by the two types of language. At this point, given the state of the relevant science, even if a complete and correct answer to the question were proposed, it is not at all clear that it would be recognized as such.

Laura Bridgman, the first educated Deafblind person in history. Photo used by permission. Perkins School for the Blind, Watertown, MA.

The Deafblind and American Sign Language

When left alone, she seems happy if she has her knitting or sewing, and will busy herself for hours: if she has no occupation, she evidently amuses herself by imaginary dialogues, or by recalling past impressions; she counts her fingers or spells out names of things which she has recently learned, in the manual alphabet of the deaf-mutes. In this lonely self-communion she seems to reason, reflect, and argue; if she spells a word wrong with the fingers of her right hand, she instantly strikes it with her left, as her teacher does, in a sign of disapprobation; if right, then she pats herself upon the head, and looks pleased. She sometimes purposely spells a word wrong with the left hand, looks roguish for a moment and laughs, and then with the right hands strikes the left, as if to correct it.

    —Samuel Gridley Howe, describing young Laura Dewey Bridgman, the first educated Deafblind person, in the Seventh Report to the Trustees of the New England Institution for the Blind

The most widely celebrated Deaf individuals in the history of the United States have also been blind, and the reason, of course, is language.

As flowers, sunshine, and thunderstorms do, language, too, must pass through the sieve of our senses. Each of us must learn to identify objects, processes, and behaviors by those characteristics that successfully make their way along our sensory pathways. For a Deafblind individual, the sieve of the senses is exceedingly fine, and many of the impressions that most people take for granted remain forever outside the experience of the Deafblind. Consequently, much of the education of the Deafblind involves making students as sensitive as possible to the input of the few senses that remain. That the sense of touch, especially, can be cultivated to such an exquisite degree of sensitivity is a remarkable testament to the determination and creativity of the students and teachers involved.

It is difficult for those whose senses of sight and hearing remain relatively intact to imagine how one apprehends the world when restricted to (at most) the senses of touch, taste, and smell: Portraits of loved ones are often reduced to the size, shape, and texture of the surrounding frame and whatever memories the frame and enclosed plate of glass invoke; mirrors, so important to so many, are, for the Deafblind, no more than smooth, cold, surfaces; sunshine, a recurrent topic in the writings of Helen Keller, is described in terms of the warmth one feels, the shadows that sunlight casts, the direction of the sun's rays, and sometimes the smells that sunshine elicits from the earth. Flowers figure prominently in the writings of Robert J. Smithdas, another prominent Deafblind author. In his autobiography he describes how, as a youth, he learned to identify different types of flowers: Smells were important, of course, as were the shapes and textures of the leaves. Tastes also helped. (It seems many of the flowers that his mother grew in her garden during his youth tasted bitter or sour.)

Language sometimes becomes a purely tactile experience for the Deafblind. Depending on the degree of one's deafness or blindness—few Deafblind are entirely deaf and entirely blind—written, spoken, or signed language, and in rare cases all three, may be purely tactile experiences. Words of sarcasm and wit, geometry and algebra, love and despair can all be communicated by touch, a situation that is, to an outsider, a continual source of wonder.

Unfortunately, few statistically precise statements can be made about the Deafblind as a social class. Unambiguous information about this group of people is not now nor has it ever been available. Estimates of the number of Deafblind in the United States, for example, vary widely. Uncertainties in the census data are caused by the existence of different definitions of deafblindness and by the difficulties encountered in identifying the Deafblind among the general population. A few facts, however, are clear. As the education of their Deaf contemporaries has been, the education of many Deafblind was also profoundly affected by the oral versus signed language debate. Second, medical technology has profoundly altered the makeup of the Deafblind as a social class. As the etiology of deafblindness has changed so have the communication needs and preferences of those who identify themselves as Deafblind. Third, because the Deafblind are such a small population and there is so much variation in the population a simple statistical description would, even if it existed, be of limited value. In this book the history of the language of the Deafblind is told as a series of individual histories, stories of interesting people living their lives in remarkable situations. Their lives illuminate much of what is interesting and unique about the Deafblind and their relationship to language.

Laura Bridgman

The social history of the Deafblind begins with Laura Dewey Bridgman, the first educated Deafblind individual. Born in Hanover, New Hampshire, in 1829, she became severely ill at the age of two. The disease, believed to be scarlet fever, killed her two older sisters. When she recovered from the initial symptoms —she was bedridden for an additional two years after the onset of her illness— she had lost her sense of hearing, and most of her senses of sight, taste, and smell. (She was still able to detect light in one eye until the age of five when she punctured her eye by walking into her mother's spinning wheel.) By the age of six, then, only her sense of touch remained intact. Nevertheless, left to her own devices and those of her immediate family, Laura Bridgman learned to sew and knit, and she developed a simple set of "home signs," idiosyncratic signs that identified family members and some of her basic needs. But communication is also a basic need, and her home signs were, by themselves, inadequate for the task. As she became older, she became exceedingly difficult to manage. As Helen Keller would so famously experience many decades later, seven-year-old Laura Bridgman experienced intense tantrums during which she had to be physically restrained.

At the age of seven, she came to the attention of Samuel Gridley Howe, the head of the recently established New England Asylum for the Blind, now the Perkins School for the Blind. Educated as a physician, Howe left for Europe upon graduation from medical school to join the Greek Revolution against the Turks. He later took part in a revolution in Poland. After he gained prominence in the United States, he lobbied strenuously and successfully for legislation promoting what he perceived to be the best interests of the Deaf, the blind, and the mentally disabled, and he was an abolitionist who contributed material support, money, and possibly guns to John Brown. But as he was during his lifetime, Samuel Howe is today best remembered as Laura Bridgman's teacher.

Howe's trip to New Hampshire to meet Laura Bridgman for the first time marked the end of a search. Howe was fascinated with the question of which ideas are inherent to the human mind and which are acquired. The topic was, in fact, one of the great philosophical questions of the time. In particular, Howe, and numerous other educators and philosophers, wanted to know whether humans are born with a conception of God. He also wanted insight into the nature of that conception, if it existed. This was also a topic on which Thomas H. Gallaudet and other faculty members at the Hartford school often wrote. Educators of the

Deaf hoped to gain insight into the question by interviewing prelingually Deaf individuals about their ideas of God prior to the time they acquired language. Howe, by contrast, had been searching for a Deafblind child who could function as a sort of ultimate test case, an individual who was almost completely unaware —unaware of language, visual and aural, and unaware of religious imagery—in the belief that such a student would enable him to distinguish learned concepts from innate ones.

Gallaudet and Howe had more in common than an interest in the nature of the untutored mind. Both were extremely articulate, socially prominent men who dedicated their lives to the education of those with disabilities. Both were interested in the education of the Deaf, and both had even been offered the position of head of the Asylum for the Blind. The trustees of the Asylum for the Blind originally offered Gallaudet the position of head of the school. Howe was offered the job only after Gallaudet turned it down.

Before learning of Bridgman, Howe had traveled to the Hartford school to meet a Deafblind student named Julia Brace, but he was unimpressed with her potential as a student. Brace was first admitted to the Hartford school shortly before her 18th birthday, too late, apparently, to overcome her language deficit. While she could sign a little and she understood some signed language by feeling the positions of the hands and arms of those who signed to her, left to herself Brace spent a great deal of time sleeping. Howe continued his search for a subject for his great experiment.

More pseudoscientist than scientist—he was fascinated with "the intellectual philosophy of phrenology"—Howe later described the Bridgmans in these words:

[the parents of Laura Bridgman were of] average height, and though slenderly built, of sound health and good habits. The father's temperament inclined to the nervous, but he had a small brain; while the mother had a very marked development of the nervous system, and an active brain, though not a large one.

They were persons of good moral character, and had received about as much culture as is common in the rural districts of New Hampshire.

The child inherited most of the physical peculiarities of the mother, with a dash of what, for want of a better name is called the "scrofulous temperament." This temperament makes one very liable to certain diseases, but it gives great delicacy of fibre, and consequent sensibility.[1]

During her early years at the Asylum for the Blind, Laura's principal instructor was not Howe but Lydia Drew. It was Drew who worked with Laura every day. They even shared a bed. Drew began by helping her young charge familiarize herself with words that were printed in raised letters and pasted onto the objects that they identified—a label with the word *fork* attached to a fork, for example. (The

Braille system, first described in an 1829 publication, did not come into general use in the United States until later in the nineteenth century.) After Laura had familiarized herself with the labeled objects, Drew separated the objects from the labels and then helped the little girl match the labels to the corresponding objects. Soon Laura, with Drew's help, learned to sequence individual letters in the correct order to identify the objects to which the labels had originally been attached, and it was during this process that Laura Bridgman perceived the connection between the raised letters and the idea of communication. She began to ask the name of each thing that she encountered, an outcome that proved the effectiveness of the method and simultaneously demonstrated its severe limitations. The method of raised letters was simply too cumbersome a means of self-expression. Laura required a more spontaneous method of communication, and so Drew taught her the manual alphabet, which she had learned from George Loring, a former student of Laurent Clerc and a former teacher at the school in Hartford. To be sure, Howe taught Laura himself occasionally, but most of the day-to-day work was Drew's. (Drew also taught Howe the manual alphabet.) Nevertheless, the highly inventive techniques and the creative concepts that formed the basis of Laura Bridgman's education were all Howe's—and so was the decision to eschew all aspects of signed language except the manual alphabet.

Although Howe had strong feelings about signed language, he never learned the language. He was familiar with the writings of Étienne Bonnot de Condillac and Roche Amboise Sicard, but was suspicious of their conclusions. Laura, Howe decided, would learn only the manual alphabet. His decision to avoid signed language was carefully justified and was an integral part of his approach to the education of Laura Bridgman.

As previously mentioned, Laura arrived at Howe's school with a small vocabulary of home signs that she used to communicate with her immediate family. These signs could have been used as a foundation upon which to build her communication skills, but Howe discouraged her from using them at all. He believed that signed language was little more than pantomime, capable only of expressing the simplest, most concrete concepts. The real test in the education of the Deafblind, as in the education of all other individuals, was, according to Howe, not whether one could learn the pantomime that he believed signed language to be, but whether one could learn "arbitrary language,"[2] by which he meant a system of symbols decoupled from the objects that they signified. He did not want Laura to translate from signed language to English. He wanted to control not only what she said, but how she thought it. Howe wanted to control the language of thought.

Howe's ideas about signed language anticipated the movement to remove signed language from American schools for the Deaf. Although he seems not to have researched the matter—his approach grew out of philosophical convictions rather experimental data—he tendered his opinions as facts, and his prominence on the American cultural scene lent a good deal of weight to what, in the end, were little more than personal prejudices about language. He seems to have believed that a healthy mind will grasp one language as readily as another, and because he believed that arbitrary language was superior to the natural language of signs, he decided that he would teach Laura English, or more precisely, written English. In his 1841 report, he expressed his understanding in these words:

> Why are words in the finger language [words spelled in the manual alphabet] so familiarly connected with thought by Laura Bridgman? Because she could use but few natural signs, or but little pantomime [upon her arrival at Perkins]; and she was prevented by her teachers from using even that little, so that the current of her thoughts, forced in a different direction, has worn for itself a channel, in which it flows naturally and smoothly.[3]

Howe went on to write that he believed that it might be possible to teach his young charge to use her voice, but decided against making the effort because "the advantage to her would not be equal to its cost in time and labor," a sentiment about the value of articulation that he shared with Charles-Michel de l'Epée, Gallaudet, and Anne Sullivan.

However one feels about Howe's ideas on language and pedagogy, as an educator of the Deafblind, there is no doubt that he succeeded where none had succeeded before, and he succeeded to a degree that few, perhaps even Howe himself, could have anticipated. By the age of 19 Bridgman was able to write the following letter to a woman who had lost her only child (the punctuation, spelling, grammar, etc., are entirely hers):

> My dear Mrs. L.:—
> I was very much surprised to hear of the decease of your darling, last Tuesday. I hoped that she would recover very soon. I trust that your little Mary is much happier at her new home than she was on the earth. I am very positive God, and his beloved Son Christ, will educate your child much better than men could in this world. I can scarcely realize that the school is so excessively beautiful in heaven. I can sympathize with you in your great affliction: I cannot help thinking of your trouble and little Mary's illness. I know very certainly that God will promote her happiness for ever. I loved her very dearly, as if she were my own daughter. I shall miss her very much every time I come to see you. I send my best love to you and a kiss. I am very sad for you. Yours, &c.
> L.B.[4]

While Howe's effect on Laura Bridgman was profound, so was her effect on him. When she was young, she was sometimes described as one of the most famous women in the world, second only to Queen Victoria. Prior to Laura Bridgman, it was an open question whether a Deafblind person could be educated, but she was brilliant, and she was pretty (a trait upon which visitors often remarked), and she was curious and cheerful, a combination that made her fascinating to many. In his annual reports to the trustees of the school Howe writes a carefully crafted narrative of an outstanding student and fascinating individual. In his 1840 report, for example, he tells how each day, when she was learning the imperfect verb tense, she would, of her own accord, compile lists of verbs that she recognized in infinitive form and present them to her teacher so that her teacher could spell the imperfect form into her hand. When her teacher informed her that the imperfect of eat was not eated but ate, Bridgman laughed and asserted that this could not be right because ate was simply *eat* with the letters permuted. The reports are filled with similar stories and bits of conversation between Laura and her teachers. In fact, virtually everything that Laura did during her early years was recorded by her teachers or by Howe. Some of it was published in the school's annual reports, and although many extra copies of the reports were published, they generally sold out quickly so great was the interest in the Asylum's most famous student.

Howe experimented on his charge as frequently and as aggressively as his humanitarian ideals permitted. He withheld from her (with her parent's permission) various ideas about God and religion and then wrote about the ideas that she developed on her own. He attached one lead of a battery to the inside of her nose and the other lead to her tongue in an attempt to stimulate her sense of taste. He had her lightly grasp smooth objects—a bar, for example—and then drew them through her grasp at varying rates to determine how accurately she could judge lengths. Each experiment was carefully recorded, and Laura, it seems, was a willing participant.

To many Americans of the time, most of whom had no interest in the pedagogy of the Deafblind, Laura Bridgman also symbolized America's humanity and philanthropy. In fact, when America's contribution to an English Great Exhibition, a forerunner of the World's Fairs of the twentieth century, was ridiculed in the British press, the Boston *Evening Telegram* published an angry editorial favorably comparing America's "Great Diamond," Laura Bridgman, with the technological triumphs of the European nations.[5] She illustrated America's willingness to educate all of its citizens regardless of social class or disability. The publicity made Laura Bridgman a great tourist attraction. Many notables came to see her. Charles Dickens wrote a long, breathless description of her. The following excerpt from Dicken's essay conveys some feeling for how her contemporaries perceived her:

> The thought occurred to me as I sat down in another room, before a girl, blind, deaf, and dumb; destitute of smell; and nearly so of taste: before a fair young creature with every human faculty, and hope, and power of goodness and affection, inclosed (sic) within her delicate frame, and but one outward sense—the sense of touch. There she was, before me; built up, as it were, in a marble cell, impervious to any ray of light, or particle of sound; with her poor white hand peeping through a chink in the wall, beckoning to some good man for help, that an Immortal soul might be awakened.[6]

Over the years, however, the public perception of Laura Bridgman changed. From an early age she showed little patience with those she considered slow-witted—a trait that impressed many as cute during her youth and as cranky during her later years. And while she was no less singular nor less impressive during her later years than she had been as a youth, she was no more singular nor more impressive, either. Interest waned. Visits from tourists—and there had been many hundreds of visitors to the Asylum each year during her youth—ceased. The public turned its attention elsewhere.

Meanwhile, Laura continued to live at the school that she had inadvertently helped to make famous, and she participated in the life of the school whenever possible. She took a special interest in other Deafblind students. Howe writes movingly of Laura's attempts to communicate with, and even teach, Oliver Caswell, a younger Deafblind student at the school, but neither Caswell nor any other Deafblind individual of her generation provided Bridgman with the conversation and company that she craved. During her life, she was unique. Despite her situation, she learned to make her solitary way in a manner that, by all accounts, brought her happiness and satisfaction. She read—her favorite book was the Bible—she wrote letters, and she maintained a lively correspondence with numerous friends. For decades after her arrival at Perkins, all Deafblind students were educated according to the model that had worked so successfully for her. In her later years, she was friends with the young Anne Sullivan, Helen Keller's future teacher, who was also a student at Perkins School for the Blind. A few years before she died, she sent a doll that she dressed herself to nine-year-old Keller.

Helen Keller

Helen Keller's story is too well-known, too well documented, to recount in any detail here. Her discovery, at the age of seven, of the connection between the exterior world and the sequence of shapes (in the form of fingerspelled words) made by her teacher, Anne Sullivan, in Helen's hand has been recounted in numerous books, theaters, and cinemas. We recount only those aspects of her story that impinge on the subject of this book.

Helen Keller (1880–1968) was born in Tuscumbia, Alabama. She contracted the disease that caused her deafness and blindness at the age of 19 months. The disease has never been identified. She was untutored for a number of years. As Helen became older, she became increasingly difficult to control, and in this, too, she resembled the by-then elderly Bridgman. Her increasingly desperate parents, learning of Laura Bridgman and how she had been successfully educated, sought the advice of Alexander Graham Bell on how to educate their daughter, and he obliged. He suggested the Perkins Institution. Samuel Howe had been dead for two years when the Kellers consulted Bell, but Howe's influence at Perkins was still strong. His son-in-law, Michael Anagnos, had taken charge of the school, and he subscribed to Howe's prejudice against signed language. Furthermore, educational trends had caught up with Howe and Perkins: By the time the Kellers sought help for their daughter, the antisigned language, oralist philosophy was the dominant philosophy in the education of the Deaf. (See Chapters 3 and 4 for a discussion of the goals of this social and educational movement.)

When the Kellers contacted Perkins for help with their daughter, Anagnos chose Anne Sullivan, a recent graduate of Perkins, to send to the Keller's home in Tuscumbia, Alabama, to educate their daughter. Sullivan, Keller's brilliant teacher, was well prepared for her assignment. She knew in a way that few of her contemporaries did that the Deafblind could be educated, because she knew Laura Bridgman personally. She also knew how to communicate with the Deafblind. In order to converse with Bridgman, she had learned the manual alphabet. Philosophically, she had already adopted the oralist philosophy of language acquisition: Make as few accommodations to the student's disability as possible and speak—or in this case fingerspell—to the student "naturally," that is, to attempt to communicate with the student just as an idealized hearing mother would communicate with her idealized hearing child.

Together, of course, Keller and Sullivan succeeded as none had previously. Keller, as Bridgman had before her, became articulate and well-read. The major difference between the two occurred later: Bridgman remained within the walls of the Perkins Institution her entire life, Keller—with Sullivan's help, and perhaps with Sullivan's continual prodding—embarked on a lifetime of travel, writing, and political activism. She became the first Deafblind individual to attend college. (In 1904, she graduated from Radcliffe College at the age of 24.) Her autobiography, published in 1903, is often described as one of the great books of the twentieth century. Throughout her life, Keller counted some of the most prominent people of her age as friends and benefactors. But Helen Keller had wanted something more: She wanted to learn to speak and to understand the speech of others.

From a technical point of view, the acquisition of speech and speech reading by a Deafblind person was something new. There were no previous case histories on which to rely. Laura Bridgman had learned to enunciate only a few words. Sullivan was skeptical of the benefits of undertaking a program to teach her famous student speech. She knew it would be extremely difficult at best—there was no guarantee of success—and the time spent in learning to pronounce words might better be spent in other pursuits. In fact, in her 1891 report for the Perkins School, Sullivan wrote that she believed the considerable time and energy that currently went into teaching speech to Deaf children at many schools for the Deaf meant that those students missed numerous opportunities to enhance intellectual development. The acquisition of speech and speech reading is slow, hard work. It was natural to suspect that these skills would be even harder and more time-consuming for Keller to acquire than for students who were deaf but sighted—in part, because of her twin disabilities but also because no one had any experience teaching a Deafblind individual these skills.

The acquisition of effective speech and speech reading skills proved to be very difficult for Keller. She used at least two different techniques for speech reading. One involved placing the tips of her fingers on the cheek near the mouth of the speaker in order to feel the motions of the lips while simultaneously placing her thumb on the individual's larynx. A second method was to place the fingers around the mouth. Both methods were awkward and later generations of Deafblind who relied on tactile speech used more efficient methods. Moreover, her speech, the improvement of which was a long-standing goal of hers, was never especially good despite years of hard work, and in this area, too, she has been surpassed by later Deafblind individuals. It is doubtful, however, that her determination to learn to speak has ever been surpassed. Helen Keller did not simply wish to speak like those around her—and virtually everyone did speak because virtually everyone around her was hearing—she was ambivalent about her use of the manual alphabet, the very medium that had first made it possible for her to communicate with Sullivan. In her book *Teacher* she describes the extraordinary efforts that she undertook simply to break herself of the habit of fingerspelling to herself after the acquisition of her (imperfect) speech. She describes the habit as a sin. "[Keller (in this passage she describes herself in the third person)] sinned . . . by spelling constantly to herself with her fingers, even after she had learned to speak with her mouth."[7] Keller, who wrote *Teacher* when she was in her 70s, reveals that she asked Sullivan to tie her fingers in paper in order to physically prevent her from spelling. Sullivan complied and cried as Keller restrained herself "day and night." The experiment was only partially successful. Even in her 70s, during times of excitement or when she woke from sleep, she continued to finger-spell to herself. She remained heavily dependent on the manual alphabet as a means of communication and used it to communicate with Sullivan and Polly Thompson, Sullivan's successor.

If Helen Keller's ideas and attitudes about language were complex, it is because language is complex. She did not have the luxury of waiting until she had refined her ideas into a coherent, easy-to-explain, logical whole. She had to live life as it was and communicate in whatever ways that were available to her, a situation that she shared with the rest of humanity. If she felt more strongly than others about language, it was because her struggle to communicate was so much more difficult than that of most others. There is little doubt, however, that she was one of the most effective communicators of her generation.

With respect to the issue of teaching speech to the Deaf, Keller was a more enthusiastic proponent of the idea than her teacher. She was not shy about exhorting the Deaf to adopt speech as their primary means of communication. She claimed to be unable to see the value of any other approach, and, although she acknowledged that another approach to educating and communicating with the Deaf existed, she demonstrated little familiarity with it. The manual alphabet was the only aspect of American Sign Language that she adopted, and in her book, *Teacher,* she expresses gratitude to Bell and especially to her teacher, Anne Sullivan, because Sullivan had an "undimmed vision . . . [of Keller] as a dweller in the world of normal humanity . . . [and not as a] deaf or blind variety of being,"[8] an apparent reference to Bell's controversial article on eugenics, "On the Formation of a Deaf Variety of the Human Race."

In a famous 1896 address to the fifth meeting of the American Association to Promote the Teaching of Speech to the Deaf at Mount Airy, Pennsylvania, home to the Pennsylvania School for the Deaf, Keller described with great eloquence her feelings about the value of speech for the Deaf. She drew on her own experiences and described the great pleasure that she derived from the spoken word, and she told the audience how that skill had brought her closer to those she loved. (She used her immediate family as an example and described how they would ask her to read to them and how she and her father engaged in long discussions. She took pains to emphasize the importance of these activities in her life.) She denigrated the value of the manual alphabet as a medium of communication and claimed that the use of the manual alphabet had been a struggle of its own kind. Prior to the acquisition of speech, she said, her thoughts "beat against my finger-tips like little birds striving to gain their freedom." In fact, she claimed that she was unable to effectively give expression to her ideas until she was taught speech. She acknowledged that the acquisition of speech was difficult and time-consuming and that her speech, in particular, was not always easy for strangers to understand, and she ended her address by exhorting the Deaf to strive to learn to speak:

> So I want to say to those who are trying to learn to speak and those who are teaching them: Be of good cheer. Do not think of today's failures, but of the success that may come tomorrow. You have set yourselves a difficult task, but you will succeed if you persevere; and you will find a joy in overcoming obstacles—a delight in climbing rugged paths, which you would perhaps never know if you did not sometime slip backward—if the road was always smooth and pleasant. Remember, no effort that we make to attain something beautiful is ever lost. Sometime, somewhere, somehow we shall find that which we seek. We shall speak, yes, and sing, too, as God intended we should speak and sing.[9]

It is a remarkable speech, but it was made in a voice that many found difficult to understand by a woman who was continually accompanied by Anne Sullivan, one of the most gifted educators of her time and who, among her many other talents, served expertly as an interpreter for Keller whenever an interpreter was needed. And Keller's speech was made to an association composed largely of hearing individuals. Although Keller spoke directly to the Deaf in her speech, her mode of communication was singularly ill suited to communicate to that very audience the ideas about which she felt so strongly. Speech reading someone on a distant podium is impossible even under the best of conditions.

The Tadoma Method

In the same way that the history of the Deafblind did not begin with Helen Keller, it did not end with her. Educational practices continued to evolve as did ideas about language. The Tadoma method, an extremely interesting innovation in Deafblind communication, was an important factor. The purpose of the Tadoma method is to enable the Deafblind user to learn to speak and to read the speech of others. The technique, the implementation of which varies somewhat from individual to individual, generally requires one to place the thumb lightly on the lips of the person whose speech one wants to read. The fingers of the hand are spread out along the side of the face and throat so that the motions of the jaw, the facial expressions of the speaker, and the vibrations of the vocal tract can all be felt. (Notice, for example, that although the letters *m, b,* and *p look* the same to a lip reader, they do not *feel* the same to someone using the Tadoma method.)

Tests have shown that individuals fluent in the method can exhibit good speech comprehension at rates of about 1/3 that of normal speech—so-called normal speech proceeds at a rate of about 100 words per minute—and some claim that fluent Tadoma users display good comprehension at even higher production rates—about 40 words per minute. In addition to facilitating communication with others, one can apply the Tadoma method to oneself, and so check one's own speech for clarity. Historically, oral educators envisioned that the Tadoma method would supplant fingerspelling among the Deafblind just as they hoped that speech and speech reading would supplant signed language among the Deaf. As one might imagine, the Tadoma method is quite difficult to learn, and it does not work for everyone, but when it does work, the results can be spectacular.

Sophia Alcorn (1883–1967) taught the first American Deafblind students the Tadoma method in the 1920s. Tad Chapman and Oma Simpson were the names of her students, hence the name of the method. Alcorn learned the basics of the method from Caroline Yale (1848–1933), who was a teacher at Clarke School in Northampton, Massachusetts, and who used the method to teach the Deaf—but not the Deafblind—speech. A June 25, 1927, article in the *New York Times* describes Chapman, then 12 years old, as the main attraction at a meeting of the Society of Progressive Oral Advocates. By this time, he had acquired a vocabulary of 2,000 words exclusively through a particularly difficult variant of the Tadoma method, one that involved placing his thumb on the speaker's face rather than on the speaker's lips. In an October 1930 article in the *Volta Review,* Alcorn explained that she had taught him this variant because some people were reluctant to have him place his thumb upon their lips. By the age of 17, he was enrolled at Perkins and communicating via Morse code and the manual alphabet as well as Tadoma. As a youth Chapman was famous, but the public eventually became used to the breathless accounts of his impressive accomplishments—and although his accomplishments remained impressive they did not become more impressive with age—and so, as Laura Bridgman had done before him, Tad Chapman also faded from public view.

At the Perkins School for the Blind, the Tadoma method was used *in place of the manual alphabet* for many years, if, in the teacher's judgment, the student could communicate without the aid of fingerspelling. These were the years when oral education was the dominant philosophy in American Deaf education, and according to Gertrude Stenquist (1912–1994), a longtime teacher at Perkins, the faculty at Perkins believed that the manual alphabet would interfere with the acquisition of speech. Stenquist perceived sign as even more of a problem. Once a child learned to sign, she asserted, he or she would have little interest in acquiring or using speech. Consequently, for many Deafblind Tadoma was not *a* method but *the* method of communication during their early years at Perkins, the school which was, and perhaps remains, the foremost institution for

Deafblind education in the world. The emphasis on the Tadoma method began to fade in the 1950s.[10]

One of the most prominent users of Tadoma is Robert J. Smithdas (b. 1925), an author and speaker and the second Deafblind individual (after Helen Keller) to receive a college degree. Meningitis was the cause of Smithdas's deafblindness. He contracted the disease at the age of five. When he recovered, he had a little residual hearing in his right ear—not enough to enable him to develop clear speech but if one spoke directly into that ear and was willing to repeat oneself, verbal communication remained possible. Smithdas's residual hearing was lost over the next few years. He learned the Tadoma method at Perkins.

Smithdas attended St. John's College several decades after Keller attended Radcliffe. The comparison between the two was an obvious one, and the elderly Helen Keller visited Smithdas just prior to the start of his college career. Smithdas's account of the meeting indicates that it was a brief one. He presented her with a corsage, and she expressed her pleasure in his accomplishments, warned him of the difficulty of the task he was about to undertake, and assured him of her confidence in his success.[11] Except for feelings of nervousness, Smithdas does not describe his own reaction to their meeting. In any case, he went on to graduate from St. John's. He has since written an entertaining and memorable autobiography and two volumes of poetry. As of this writing, he is associated with the Helen Keller National Center for Deaf-Blind Youths and Adults, where he has been a part of the staff for many years.

Thanks, in part, to the Tadoma method, Smithdas's speech is much clearer than Helen Keller's ever was. Smithdas's account[12] of his experiences learning the Tadoma method indicates the initial work was arduous and intimate. He was not allowed to use the manual alphabet during the lessons. He placed his fingers inside the teacher's mouth, for example, to feel the position and tension in the tongue associated with various sounds. He had to hold his hand in the difficult position characteristic of the Tadoma method for extended periods of time. Months passed before he was able to understand even the simplest sentences, and 15 years would pass before he could confidently deliver a lecture.

Some Deafblind individuals acquire a fair amount of speech before losing their hearing. In these cases, the acquisition of the Tadoma method is to some degree a matter of substituting that method of communication for a previously acquired one. These individuals acquire their knowledge of language in the usual way so it was "only" a question of switching modalities. They substituted a tactile medium for an aural one. There are other instances, however, involving prelingually Deafblind individuals, in which the Tadoma method was, in effect, their first language in the sense that it was via the Tadoma method that they were initially exposed to spoken language. Despite the sometimes astonishing successes made possible by this mode of communication, the Tadoma method is rarely taught today, and the number of users continues to decline. Some contemporary estimates have the total number of users at about 50 worldwide, half of whom live in the United States. (As of this writing, there is one student currently at Perkins who is skilled in using the Tadoma method.)

Tactile American Sign Language

American Sign Language is far more widely used among the Deafblind than the Tadoma method. The intellectual tradition represented by Bridgman, Keller, and Smithdas, a tradition that eschews signed language in favor of the manual alphabet and (insofar as possible) the manual alphabet in favor of speech, affected one small, but particularly famous, segment of the Deafblind population. There is another segment of the Deafblind whose relationship to American Sign Language is far more complex. They have always been present, but they have become increasingly prominent of late. To understand why, it helps to know a little about changes that have occurred in the Deafblind population.

As noted in the beginning of this chapter, the etiologies of deafblindness have changed a great deal since the time of Laura Bridgman. On the one hand, many previous causes of deafblindness have been brought under control. Scarlet fever, rubella, and meningitis, for example, once significant causes of deafblindness, are not as common as they once were thanks to antibiotics, routine vaccinations, and better treatment protocols. One might think, therefore, that the number of Deafblind has decreased, but that is probably not the case. Improvements in medical technology have also meant that children with severe disabilities, children who previously would not have survived, are alive today. Some of these individuals are Deafblind. The geriatric Deafblind are also an increasing segment of the Deafblind population, but it is difficult to make either of these statements precise. Statistics on the number of Deafblind in the United States are incomplete, and consequently, generalizations are, whenever possible, best avoided. The best source on the Deafblind population in the United States is the Deafblind census, which provides a fairly complete picture of that segment of the population between the ages of birth and 22 years of age but nothing beyond the age of 22. The Deafblind census indicates that there are about 10,000 individuals in this age group. From this information, Nancy O'Donnell of the Helen Keller National Center for Deaf-Blind Youths and Adults estimates that there are at least 50,000 Deafblind individuals throughout the United States.[13]

One important component of the Deafblind population that has remained relatively constant in numbers during recent years, a group of particular interest to readers of this book, is comprised of individuals with Usher syndrome, a genetic condition that causes both hearing and vision loss. Individuals with Usher syndrome compose a major segment of the Deafblind community, although (again) it is difficult to be precise about the details. A reasonable estimate is that approximately one-fourth of all American Deafblind have Usher syndrome. Many individuals with the condition use American Sign Language as a first language, and it is to this group and the way that those with Usher syndrome use signed language that we now turn our attention.

There are three types of Usher syndrome, Types I, II, and III. Types I and II together comprise over 90 percent of the total. The relatively rare type III is responsible for the remainder. We confine our remarks to the first two types. The symptoms characteristic of Usher syndrome include hearing loss and balance problems (but not any cognitive disabilities) and tend to be more severe among those with type I than type II. Individuals with type I often have American Sign Language as their first language, and some individuals with type II also use American Sign Language as their first language.

Usher syndrome manifests itself over many years. The affected individual is born hearing impaired and with a visual condition called retinitis pigmentosa, which is not immediately apparent. Individuals with retinitis pigmentosa are born with good vision, but over time their night vision begins to fail. Night blindness generally occurs while the individual is relatively young, usually a teenager or young adult. Concomitant with the loss of night vision, the individual also begins to lose peripheral vision. Loss of peripheral vision, a condition sometimes called tunnel vision, proceeds at a slower rate, and the individual generally becomes entirely blind in middle age. As of this writing there is no cure.

Historically, individuals with Usher syndrome have often been educated alongside their Deaf (sighted) counterparts, because when they are young, deafness is the dominant condition. Vision problems are not initially severe enough to significantly affect one's lifestyle. This is why American Sign Language is often the primary language of those with the condition. As these individuals become older, however, understanding signed language becomes increasingly difficult. The loss of peripheral vision reduces one's view to what one would obtain by looking through a long narrow tube. Initially, one's expressive signed language is unimpaired. (Expressive difficulties, if they occur, arise later because one is unable to view one's own signs, and without feedback, signs sometimes become less clearly articulated.) The more immediate problem occurs in the area of signed language comprehension.

It is an oft-made observation that individuals fluent in signed language watch each other's faces rather than each other's hands while signing. In order to sign effectively, signers depend heavily on their peripheral vision. Signing space, the region about the body where one produces signs, is fairly large. It extends slightly above the top of one's head and is bounded below by one's waist; laterally, it extends somewhat past one's shoulders, and in terms of depth, it is roughly bounded by a plane tangent to the front of one's body and a second, parallel plane placed at a distance of about two-thirds of the length of one's arms when they are extended straight out. Fluent, expressive signing involves making full use of this space, but for an individual with little peripheral vision seated at a normal conversational distance from a signer most of the signing space is out of sight.

The loss of peripheral vision happens slowly, almost imperceptibly, but the process is inexorable. The older the individual with Usher syndrome becomes, the smaller is his or her field of vision. It is a paradox: For a young person with Usher syndrome, American Sign Language is often the natural choice. It is easy to learn, expressive, and enabling. As one becomes older, however, and one's vision diminishes slowly and predictably, signed conversations become increasingly difficult to understand. Each affected individual solves and resolves the problem of signed language comprehension as his or her vision continues to diminish.

Solutions to the problem of a diminishing field of view depend on the individual and the extent to which the visual field has contracted. Initially, it might be enough to increase the distance between the two individuals engaged in conversation. Early in the progression of the syndrome, the affected individual can simply step back and continue to view signing space with few or no modifications on the part of the signer, because under these conditions signing space occupies a smaller part of one's field of view. Stepping back enables the individual with Usher syndrome to "fit" signing space into the region of space still visible to them. Alternatively, the Deafblind person might prefer that the signing partner remain closer and simply modify all signs in such a way that each sign is made within that part of signing space visible to the Deafblind individual. This technique, too, has its limitations. As signs are made in an ever-smaller region of space, clarity is lost as certain previously easy-to-distinguish signs become indistinguishable. Signs that are distinguished solely by their place of articulation are the hardest to tell apart under these conditions, because in order to fit the signs into an ever-smaller signing space, the signer must dispense with the sign's place of articulation. This difficulty can, however, be addressed by fingerspelling more and signing less. Because fingerspelling occupies a relatively small region of space, one need be sure only that one places one's hand in the Deafblind individual's field of vision before beginning. Because the vision of an individual with Usher syndrome continues to deteriorate, all of these techniques eventually fail.

One often signs *to* a Deafblind individual fluent in American Sign Language and with no residual vision in the following manner: The Deafblind individual rests his or her hands lightly on the hands of the signer. (Some individuals prefer to use one hand only. For specificity this chapter treats the two-handed case, but one-handed sign reception is similar to that described here.) Their hands remain in contact for as long as the signing party continues to sign. The Deafblind individual's partner-in-conversation signs as normally as possible and in the process moves the Deafblind individual's hands through a sequence of gestures. In this way, the Deafblind individual reads the signs by feeling the motions, hand configurations, and places of articulation of the signer's hands. The Deafblind individual responds by signing, and because there are no unusual constraints on the signing of the Deafblind individual, communication from the Deafblind person to the other (sighted) participant proceeds in a more or less familiar way. (With obvious modifications, the techniques described here also enable two Deafblind individuals to sign to each other.) Signed communication *to* the Deafblind individual may be somewhat slower than signed communication to a sighted individual, but variations in the signing rate are large and depend on the individuals involved.

What happens to American Sign Language when it is expressed tactilely? (To prevent confusion the term American Sign Language is, for the remainder of this chapter, reserved for the version of the language used by sighted signers, and the term tactile signed language is used to refer to that version of American Sign Language used by the Deafblind.) To be sure, fluent, sighted signers have little difficulty recognizing tactile sign as a form of American Sign Language, and these individuals are usually able to carry on conversations with fluent (Deafblind) tactile signers, but, not surprisingly, accommodations must be made for the change in modality. Conversations do not always go smoothly for inexperienced sighted signers interested in conversing with tactile signers. To convey a little of what makes this type of signing unique—and uniquely difficult—we consider how tactile signers deal with three aspects of American Sign Language.

First, recall that American Sign Language is often described as a dual channel activity (see Chapter 7) in the sense that much of the information is conveyed nonmanually. The difference between asking a question and issuing a command in American Sign Language, for example, often depends principally on one's facial expressions. But in tactile sign, facial expressions are literally beyond reach. Similarly, negation in American Sign Language is often conveyed via a shake of the head while *simultaneously* signing the sentence to be negated. In this case, it is clear that without some modification of the form of the initial utterance all that will be conveyed to the tactile signer is the unnegated sentence. Meaning will be lost.

For tactile signers, then, one common source of difficulty involves distinguishing between questions and statements—especially when their interpreter or conversation partner is inexperienced in tactile sign. Among fluent tactile signers, the problem is often solved by first pointing toward the Deafblind individual and then formulating the question. Furthermore, that part of the utterance following the pointing gesture will generally include an explicit manually produced interrogative. Consider questions that are formulated so as to permit only a yes/no response. In this case, it is not uncommon for tactile signers to complete the question with a sign that is used almost exclusively at the end of questions. It is made by crooking the index finger (sometimes described as crooking the finger in the shape of a question mark) and wiggling the end of the finger. This "question sign" is used in American Sign Language as well, but less frequently and usually only for emphasis—a questioning facial expression is generally considered sufficient. Tactile sign simply transfers, via this sign, information from the face to the hands where the nature of the utterance can be more readily perceived.

Another example of an important difference between American Sign Language and tactile signed language is the way that the receiver provides feedback to the signer as information is conveyed, a phenomenon sometimes called "back-channel feedback." Consider, for example, the case of two English speakers engaged in conversation. While the speaker is talking, the listener may simultaneously convey agreement with the speaker by saying a few words or even merely a few syllables—for example, "right" or "uh-huh." These or other words or syllables might also be used to convey the idea that the listener understands the intent of the speaker independently of whether there is agreement between the two parties. What is important is that these brief utterances occur simultaneously with the speaker's utterances and that they not interrupt the flow of information from the speaker. A similar phenomenon occurs in American Sign Language. There are even a few signs that are used almost exclusively in this context—probably the most common is the Y hand shape (produced palm down or sometimes used with the palm facing outward) that is "bounced" up and down lightly and only occasionally to signify that the listener is following the speaker.

Introducing back-channel feedback in tactile signed language must be done in such a way that it can be expressed while the receiver's hands are in contact with the speaker's hands but without interrupting the speaker's own narrative. This is the difficulty: Once hand contact is broken, so is communication. Furthermore, contact between the hands of the two parties is not symmetric. The receiver's hands are placed lightly on top of the signer's hands making it difficult to convey specific hand configurations from receiver to speaker. The solution is for the receiver to tap lightly on the top of the speaker's hands—sometimes with one finger and sometimes with all four—at varying rates, repetitions, and degrees of emphasis. These tapping motions do not interrupt the flow of the narrative; they can be executed simultaneously with the narrative, and they function in the same way as the forms of back-channel feedback for English or American Sign Language previously described. Steve Collins and Karen Petronio[14] write that these forms of tactile feedback are practiced un-self-consciously by fluent Deafblind signers from different areas of the country. Indeed, when it was pointed out to a group of tactile signers that they were using these utterances, they were surprised, as they had not consciously been aware of the construction.

While much of American Sign Language carries over without difficulty to tactile sign, and some of the rest can be adapted to the sense of touch, there are certain aspects American Sign Language that remain problematic when expressed tactilely. One of the more important of these traits involves comprehending signs made near the face.

Individuals fluent in sign generally focus their attention on the face of the signer and rely on their peripheral vision to supply the remainder of the information. As a consequence there are many signs made on or near the face that differ only slightly in their place of articulation or in the movement that distinguishes them. (By contrast signs made on the torso are generally larger and do not depend so much on subtleties of placement to distinguish them.) For example, the sign that is sometimes translated as "dry" is made on or near the chin, and the sign that is sometimes translated as "summer," which is identical in movement and hand shape, is placed on or near the forehead. Furthermore, if the sign often used to convey the idea of "ugly" is made with one hand—and it often is—it is identical in hand shape and movement as "dry" and "summer," but is placed directly in front of the nose. These subtle differences between signs are difficult to convey in tactile signed language and may result in confusion.

One solution to the problem of conveying signs that "feel the same" to the tactile signer involves fingerspelling a one-word synonym for the sign in question. Of course, fingerspelling tends to be slower than signing, and it involves substituting an English word for an American Sign Language sign so it entails a certain amount of awkwardness. Another solution is to rely more on the context in which the sign appears. What is important to bear in mind is that the adaptations made by each Deafblind person are sometimes unique to that person. It is a truism that each individual, no matter the language used, employs language in a way that is characteristic of that individual. Nonetheless, the range of variation of communication techniques among the Deafblind is almost certainly greater than that which one finds among most other groups and is out of all proportion to the size of the population.

The statistics of American Sign Language use among the Deafblind are not especially reliable. Etiologies and times of onset of the condition of deafblindness vary widely among individuals—and these factors have profound effects on language acquisition—so the language differences among those in this relatively small group are large. Even among that subset of the Deafblind population consisting of those with Usher syndrome, there is great individual variation in language use. Because the value of the available statistics is so suspect, it is more instructive to consider the insights and accomplishments of a single Deafblind individual. No claim is made that his story is typical, in part, because it is not certain what typical means in this context. But his story is interesting and demonstrates how one individual with Usher syndrome learned to make the transition from a life based on sight to one based on touch and from a visual version of American Sign Language to a tactile one. It is an example of how one person has learned to live a vital and productive life under circumstances that most people would describe as difficult.

Harry C. Anderson

Harry C. Anderson (b. 1936) has Usher syndrome.[15] Born in Moorhead, Minnesota, Anderson was educated at the Minnesota School for the Deaf in Fairbault. He received a Bachelor's degree in Business Administration from Gallaudet College, now Gallaudet University, and Master's degrees in Deaf Education and Guidance Counseling from Gallaudet and the University of North Florida, respectively.

Anderson identifies English as his first language, but he has spent his life in environments where American Sign Language is the dominant language. This is as true of his personal life as it is of his educational and professional lives: An older sister has Usher syndrome, and they have always signed together; his wife, Elaine Anderson, is Deaf, and their two sons are also Deaf.

At the age of 13 Anderson began to encounter difficulty seeing in movie theaters and other dimly lit environments. Adjusting to sudden changes in lighting conditions also proved increasingly difficult for him. As his peripheral vision began to diminish, he initially compensated by increasing the distance between himself and those with whom he conversed—preferring to stand six to eight feet away instead of a more common distance of three to four feet. If the situation was such that it was not possible to maintain the greater distance, he concentrated on the signer's hands rather than the signer's face because his diminished peripheral vision made it impossible for him to see both simultaneously. As he became older, he continued to search for ways to compensate for his fading vision—more powerful lenses for his glasses, holding printed material ever closer to his eyes, and sometimes simply pretending to understand conversations that he could not see. These experiences are common among those with Usher syndrome as they make the transition from being Deaf to being Deafblind.

It was not until he was 36 years old that Anderson was diagnosed with Usher syndrome. (Such a late diagnosis is now atypical. Increased awareness on the part of health professionals and breakthroughs in genetics make earlier diagnoses more the rule than the exception today.) His initial concerns subsequent to the diagnosis were for his marriage, his relationships with his sons, and his career. His had been a visual world. He had not, for example, used hearing aids prior to the diagnosis, a situation that soon changed.

Because there is no cure for Usher syndrome, one can only adapt to what one knows is the outcome. As his vision faded, Anderson's family life remained strong. This is not always the case for those with Usher syndrome, and in correspondence with the author Anderson's remarks about his wife strongly convey not just love but appreciation. After the diagnosis, Anderson ceased working as a classroom teacher of the Deaf. He made the transition to a counselor at the Florida School for the Deaf and the Blind. He later left his job as counselor to work as the research coordinator on a three-year federal grant on the educational, employment, transportation, and housing needs of the Deafblind in Florida. After the grant expired, he worked as an assistant director of a rehabilitation center for blind individuals with multiple disabilities before returning to the Florida School for the Deaf and the Blind, where he worked until his retirement as a guidance counselor for children with multiple disabilities.

Throughout his life Anderson has had to solve and resolve the problem of communication. Switching from a visual form of American Sign Language to a form of American Sign Language based on touch occurred in steps. At first, he used tactile sign only in dimly lit environments. As his condition progressed, however, he employed tactile signed language in an increasing number of situations, and eventually, he had no choice but to use tactile signed language in all those situations in which he had previously communicated visually. Anderson does not seem to regard the change in modality as particularly significant of itself. The tactile mode, he asserts, does not even require more concentration. As previously described in this chapter, to communicate via tactile sign, he places his hands on the hands of his partner in order to follow the manual component of the language. He says that the tension in the signer's hands and arms, the tempo of the signs, and the force with which the signs are made all help him to visualize various nonmanual components of the other party's sign. It is a method of communication with which he has become comfortable, and he remains a proficient and entertaining conversationalist as well as a noted storyteller in American Sign Language.

But it was not simply a matter of changing from a visual to a tactile language that made the difference for Harry Anderson. Technology has enabled him to make the transition to a new way of living. Technical innovations of all sorts play an increasingly important role in his life and in the lives of many other Deafblind. In Anderson's case, he began to use the best hearing aids available (as previously mentioned, he had not depended on hearing aids until after his diagnosis with Usher syndrome), because his level of hearing remained constant even as his vision went from bad to worse—a situation that is typical for those with type II Usher syndrome. In addition to his hearing aids, he now owns a personal FM system that enables him to listen to a (wireless) transmitter from a distance not exceeding a few hundred feet. And should his hearing fail to the extent that hearing aids no longer help, he remains ready to opt for a cochlear implant "at the earliest possible opportunity." (Cochlear implants are surgically implanted devices that bypass parts of the normal hearing apparatus in order to directly stimulate the auditory nerve of the user. See Chapter 9 for more information.) In addition to various assistive devices that enable him to better hear his surroundings, his computer is equipped with software that converts printed text into voice output and so enables him to use e-mail and other applications.

For many with type I Usher syndrome, where hearing loss is more severe than that experienced by those with type II, neither hearing aids, FM systems, nor cochlear implants are normally of much use. Still other devices exist, however, that turn computer text files into Braille files, and, provided that the individual is ready and able to learn and use Braille, these other devices may prove to be of some use. There are even devices that enable the Deafblind to use the telephone. These machines are modeled on similar devices used by sighted Deaf, called text telephones or TTYs (sometimes called telecommunication devices for the Deaf or TDDs). TTYs convert typed input into acoustic signals that are sent over the phone lines to another TTY; the receiving device then converts the acoustic input back into typed output. Such machines are useless to those without vision. The devices used by the Deafblind are modified to convert the received signal into Braille output.

Much has changed for the Deafblind since the days of Laura Bridgman. Etiologies have changed as have educational philosophies, assistive technologies, and expectations about life's possibilities. Language use among the Deafblind has changed. The composition of the Deafblind as a social class has also changed. With respect to those Deafblind fluent in American Sign Language—principally those with Usher syndrome, a group that comprises perhaps 2 to 3 percent of all Deaf in the United States and perhaps 25 percent of all Deafblind—there are now well-marked paths, pioneered by individuals like Harry Anderson, that illustrate how one can maintain one's language and other aspects of Deaf culture and continue to contribute to society during and after the difficult transition to life without light.

Nine

Some Contemporary Trends Affecting American Sign Language

The educated deaf differ from other people merely in the lack of hearing. They seek neither pity nor charity...but just a square deal in their relations with the hearing community.

—Thomas F. Fox[1]

For those unfamiliar with Deaf culture and the culturally Deaf, it is often difficult to appreciate the idea that many Deaf do not perceive deafness as a disability. These Deaf reject the label "handicapped," as they reject the necessity of a technical fix for the physical characteristic that many outsiders perceive to be their defining trait. Theirs is Deafness as culture, and to be culturally Deaf is, in this view, not a bad thing at all. In fact, many Deaf now celebrate their Deafness and describe their lives as filled with possibilities rather than limitations. Knowledge of Deaf history is widespread among this group, and these (adult) Deaf can, consequently, point to successful, historically important Deaf individuals who have contributed to any number of fields. As this text has indicated, there is no shortage of interesting, historically important individuals, and to be part of this heritage is, for many, a source of pride.

Today, many Deaf would be who they are, and this is new. The abbé de l'Epée, Pierre Desloges, T.H. Gallaudet, Laurent Clerc, A.G. Bell, William Holland, Helen Keller, John B. Hotchkiss, Alice Terry,...virtually everyone involved in this history, until recent times, agreed on one assertion, and none of them were shy about saying it out loud: Deafness is a misfortune borne by those who evince the trait and by their families. The nature of signed language, its role in the lives of adult Deaf, the use of American Sign Language in the education of Deaf

Discussing art in American Sign Language. This unique language is rapidly evolving in response to changes in law and educational philosophy. Courtesy of Gail Christian and Leela Christian-Tabak.

children, and every other issue associated with the Deaf and their language has always been open to often rancorous debate, but the disagreements centered on how best to alleviate the effects of deafness. There was no disagreement on what they perceived as the tragic nature of the condition itself. But it is no longer uncommon to encounter Deaf individuals who explicitly reject the characterization of deafness as a tragedy. They perceive deafness in terms that are primarily linguistic—their first language, American Sign Language, is different from that of the majority—and cultural, because Deaf culture involves practices, values, and traditions that are somewhat different from the mainstream. The analogy, described in Chapter 4, between the Deaf and certain ethnic groups whose first language is not English has never been more enthusiastically embraced. To understand the response of many Deaf to certain trends in education and medicine with the potential to impact the future of their language and culture, one must first appreciate a linguistic and cultural conception of deafness.

Few individuals not intimately familiar with Deaf culture are aware of how thoroughly a cultural and linguistic description of deafness has come to pervade the perceptions of many Deaf, and they express surprise when first learning of it. There is, after all, much in contemporary American culture to militate against such a positive view of deafness. Today, many scientists, physicians, and, more recently, biomedical engineers spend their professional lives attempting to "cure" deafness. These individuals see deafness in the narrowest possible terms; that is, they perceive deafness as a physical defect resulting in a communication disorder. Indeed, one of the institutes that comprises the National Institutes of Health is called the National Institute on Deafness and Communication Disorders (NIDCD), and its motto is "improving the lives of people who have communication disorders." Those researchers employed at the NIDCD seek a cure for deafness just as other health professionals seek cures for cancer, multiple sclerosis, or sickle cell anemia. Never mind that the condition of deafness is hardly fatal and that many Deaf—who are, after all, best positioned to evaluate the seriousness of their condition—not only reject a surgical cure for their condition but cannot be bothered to wear hearing aids even when they know from their own experience that they hear better with them than without. How seriously can such individuals regard their "disability?" How worried can they be about their "disorder?" Is research at the NIDCD distorted by a lack of awareness of how the Deaf themselves see their condition? As of this writing, for example, there is nothing on the NIDCD Web site that portrays the Deaf as capable individuals who live interesting lives as Deaf people—not interesting lives *in spite of* their deafness, but interesting lives *as* Deaf people—rather, the view at the NIDCD is of the Deaf as victims requiring aggressive curative treatments.

There have always been these two competing perceptions of deafness—deafness as a deficit and deafness as a cultural and linguistic heritage—and views about the meaning of deafness have never been more polarized than they are today. Among health-care professionals, those perceptions are often ahistorical. In effect, far too many doctors, scientists, and biomedical engineers work in a vacuum. They are sure that their perceptions of the meaning of deafness in the lives of the Deaf are correct, but they are unable to assess the value of their perceptions relative to those of others because they have never bothered to familiarize themselves with ideas different from those they acquired during their own educations. Incredibly, there are many individuals involved in the most intimate and profound issues specifically affecting the lives of the Deaf who have never had meaningful contact with Deaf adults.[2] Unaware of the great harm that was done to previous generations by those who also subscribed to a medicalized view of deafness, they are bewildered by the hostility that their views engender in those who have suffered from the well-meaning efforts of previous generations of such professionals. This view of deafness as disability, uninformed as it usually is by knowledge of the Deaf and the history of the Deaf, is shared by many outside the health-care field as well.

But if so much of society perceives deafness so negatively, how can so many culturally Deaf individuals be positive about their situation? First, it is important to understand that the assertions of the Deaf are sincere. Many Deaf adults hope, for example, to have Deaf children. They neither fear nor regret their Deafness, and consequently, they wish to share it. These individuals, who understand Deafness in ways that most hearing people never can, have decided that Deafness is worth sharing with those they love the most and for whom they are the most ambitious.

Second, many Deaf understand that deafness of itself does not preclude one from an interesting and successful life. Although this has been true in the United States from the time that the Hartford school first opened its doors, it is also true that Deaf Americans currently live during a time of unprecedented opportunity. There are now successful Deaf attorneys, Deaf architects, Deaf actors and actresses, Deaf engineers and Deaf scientists, Deaf business owners, Deaf teachers, and Deaf individuals at all levels of government service. With so much individual accomplishment, how serious a disability can deafness be, and how much should be done to correct it? There is, of course, no simple answer to the preceding question, but the topic generates much interest among the Deaf. (Would that it generated nearly so much interest in those interested in curing deafness.)

Third, many Deaf now explicitly recognize that aural acuity is just one trait among many physical characteristics, that statistical variation in each such trait is unavoidable, and that no individual is defined by any one trait. Many feel that variations in the level of acuity of one's hearing should be accepted rather than eliminated just as one might accept naturally occurring variations in height, eye-hand coordination, skin tone, intellect, courage, physical endurance, and visual acuity. How homogeneous a society are we willing to accept? How homogeneous a society is healthy? Certainly, many Deaf question whether so much effort and time should be expended in the attempt to match one's level of hearing and speech to some statistical average. There are other activities that provide many Deaf with more satisfaction and insight than speech therapy.

This is the paradox: While many Deaf adults find the demands of home and career, the company of friends, or the personal satisfaction generated by the pursuit of hobbies to be more absorbing than the problem of how best to pass for a hearing person, the livelihoods of many, usually hearing persons, depend on solving precisely this problem. And because Deaf adults generally express little interest in "curative" products and services, the products and services are marketed to the parents of Deaf children with the following goal: To train Deaf children to act as nearly the same as hearing children as they can be made to act, where "as nearly the same" is measured in terms of their speech, their ability to speech read, and their ability to use what hearing they have. Today, achieving that goal may also include the implantation of devices in the head of the recipient—again, usually a child—to directly stimulate the auditory nerve. (These devices, called cochlear implants, are described later in this chapter.)

Finally, it would be wrong to imply that the only new aspect of the debate is the further radicalization of both sides. The debate over the nature of deafness in the lives of the Deaf has also been enriched by new ideas about equal opportunity. For many years American Deaf had an uncomplicated notion of fairness as it related to deafness. They routinely opposed "favors." As described in Chapter 4, for many years, groups of Deaf successfully opposed tax breaks for themselves because they wanted no special treatment from the government. Paying their share of the tax burden was a powerful statement that they were equal to hearing citizens and so deserved equal access to the rights and duties associated with citizenship.

But tax law is a blunt and not an especially effective mechanism for helping those that some identify as disabled. And if the tax breaks are not too large, they can be opposed without too large a penalty, and until the last few decades, tax breaks were what the government had to offer. Access to technology was not valued because available technology was relatively crude, and full access to that technology—even assuming that full access were possible—would have provided only modest benefits. That has changed. New technology, new legislation, and higher expectations have altered the context in which conversations about the meaning of deafness take place. In fact, Deaf rejection of the characterization of deafness as a disability is somewhat undermined, or at least complicated, by the mechanism so many Deaf now use to gain equal access to so much of American culture. The Americans with Disabilities Act (ADA) has made a tremendous difference in enabling the Deaf to have access to a wide variety of legal, medical, educational, and cultural institutions and services. This law, passed in 1990, is an ambitious and complex piece of legislation that has had a profound effect on the lives of Deaf Americans. (The scope of this law affects many people classified as disabled. Only its impact on the Deaf is considered here.)

The ADA prohibits discrimination in employment, places of public accommodation, and all activities of state and local governments. It has been used to obtain interpreters for the Deaf at hospitals, courts, and various public meetings and to require television broadcasters to provide closed captions for much of their programming. Telephones, once one of the great barriers to full integration of the Deaf in American life, have become considerably more accessible with the introduction of relay services, a service that became mandatory with the passage of the ADA. [The relay call consists of three parties: a user of a TTY or text telephone, a text-based telecommunications device common in many Deaf homes, a second (hearing) party, who lacks a TTY, and a third party, the calling assistant, who relays messages between the other two parties. One user dials the number of the calling assistant who then contacts the other party. The Deaf individual types text to the calling assistant, who reads the text to the other (hearing) party and, finally, types the hearing party's reply. The process sounds laborious, but it was an enormous improvement over life before the existence of the relay service because the service finally made the entire telephone system—not just those parties with TTYs—accessible. More recently, the TTY relay system has been supplemented by video relay system that enables the Deaf person to sign directly to an interpreter, who takes the place of the calling assistant. Under these conditions, conversations take place at a more normal rate.] Note one more example: Deaf now have access to virtually any college in the country, because under the ADA these institutions are required to hire interpreters in order to make their classes accessible.

The level of accessibility for those classified as disabled is much higher than ever before. Deaf Americans, provided they are willing to explicitly or implicitly self-identify as disabled, have a powerful tool for obtaining access to a broader range of opportunities and technologies than they previously enjoyed, and given the scope of the ADA and its strong language, few Deaf are reluctant to appeal to the law when searching for a mechanism to acquire access to a particular service or event. In fact, American Deaf have an excellent record of using the ADA in creative ways to obtain increasingly higher levels of access. But in the argument over how the concept of disability applies to the Deaf, the ADA is a two-edged sword: While it is a powerful tool, it requires those who seek to apply its provisions to self-identify as disabled. The ADA has changed what it means to have equal access and to receive equal treatment. Its effects have been so positive and so profound that very few Deaf, whatever their feelings about being labeled "disabled," argue against its application to the Deaf because very few want to return to a time before the ADA went into effect.

Least Restrictive Environments

At some level all parties in the debate over the value and the meaning of American Sign Language in the lives of American Deaf recognize that at the heart of the dispute is the nature of the relationship between Deaf adults and the broader society. But because Deaf adults have already-established lives in the broader society and are unlikely to change those lives and the relationships they entail in response to the abstract philosophies of third parties, the dispute is expressed in terms of the best ways to educate Deaf children, who are perceived as the clean slates on which tomorrow's Deaf history will be written.

This is key: The future of American Sign Language as a language depends on Deaf children. This is not to imply that children who exhibit the trait of deafness have any obligation to learn American Sign Language or to become part of what is sometimes called the Deaf community. Nor is it to say that they are free to do as they choose; as minors these crucial decisions are not theirs to make. They benefit, or not, from the decisions that are made for them by their parents, and the decision of whether they will learn American Sign Language is one of the most important that their parents will make for them. It will have a profound and permanent effect on their lives. Conversely, the future state of American Sign Language as a language in which art, science, opinions, affection, and the minutia of ordinary life are expressed will deeply and permanently affect the lives of all who depend upon it as their primary language.

One remarkable trend affecting Deaf children and their relationship to American Sign Language is the practice of mainstreaming, which involves placing Deaf students in "regular" classrooms, where, in particular, the majority of students are not Deaf. Because deafness is such a low incidence phenomenon, mainstreaming a Deaf student often means placing a Deaf student in a class in which there are no other Deaf students present. The practice of mainstreaming is now widespread. (Children of many different backgrounds are mainstreamed, but only the practice of mainstreaming Deaf students is examined here. Also, the term "mainstreaming" is sometimes used in a technical sense by some authors to differentiate a specific form of the practice from other related practices such as "full inclusion." No such distinctions will be made here because it is only where these various practices overlap—that is, it is only the situation when a Deaf child or Deaf children simultaneously share a common classroom and teacher with their hearing peers —that is of interest here.)

Mainstreaming is not a new idea. Alexander Graham Bell remarked (see Chapter 3) in testimony before the Royal Commission of the United Kingdom on the Condition of the Blind, the Deaf and Dumb that he considered the ideal educational environment for a Deaf student to be one Deaf student per school. Because all of the other students would be hearing in this environment, signed language would be largely useless, and the full force of his theories on the importance of speech and speech reading could be brought to bear upon the isolated student. Although mainstreaming is currently characterized as a method for *integrating* the Deaf student, Bell believed that it was valuable because it *isolated* the Deaf student from other Deaf students. The mainstream environment, he believed, was the ideal environment for breaking the transmission of signed language from one generation to the next and for eliminating the Deaf as a social class. By surrounding the Deaf student with hearing students and teachers, Bell sought to force the student not just to use English but to think English. In this manner Bell sought to control the language of thought. For reasons not clear from his testimony, Bell concluded that the one-student-per-school model, though desirable, was not practicable. Today, however, it is quite common.

Modern mainstream practices as well as important supplementary laws and enabling regulations have evolved out of a 1975 federal law called the Education for All Handicapped Children Act but better known as P.L. 94-142. (The current version of P.L. 94-142, numbered 108-446, has not substantively changed the situation for most mainstreamed Deaf students.) P.L. 94-142 orders schools to

> ...assure that, to the maximum extent appropriate, handicapped children, including children in public or private institutions or other care facilities, are educated with children who are not handicapped, and that special classes, separate schooling, or other removal of handicapped children from the regular educational environment occurs only when the nature or severity of the handicap is such that education in regular classes with the use of supplemental aids and services cannot be achieved satisfactorily....

First, notice that although many Deaf subscribe to the view that the Deaf are a linguistic and cultural minority and reject the notion that the Deaf are handicapped, P.L. 94-142, which is applied to Deaf children throughout the country, makes no distinction between Deaf children, children in wheelchairs, blind children, and children with severe intellectual impairments. All such children, and many others, are described by the single word "handicapped." It is a remarkable label because the children who fall into this class have as much—and as little—in common with each other as they have with the broader student population. In this context, the word handicapped conveys little beyond a general societal perception of otherness, and it illustrates just how artificial a category the word handicapped denotes.

Second, notice that the authors of the law consider "special classes" and "separate schooling" to be highly undesirable. The law encourages—but does not require—local school systems to limit their students' exposure to these learning environments and, in fact, the law makes it clear that separate schools are a last resort. It should come as no surprise, therefore, that enrollment at residential schools for the Deaf began to drop in the years subsequent to passage of P.L. 94-142, and this is precisely what happened. In 1975 about 42 percent of all Deaf students attended residential schools for the Deaf. Twenty years later, after a period of steady decline, only about 22 percent of all students attended residential schools. It remains at roughly 20 percent today. Low enrollment has increased per pupil expenditures and reduced the ability of the residential school to provide an immersion environment where Deaf students meet a large number of peers all of whom share a common language. Many of the large residential schools for the Deaf that once formed the backbone of the Deaf education system in the United States are now struggling to survive.

The motivation for the mainstreaming of Deaf students, an educational option that has largely replaced the residential schools where Deaf culture and language are often celebrated, is based on the concept of "least restrictive environment." In practice, the least restrictive environment is defined to be an ordinary classroom consisting of hearing students of roughly the same age as the Deaf student. Deaf students who require fewer and less intrusive accommodations are generally considered to be more mainstreamed than Deaf students who require more and more intrusive accommodations. The greater the number and extent of the accommodations that must be made for the Deaf student, the more restrictive the environment the student is said to inhabit. Students who are removed from class for part of the day to attend separate classes taught by a special education teacher inhabit a more restrictive environment than students who, because they are not scheduled for special education classes, are able to spend the entire day in the regular classroom. Under this definition, students who attend a residential school occupy the most restrictive environment, a situation that, according to the law, should be avoided whenever possible.

As a practical matter, then, the concept of least restrictive environment identifies architecture with environment: The regular classroom environment is best; the special education classroom is second best, to be used when necessary, and the separate residential school is the least desirable of the three environments. This hierarchy is easy to understand, largely unquestioned, and as solidly entrenched as the bricks and mortar in which it is expressed. There is, however, another type of environmental restriction experienced by Deaf children in mainstream classrooms. It is less remarked upon because it is less visible. Indeed, it seems to be quite invisible to many nonsigning professionals involved in the education of these children. It is the linguistic environment inhabited by the Deaf child.

A lone Deaf child (or the few Deaf children) in a hearing classroom filled with hearing children is immersed in an environment that was designed for the hearing children. In theory access to this environment is provided by an interpreter for the Deaf, but even with an interpreter much of this environment is inaccessible to the Deaf. Announcements on loudspeakers, for example, often occur simultaneously with conversations between classmates. A hearing student may initially "sample" a few information sources in such a noisy environment and then choose to concentrate on the most interesting source of information, but even with an interpreter, most of these language streams are inaccessible to the Deaf because no interpreter can interpret more than one conversation at a time. Consequently, the Deaf student cannot sample the sources and decide which one is worthy of attention. The choice of information source is generally left to the interpreter. Similarly, there may be classroom exercises in which a hearing student reads a text aloud while other students follow along in their texts. This experience is also inaccessible to the Deaf student even with an interpreter. A Deaf student must always choose whether to watch the interpreter or read the text because for a Deaf student these activities are mutually exclusive. Choosing to watch the interpreter enables the student to follow the rhythm of the class but only to receive an *interpretation* of the text. Alternatively, if the student reads the text and does not watch the interpreter, the student embarks on a brief program of independent study, accessing the text at a speed and in a manner quite different from that of the other students. There are a host of similar situations and activities that occur daily in a mainstream classroom from which the Deaf student cannot help but be disenfranchised. In a mainstreamed classroom, the Deaf student occupies a linguistic environment very different from that of any hearing student. To be sure, all students occupy the same physical space, but Deaf students experience it in ways that would be very foreign to their hearing classmates. They experience the linguistic environment of their classroom in ways that would probably be surprising and even unacceptable to their parents if their parents could experience the class as their children do. The linguistic restrictions that Deaf students encounter in the mainstream environment are profound and fundamental.

Deaf students in a mainstream classroom also experience extraordinary restrictions on their opportunities to use expressive and receptive language in the sorts of informal situations that most hearing people take for granted. Hearing children learn a great deal of their language through peer-to-peer interactions. Because there are so few Deaf students in most schools—deafness is a low incidence phenomenon—the Deaf student is generally surrounded by children, few, if any, of whom are fluent in American Sign Language.

It is often the case that a few hearing students will learn a modest number of signs and perhaps learn to fingerspell slowly in order to communicate with their Deaf classmate. These attempts to learn signed language, which are generally undertaken with the best of intentions, are usually insufficiently expressive for the Deaf student to engage in open and unrestrained conversations; that is, neither party experiences the situation in which language becomes invisible and both parties are able to devote their energies to the content of the conversation. They do, however, demonstrate how difficult it is for a student—in this case the hearing child—to learn a language when not immersed in it. Despite their lack of fluency, it is often the case that on the playground, and sometimes even in the classroom, these minimally skilled hearing children fall into the role of interpreter for the Deaf student. Their signed language, because it is inadequate to the task at hand, often leads them to express ideas simply and crudely, even when the language that they are attempting to interpret has neither of these features. This leads to what Claire L. Ramsey[3] calls "caretaker language": Interpreted conversations reduce to "pay attention," "sit," "be quiet," "good," "bad," "yes," and "no." This is not an environment conducive to learning language of any type. Ordinary, nuanced conversations in American Sign Language are often impossible and always painfully rare for many mainstreamed Deaf students.

In addition to the reasons already enumerated, there are still other reasons that signed language interpreters are overvalued as solutions to the problem of classroom accessibility. The judicious use of an interpreter requires a certain linguistic maturity on the part of the user that most children, hearing or Deaf, are still in the process of acquiring. Contrary to the apparent expectations of many, Deaf children are not born proficient in American Sign Language, and, as already discussed, the mainstream environment offers few opportunities to learn. Proficiency in the language must be developed over time in an environment that permits practice and experimentation, something that early scholars recognized. Thomas H. Gallaudet, for example, wrote with a mixture of pleasure and wonder at the rapidity with which newly arrived Deaf students acquired proficiency in what was then called "the natural language of signs" once they were immersed in an environment where the student's peers and teachers signed. A culturally Deaf environment was, in Gallaudet's view, the least restrictive environment:

> After a short residence in the family [of Deaf at the Hartford school], he [the newly arrived student] makes rapid progress in this natural language of signs, enlarged as it is, by culture, into greater copiousness, and marked by more precision and accuracy than in those detached families throughout the country in which insulate deaf-mutes exist; and improved in a somewhat regular system by the skill of those who have been engaged, for a long course of years, in this department of education.[4]

Immersion in Deaf culture and language is, according to Gallaudet and many today, the least restrictive environment, although, of course, he did not use that term. It is not difficult to see that because of their age and because there are relatively few opportunities for young children to learn American Sign Language in a mainstream environment, the role of the interpreter is reduced to interpreting from English, a language that the student has only begun to study, into American Sign Language, a language in which the student has little formal experience.

Watching an interpreted version of a lecture does not offer the same type of language-learning opportunities as watching a similar lecture delivered in American Sign Language by a teacher fluent in American Sign Language. Interpreters must adjust the rhythms of their signs and the manner of presentation to what they hear. A good interpreter can often turn a natural sounding phrase in English into a natural sounding phrase in American Sign Language and vice versa, but not as often as one might think. Sometimes a lecture that is effective in one language is simply not as effective after it has been interpreted into the other, even when the interpreter has done a credible job. This is especially true if the language of the lecture depends heavily on the use of certain specific words or certain types of word play that have no easily expressed analogues in the recipient's language. This is not the interpreter's fault nor is it the lecturer's fault. A good lecturer cannot help but use those often-unique aspects of language that in the lecturer's judgment are best suited to convey the intended meaning in the language familiar to the lecturer. The question of whether the resulting lecture translates well into the target language is generally beyond the lecturer's competence to answer. Interpreting between languages often involves some loss of meaning. It is the interpreter's job to minimize the loss. It is unreasonable to expect more. To experience an interpreted lecture is a very different matter from experiencing the lecture in the language in which it was delivered, and experienced adult consumers of interpreting services are very aware of this. Most Deaf children, of course, have no basis for comparison.

Finally, it is widely acknowledged that there have never been sufficiently many skilled interpreters to fill the classroom positions created by mainstreaming. This is still the case, and there is no indication that there will be enough skilled interpreters at any point in the foreseeable future. The result is that as linguistically restrictive as mainstreaming practices are in principle, in practice the situation is usually somewhat worse. The linguistic restrictions that are so much a part of the Deaf child's mainstream environment bode ill for the future of American Sign Language.

Cochlear Implants

Another source of controversy among many Deaf individuals has been the introduction of the cochlear implant, a device designed to bypass certain parts of the auditory system in order to provide direct electrical stimulation of the auditory nerve and in the process produce in the user the sensation of hearing. That a medical procedure should be viewed by many Deaf as a threat to Deaf language and culture has left many inside and out of the medical community bewildered. Rather than attempting to understand Deaf skepticism, however, medical professionals and audiologists have often acted as if these Deaf adults and Deaf organizations simply do not matter. In particular, those involved in implanting these devices and in training the recipients in their use have generally failed to respond to skepticism about the value of the implants in a way that facilitates dialogue or that indicates understanding of the point of view of these Deaf, who are, after all, members of the very group that the professionals claim to be interested in helping.

In a historical sense, the issues involved in cochlear implantation are hardly new, and Deaf skepticism of this most recent attempt to treat deafness as a pathological condition is not hard to appreciate. Beginning in the latter half of the nineteenth century, American Deaf have suffered numerous sustained attempts to coerce children who could not hear to act as if they could. The treatments for deafness, which began with ear horns and speech and speech reading lessons and progressed to electronic hearing aids and speech and speech reading lessons, were available to all, but most Deaf adults did not avail themselves of these techniques and technologies. Deaf children, by contrast, were often forced to spend long hours attempting to learn to make their voices, which they could not hear, sound like the voices of hearing people, who, of course, they also could not hear. They were drilled in speech reading techniques hour after hour and day after day, and they were often punished when they attempted to communicate via signed language, the one modality that offered them the freedom to express themselves in a way that was effortless and graceful. Even today, years after many oral-only schools have either permanently closed their doors or abandoned the oralist philosophy, it is not difficult to find many mature Deaf adults who still speak bitterly of their experiences in these institutions.

Hearing aids were the technical fix of choice for deafness for many years, and they remain an important technology in this regard. But hearing aids provide the Deaf child with a very different experience from what they provide a hearing adult who loses some hearing later in life. A Deaf child does not know *how* to hear. The amplified sounds that may stimulate the Deaf child's auditory nerve simply do not carry the same information that they provide to a late-deafened adult. Deaf children, when they can benefit from the use of hearing aids at all, must first learn to use the input the devices provide. The effective use of hearing aids by Deaf children requires substantial practice, and the improvements in receptive and expressive spoken language that have been obtained through the use of these products, especially the earlier models, were, when they occurred at all, generally quite modest. Moreover, depending on the nature of the child's hearing loss, hearing aids might not provide any additional sensation of sound. Nevertheless, for many years, virtually all Deaf children were provided with hearing aids, and all were required to use them. In retrospect, the early devices were crude; they were expensive and difficult to maintain; they required the use of uncomfortable ear molds; they often provided as much feedback as usable sound; they were useless in noisy environments even when they worked as envisioned by the designer, and many children gained little or no benefit from them. All of this raises the question of why hearing aids were used so widely on children in the first place.

Audiologists, speech therapists, and oral educators have always held out the hope to the parents of Deaf children that given enough practice, enough hard work, and enough talent on the part of the children involved, their offspring could be taught to act as if they could hear—or at the very least, they could be taught to act less Deaf—and to the parents of these children, most of whom were hearing and most of whom had little knowledge of Deaf history and no personal acquaintance with any Deaf adults, this was, indeed, an attractive proposition. Moreover, each generation of audiologists, speech therapists, oral educators, and physicians, would, if they looked back on the efforts of their predecessors at all, assure the parents that while previous generations had not been as successful as they might have wished, this time—this generation—had finally gotten it right. It is a pattern that extends back well over a century in the United States and even further in Europe. (See Chapter 1.) The Deaf have never stopped pointing out the fallacies involved in these efforts at ameliorating the condition of deafness, but for the reasons described in Chapter 4, they have never been very successful in bringing their sensibilities to the fore. This is, again, the situation today with respect to cochlear implants.

The cochlear implant is the latest technology used to treat deafness. It is an extremely aggressive treatment where success is measured by the most undemanding of metrics for a condition that is not life threatening. The technology is quite complex, much more so than in a hearing aid, but the idea is simple enough: Sometimes hearing loss is caused by problems within the inner ear. The inner ear acts as a sort of bridge, converting the mechanical sound waves that enter the outer ear into the electrical impulses that are transmitted along the auditory nerve to the brain where the experience of hearing is interpreted. In those individuals whose deafness is caused by a failure of the inner ear to stimulate the auditory nerve—even though the auditory nerve is fully functional—a cochlear implant is increasingly recommended in an attempt to bypass the nonfunctioning inner ear and directly stimulate the auditory nerve, which, then, passes the signal to the brain. It is the implant that takes over the job of changing sound waves into electrical impulses. To accomplish this goal certain parts of the device are implanted permanently in the head of the recipient. Other parts of the device, including a microphone, power source, and speech processor are worn on the outside. The implantation operation is performed under general anesthesia on both children and adults. Some recent innovations include implanting infants less than one year old,[5] and, for those with nonfunctioning auditory nerves, experimental procedures have been carried out that involve bypassing the auditory nerve as well as the inner ear and directly stimulating the brain.[6] The implant does not produce normal hearing. It is a tool that one must learn to utilize, and as with hearing aids, an implant that is not accompanied by intensive and time-consuming therapy is of little value to the recipient.

How well does an implant work? From the point of view of the physician and the audiologist, the answer is always the same: better. Performance would be better if the child had been implanted at an earlier age, or with a more modern device, or if the child had received more postoperative therapy, or if the child's parents had been more engaged in the process. This has always been the answer to explain the modest results obtained by each new technical fix for deafness by those who seek to implement it. The failure to recognize this simple historical fact is, in large part, responsible for the inability of physicians, audiologists, and others involved in the field of cochlear implants to meaningfully respond to the skepticism and occasional anger that the implantation of these devices in the very young has sometimes engendered among the Deaf.

And just as the debates between those supporting a purely oral education and those supporting the use of signed language in the education of Deaf children usually failed to explicitly consider the opinions of the Deaf children they claimed to serve, there have been very few contemporary attempts to interview young recipients about their experiences with implants. A remarkable exception is the 2005 paper by Gunilla Preisler, Anna-Lena Tvingstedt, and Magareta Ahström[7] describing a longitudinal study of 11 children, each of whom was between 8.5 and 10 years old when they were interviewed and each of whom had between 5 and 7.5 years of experience with implants. These Swedish children were questioned about their experiences with their implants. All of the children indicated that their implants enabled them to better monitor their environment for sounds. Some of the children were able to have one-on-one discussions with their teachers in a quiet room, and none of the children was able to effectively follow either classroom discussions or classroom lectures using their implants alone. It is not enough to ask whether this represents a substantive improvement over what the children would have experienced without the implants. It must also be asked, as Desloges and de l'Epée knew over two centuries ago, whether the children's time might not have been better spent developing their imagination, their skill in art, or their insights into mathematics and science rather than their proficiency in using an implant.

How accessible is the classroom to postimplant children? In a survey of parents of implanted children, John B. Christiansen and Irene W. Leigh[8] discovered that 40 percent of the implanted children used signed language interpreters in the classroom and another 13 percent used oral interpreters. (In oral interpreting the interpreter is placed near the child and repeats what the speaker is saying, usually without voice, in order to facilitate speech reading.) The schools continued to provide a great deal of support to many of these children in addition to interpreting services including, but not limited to, the provision of media captioning, teacher aides, classroom amplification in addition to the cochlear implant, tutoring, and notetakers. Again, were the operation, the subsequent therapy, the time spent in maintaining the device, and all the other factors involved in making optimal use of the implant worth the results so obtained? Or would a program that catered to the child's strengths rather than to his or her perceived pathology have contributed more to the child's happiness and success? These are the same questions that have been asked for over two centuries, and it is worth noting that the Deaf, whose best interests these professionals claim to have at heart, are no more consulted today than they were 200 years ago.

American Sign Language as an Educational Option

The debate about signed language in the lives of the Deaf has not ended. It is part of a larger ongoing debate about the meaning of deafness: Should the Deaf strive to adopt the perceptions and behaviors of hearing people, or, instead of "overcoming deafness," should the Deaf embrace Deafness and explore the world from a point of view that is informed by the language and culture of a people with, in the words of Lucerne Rae, "a history peculiar to themselves, extending back for many centuries into the past, and sustaining relations, of more or less interest, to the general history of the human race"? Conceptually, at least, questions about the meaning of deafness and the role of American Sign Language in the lives of the Deaf have not changed in over two centuries, but the *context* in which those questions are asked continues to evolve. This context has been profoundly affected by legislation, technology, and changing educational philosophies, and it has already dramatically influenced the evolution of American Sign Language. While one may eventually celebrate—or perhaps mourn—the outcome of such complex and often conflicting social and scientific developments on American Sign Language, it is doubtful that anyone can predict what that outcome will be.

It would be interesting to know how Gallaudet and Clerc would perceive the current state of the debate. But while these two individuals, who probably remain two of the most influential figures in American Deaf culture, cannot be polled, their successor, the current executive director of the American School for the Deaf, the institution that Gallaudet and Clerc founded, is available for questioning. His name is Harvey Corson, and I went to the American School for the Deaf to interview him.

The American School for the Deaf, the institution that Corson directs, left its original Hartford campus in 1921—the site is now occupied by The Hartford Insurance Company—and relocated to a spacious site in West Hartford. The grounds of the school are immaculately maintained, and the main building, called the Gallaudet Building, faces the main road from the end of a long straight driveway that cuts through an expansive lawn. The junior and senior high schools are located in the Gallaudet Building. There is a residential hall named after Clerc. The elementary school, located far to the rear of the Gallaudet Building, is called the Cogswell Building. There are a number of other buildings on campus including one that houses the National Theatre of the Deaf, which moved to the campus in 2004. At the front of the school is a bronze statue showing Gallaudet as a young man together with the much younger Alice Cogswell. Most Deaf are familiar with the statue. It is one of two such statues—the other is located at

Gallaudet University—and the dedication of each was an important historical event. The Hartford statue was dedicated in 1925 by the National Association of the Deaf and the American School for the Deaf Alumni Association. There is also a less familiar bust of Laurent Clerc, placed at the front of the Gallaudet Building, and not far from the Clerc Dormitory. The bust of Clerc was moved to the West Hartford campus from the former Hartford campus, where it was dedicated in 1873. This is an institution that is acutely aware of its place in the history of the Deaf.[9]

Dr. Corson is the third generation of his family to be Deaf, and he is the third generation of his family to attend the Pennsylvania School for the Deaf. He graduated from Gallaudet College with a B.A. and an M.A., and he received a second M.A. from California State University at North Ridge. He obtained an Ed. D. from the University of Cincinnati in Special Education Administration, and he has spent his life working in the administration of various schools for the Deaf. Prior to arriving at the Hartford school, he worked as superintendent at the Kentucky School for the Deaf and the Louisiana School for the Deaf, and he worked as the Vice President of Academic Affairs at Gallaudet University. A thoughtful man, who at the time of our interview was approaching retirement, he expressed himself using the measured language characteristic of his profession. His responses revealed an intimate familiarity with the issues described in this book as well as a finely honed cautiousness. These topics are still highly emotive; they were controversial long before Corson was born; he has struggled with them throughout his professional and personal life, and they will in all likelihood remain controversial long after his retirement. Harvey Corson has lived Deaf history.

Corson's office is spacious and comfortable. Hung on its walls are one portrait of Gallaudet, one of Mason Cogswell, and two of Laurent Clerc. We sit at a large conference table, and I begin, as I always do, by asking him why signed language is used at the American School for the Deaf. (American Sign Language is used throughout the school, in classes, dormitories, and informally among the students, teachers, and staff.) He provides the briefest response of any that I encounter, written or oral, during the preparation of this book. "For most of those with severe and profound hearing loss, this is probably the clearest visual symbol system that these students can use for effective communication." And that was it, a kind of minimalist doctrine on the use of signed language in education.

Corson's answer can be found, albeit in more effusive language, in the works de l'Epée and Desloges and hundreds of other writers over the last two centuries, but normally it was part of a much more extensive set of ideas and beliefs about the nature of the relationship between the Deaf and visual language. That is not the case here. Unlike his predecessors Clerc and Gallaudet, Corson does not expand on the idea that proficiency in signed language enables one to establish a meaningful relationship with God or with one's peers—although during our conversation he shows that he is familiar with both of the notions, and unlike his contemporary, Sharon Gold-Johnson at the Austine School (quoted in the Introduction), Corson does not expand on the idea that the acquisition by the Deaf of a visual language leads to greater freedom and autonomy. Instead, he reduces his description of signed language to a visual symbol system of particular value to "those with severe and profound hearing loss." It is a surprisingly sparse defense of a language that has engendered so much passionate debate. We returned to the question about the value of signed language at various times during our two-hour conversation, and he recited his answer—almost word-for-word—each time. Harvey Corson has answered this question before, and he is comfortable with his answer.

I ask Dr. Corson about the Deaf perception of themselves as a linguistic community and the rejection by some Deaf of the characterization of deafness as a disability, but he prefers to discuss the perceptions of parents: ". . .the striving for a cure [for deafness] will never fade away. Practically all parents, when they find out that their baby is deaf, will mourn the loss of a perfect child. That is part of the human condition, and we need to recognize that and work with the families—recognize that they need to go through the grief in order to move on—and we need to help them through this and then talk about how they can work with their child who has some hearing loss. We need to help them understand that this is not the end of the world." I am struck, again, by the measured tone of his response. He does not engage in the debate about the characterization of deafness as a misfortune, preferring to simply observe that deafness is "not the end of the world."

On the subject of the relative value of obtaining an education in a residential school versus the value of mainstreamed education, he is, again, surprisingly demur. Some students may benefit from a mainstreamed education, he says, it depends on the individual student as well as the degree of hearing loss evinced by that student. During our conversation he acknowledges that mainstreamed students may experience significant social, academic, and linguistic isolation in their academic environment even with an interpreter, but he does not condemn the practice. For him, the key concept is access: "Access to the linguistic environment [is critical]. Access is important in considering the proper placement of a Deaf child. You need to consider access to the general curriculum and access to language and communication. . .I think," he continues, "it is important to have educational options available for children because all children are different, but educational placement must take into account the learning environment, language exposure, and culture." I press him for a stronger statement on the limitations of mainstreaming. Certainly, I say, he has noticed the difference between the signed language of mainstreamed students and those educated at residential schools? "Yes," he acknowledges, "it [the signed language of mainstreamed students] is not as fluent." But when I ask if he believes this to be important, he responds by saying, "I think it is important to have all educational options available." Should parents decide to place their Deaf child in a mainstream environment, he asserts, that choice needs to be respected, but equally, should parents choose to place their child in a residential school for the Deaf, that choice should be respected as well. "I suppose that is part of living in American society. People have choices. Parents make choices for the children, and we have to respect the choices made by the family."

Respect is particularly important when the choices so often favor options other than the residential school. Parents, who often have little knowledge of deafness, must decide for their children, and in this sense, little has changed. What is different now is that the time frame for making these important decisions is much shorter than it has ever been. Deafness is now often diagnosed in infancy, and in the event that tests uncover a substantial hearing deficit, many physicians and audiologists will argue for almost immediate implantation of cochlear implants.

And with or without implantation, children are now routinely enrolled in local programs long before they are old enough to attend a residential school. Such placements often work against later placement in residential schools. In fact, the pressure on parents to make early (and sometimes irreversible) decisions about their child's future often works against the development by the parents of social relationships with Deaf adults and so familiarizing themselves with Deaf culture and language prior to making these decisions. There is simply not enough time. Under such circumstances, they are much more likely to be guided by so-called experts in deafness.

"The parents want to raise children like them," Dr. Corson said in a practiced and resigned way, "[but] while raising a child to be like them, they can allow recognition of children's self-esteem through knowledge of Deaf history and Deaf culture. They need to understand Deaf people's struggles and achievements through history."

What of residential schools? What is the particular contribution of residential schools to the future of Deaf students and their language? I remind him that Gallaudet wrote enthusiastically about the beauty of the signed language used at the Hartford school and the liberating effect it had on newly arrived students, but Corson's language is considerably more circumspect. "A residential school has one advantage [relative to mainstreaming environments]. It is a community, a community of signers. We create a linguistic community, where people can sign as well as use English. The children are surrounded by sign language as well as English, and that [situation] can be used to the child's advantage...Language is used more consistently [in residential schools] than you may find in the public schools."

Certainly, I think, there is more to be said. Corson's justification is part of every justification that has been advanced for the establishment and preservation of residential schools that use signed language as the language of instruction, but historically most advocates of such schools have gone further. They describe the value of the language to those who become proficient in its use, the beauty of a well-turned American Sign Language phrase, and the sense of satisfaction derived by the one who utters it. They enthuse over the elegance of the language when used by an expert, but Corson says none of that. In his view, American Sign Language is one of several educational options: "You know that we have new technology. More and more children use hearing aids. What works from some children doesn't work with others. We happen to have children from all over the state, and we have a diverse population. So we can't use one approach with the children. That is why we use total communication:[10] sign language, finger spelling, speech, speech reading, and auditory training so that we can reach all children. We try to be flexible. We accept all kinds of communications approaches. We try to develop communication techniques to the maximum ability of each individual student."

Today, many educators are in agreement with Corson in characterizing American Sign Language as an educational option. They perceive it as just one choice among many. To be sure, the much older idea, that American Sign Language is *the* language of the Deaf, still has its adherents who believe that the language of the Deaf is essential because it is empowering and liberating in a way that no other "option" can ever be. In this view American Sign Language is no more an option for a Deaf student than is English, math, science, or art. By contrast, Corson's position on the use of American Sign Language in schools is much weaker. In fact, he uses the most dispassionate language that I encounter during the preparation of this book, and as I leave Hartford I wonder if, given the history of Deaf people in America, and given the success of the graduates of his institution over the last two centuries, the use of American Sign Language in school might not warrant a more vigorous defense. Certainly, the founders of the institution that he serves would never have characterized signed language as an option for their students.

Those interested in American Sign Language often overlook the fact that the program undertaken by Gallaudet and Clerc almost two centuries ago was radical in the extreme. The reason for the oversight is not hard to identify. By all accounts Gallaudet and Clerc were articulate, sincere, polite, generous, and extremely likable nineteenth century gentlemen who inspired many by their words and deeds. Including the nine years that he taught at the Paris school, Clerc taught young Deaf people and aspiring faculty members for a total of 50 years. Gallaudet, whose health was never especially good, nevertheless devoted a great deal of energy to the education of the Deaf, to the welfare of Deaf adults, and to the study of the natural language of signs. Both were motivated by compassion for a group of individuals who had previously been ignored—even dehumanized —and they received numerous accolades during their lives for their work. All of this tends to overshadow the radical nature of their approach.

Gallaudet and Clerc believed that the Deaf were best understood as a separate social class with its own culture and language. Their solution to the problem of educating the Deaf was to create a separate subculture for the benefit of the Deaf, and out of their work grew Deaf religious, educational, political, and social institutions held together by a Deaf press that sought to participate in the broader society *on equal terms* with other constituent groups. These early Deaf pioneers had no expectation, *no desire,* that anyone should mistake the Deaf as hearing. (Think of how Clerc lobbied a U.S. president and a number of U.S. congressman without ever using his voice.) Instead, they looked inward. Clerc and his successors *taught* their students signed language—they did not allow their students to just "pick up" the language as best they were able or to pursue other communications options in place of the natural language of signs. Rather, they instructed them in the use of signed language in the same way that hearing students are taught English. They showed explicitly in their writings and implicitly in their actions that they believed the natural language of signs to be a language on par with any spoken language. Their teaching reflected these beliefs. Under Clerc and Gallaudet, the relationship between the two languages was far more symmetric than is usually the case today. Theirs was an uncompromising approach that is not currently in wide use.

In the 100 years that followed the Civil War, the Deaf were largely without the kind of powerful, dignified, and intellectual support that had been provided by Clerc, Gallaudet, and their contemporaries, but with respect to creating and maintaining an organization a good enemy is almost as useful as a good friend, and the oralists provided a force against which to organize. Had the oralists not been so disrespectful, so disdainful, and so brutal in their treatment of Deaf children, it is doubtful that there would have been so much interest by the Deaf in creating organizations for the their own use. Over 2,000 Deaf attended the 1926 National Association of the Deaf convention in Washington, D.C., and attendance was high at National Fraternal Society of the Deaf conventions as well. Local organizations and alumni associations of residential schools often had the support of a broad and enthusiastic membership. Much of this solidarity has faded as the "pure" oralist philosophy has fallen into disrepute.

Although there are now many residential schools for the Deaf where American Sign Language has become a "communication option," it does not matter as much—most American Deaf students are educated outside of the traditional institutions in mainstream classrooms, usually by teachers who know little if any Deaf history and who have neither the time nor the opportunity to correct the deficit. As a consequence, Deaf children can grow up without ever having a meaningful relationship with a Deaf adult. Many do just that. There are few opportunities for these students to develop a sense of belonging to a historically significant linguistic and cultural group. What are the effects of this sort of isolation—the linguistic, the cultural, and the personal isolation that are the consequences of so many mainstream environments? Time will tell. According to those interviewed during the preparation of this book, young people are generally absent from Deaf clubs and Deaf social events, and the signed language of most of those educated in mainstream classrooms is distinctly different from, and less expressive than, the signed language of those educated in residential schools.

As the Deaf have become socially and linguistically more isolated from one another, they have simultaneously achieved more access to a wider variety of services and personal and professional opportunities. Legislation and technology are more favorable to the Deaf than ever before, and many Deaf are making full use of these possibilities to attend colleges of their choice, to keep in touch, and to qualify for sought-after employment opportunities and professional advancement. What is the effect of this combination of factors on the future of American Sign Language, a language "whose chief power and charm...shall [for the Deaf] be in expression"? The answer is not clear.

The Future of American Sign Language

Interpreters call Elizabeth L. Broecker, a vivacious and attractive 75-year-old, "hell on wheels." She is a regular and a long-time user of interpreting services, and she has never been one to suffer perceived incompetence in silence.

We meet in a coffee shop not far from her home to talk about the future of American Sign Language. She is, as she has always been, an activist, a writer, a trailblazer, and someone who, while she works hard to make things better, is not reluctant to point out shortcomings in her efforts or in the efforts of others. Elizabeth L. Broecker is not sentimental.

I traveled 400 miles to meet Ms. Broecker because I think that she is a transitional figure, a bridge between old ideas about signed language and deafness and contemporary ideas. When I share this characterization with her, she concurs. Unlike most of her contemporaries, Broecker attended a public primary school— hers was located in Vineland, New Jersey—until the sixth grade. No support services were available. During this time her parents sought a cure for her deafness. She spent sixth grade at the Marie Katzenbach School for the Deaf, West Trenton, New Jersey. At the time, the language policy of the Katzenbach School allowed students to use signed language in the dorms but not in the classroom, where all communications occurred via spoken language or in writing. Dissatisfied with the academic environment at the school—she found it too easy—she returned to Vineland for the seventh grade and remained in the Vineland schools until she graduated from high school. By her own account, she did not "fit in" with the other students because of her deafness, but whatever her social difficulties, she successfully graduated from the high school with no support services and no further contact with Deaf children or adults.

After high school she enrolled at Gallaudet College, now Gallaudet University, with the intention of becoming a teacher. It was a difficult experience. What signed language she had learned at the New Jersey school during the sixth grade had been forgotten. She remained at Gallaudet for one year and a half before returning to Vineland to work in a glass factory. She eventually married a man she had met at Gallaudet. In 1965, divorced and with four young children, she returned to Gallaudet to study sociology. It was during this time that she became active in issues affecting the Deaf: She was instrumental in bringing back the then-defunct *Buff and Blue,* a Gallaudet student publication whose readership and influence had once extended beyond the college's campus, and she advocated for the establishment of the National Technical Institute for the Deaf, a controversial position at Gallaudet, an institution with a long history of resisting innovation in any form.

Upon graduation she found work at Gallaudet but left in a dispute over whether she should be paid the same as a hearing employee performing the same job. She worked for the former Health Education and Welfare Department in New Orleans, where she finally became proficient in American Sign Language, and later moved to Philadelphia, where, in 1976, she helped establish an innovative program for the Deaf at the Community College of Philadelphia. One of the projects at the College involved giving away free text telephones (TTYs) to local Deaf individuals. (The TTY had been invented in 1964, but for a number of years, Deaf people found little use for them. There was no one to call.) In addition to providing TTYs, the program offered typing classes taught by Deaf teachers to Deaf residents of Philadelphia. This program also included an outreach program to explain to the recipients of the TTYs how to use the machines and what to expect with respect to phone bills, because prior to this time many Deaf simply lived without phone service. The program also offered literacy classes and a transition program to make it easier for the Deaf to become involved in college life. It was important work. She eventually left the program she helped establish, but she continued to perform work of special interest to the Deaf. One job bears particular mention here: She worked for the state of New Jersey ensuring that hospitals and other public institutions were accessible and conformed to the provisions of the Americans with Disabilities Act (ADA).

When I asked her about the lack of engagement of young Deaf people in traditional Deaf institutions, she agreed that young Deaf people were simply not as involved in traditional expressions of Deaf culture as their predecessors. She did not care. "I don't think," she shrugged, "there is any way to save the 'good old Deaf culture.' I think there is a new Deaf culture."

As Deaf people became less engaged in traditional Deaf institutions, she asserted, they simultaneously became more engaged in the broader hearing society. The Deaf were not losing their cultural bearings as much as they were trading the old bearings for new ones, and she began to list examples.

1. Deaf Clubs. The Deaf regularly congregated in clubs throughout much of the twentieth century. Some continue to get together, but the reasons for doing so are now fewer and less compelling. One of the old reasons to congregate in a club, she pointed out, was to watch captioned films. Deaf clubs were, for a long time, the only place to watch captioned films. That is no longer true. Caption films are now available on television and DVD. Some movie theaters now offer special open caption performances of first run films, and more recently, a new method of producing the equivalent of closed captions has been developed for use in public theaters as well. And with videophones ever more widely available, face-to-face conversations are not as necessary as they once were.

2. Higher Education. For a long time most Deaf students who wanted to attend college attended either Gallaudet or the National Technical Institute for the Deaf. They made friendships at these institutions that sometimes lasted a lifetime. But what most people forget, she pointed out, is that the Deaf often attended these particular schools because no one else would have them. There were no provisions for hiring interpreters at most colleges or universities, nor were there any other provisions for making these institutions accessible to the Deaf. But, she continued, with the passage of the ADA, Deaf students can attend virtually any college in the country. She acknowledged that most Deaf students were no longer able to experience Deaf culture as she had experienced it at Gallaudet, but they are now able to study any subject they wish at any place they want, and they can still attend these traditionally Deaf institutions if it is their desire to do so. Now they can do what they want.

3. Mainstreamed Students. Richer towns are willing and able to spend what is necessary to provide access to mainstream classrooms for their Deaf students she asserted. For this reason those students tend to stay in town for their education. The poorer towns are often not able to do as much. They often do not offer the same quality of program or the same levels of access. As a consequence, residential schools, she claimed, are no longer able to enroll a cross-section of young Deaf people. The mainstream classrooms have their problems, she acknowledged, but the residential schools can no longer offer the same experience that they once did, either, and in any case, she had toured a number of special education classes and observed the educational environment of the Deaf students. The teachers of the Deaf signed competently, she said, although the interpreters left much to be desired.

Throughout our conversation Broecker never stopped reiterating that times had changed.

There was, she insisted, no point in getting sentimental about it. Something new was happening. It was irreversible. Deaf culture and language were evolving rapidly.

Toward the end of our conversation, Broecker told a story about a young Deaf girl she had met while visiting mainstream classrooms for the Deaf. The girl was sitting by herself crying. Broecker asked what was wrong, and the girl complained that she had to watch the interpreter. Hearing students could watch the teacher, or write, or draw, or talk among themselves, or stare into space and still hear what the teacher was saying, she told Broecker, but she had to watch. It was unfair. Broecker told the girl that everything she had said was true, "But," she said, "*we* must watch the interpreter. It's true that hearing [students] can look away. *We* cannot. Watching the interpreter is what *we* must do. We have to 'go with it,'" Broecker asserted, "because there is no other choice."

I did not like Broecker's story, and while I believe that most of what she said is true, I am not sure that it is true enough to be useful. In particular, I do not agree that "there is no other choice." By becoming aware of Deaf history, we can identify alternatives and make choices. Not all the choices have already been made, and history demonstrates that past choices, good and bad, have made important differences in the lives of many Deaf Americans. I hope that this history provides some insight into the choices that have already been made with respect to American Sign Language and that it assists the reader in making additional choices for the future.

Chapter 1

1. Charles-Michel De l'Epée, *The Method of Educating the Deaf and Dumb: Confirmed by Long Experience* (London: George Hill Publisher, 1801).

2. Collins Stone, "Address upon the History of Deaf Mute Instruction," *American Annals of the Deaf* 14 (April 1869).

3. Charles-Michel De l'Epée, "The True Method of Educating the Deaf Confirmed by Long Experience," in *The Deaf Experience*, ed. Harlan Lane, trans. Franklin Philip (Cambridge, MA: Harvard University Press, 1984), p. 52.

4. Ibid.

5. Pierre Desloges, "A Deaf Person's Observations about an Elementary Course of Education for the Deaf," in *The Deaf Experience*, p. 35.

6. Christopher B. Garnett, Jr., *The Exchange of Letters between Samuel Heinicke and Abbe Charles Michel De l'Epee* (New York: Vantage Press, 1968), p. 17.

7. Ibid., p. 32.

8. Étienee Bonnot de Condillac, "The Language of Action," *American Annals of the Deaf* 31, pp. 35–41.

9. Garnett, *The Exchange of Letters*, p. 31.

10. Ibid., p. 33.

11. De l'Epée, *The Method of Educating the Deaf and Dumb*.

12. Desloges, in *The Deaf Experience*, p. 36.

13. Ibid, p 37.

14. Ibid., p. 40.

15. Helen Keller, *The Story of My Life* (New York: Doubleday, Page & Co., 1903), p. 388.

Chapter 2

1. Laurent Clerc, "Laurent Clerc," in *A Tribute to Gallaudet, A Discourse in Commemoration of the Life, Character and Services of the Reverend Thomas H. Gallaudet, LL.D., Delivered Before the Citizens of Hartford, January 7th, 1852,* ed. Henry Barnard (Hartford, CT: Brockett and Hutchinson, 1852), p. 108.

2. "To the Editor of the Christian Observer," *The Christian Observer* 18 (October 1819): 646–50. Signed "G," this article was surely written by Gallaudet, as it contains references to the author's work as a teacher of the Deaf, and the fact that whole sections are identical with his handwritten manuscript, "Essay on Signs," on file at the Library of Congress, Manuscript Division, including his eyewitness account of the conversation between Laurent Clerc and the unnamed Chinese visitor.

3. Rae, Luzerne. "The Philosophical Basis of Language," in *Proceedings of the 3rd Convention of American Instructors of the Deaf,* Columbus, 1853.

4. K. "Connecticut Asylum for the Deaf and Dumb, *The Christian Observer* 19 (January 1820): 64–65.

5. Ibid.

6. Ibid.

7. Thomas H. Gallaudet, "Essay on Signs," Manuscript Division, Library of Congress. This manuscript is labeled "ca. 1830."

8. Ibid.

9. Ibid.

10. Thomas H. Gallaudet, "Language of Signs Auxiliary to the Christian Missionary," *The Literary and Theological Review* (New York: D. Appleton & Co., 1834), pp. 204–5.

11. Charles P. Turner, "Expression," *American Annals of the Deaf* 1 (January 1848).

12. Thomas H. Gallaudet, "On the Natural Language of Signs; and Its Value and Uses in the Instruction of the Deaf and Dumb I," *American Annals of the Deaf* 1 (October 1847).

13. "To the Editor of the Christian Observer," pp. 646–50.

14. Anonymous, Untitled, *The Christian Observer* (August 1818): 515.

15. Rae, Luzerne. "Introductory," *American Annals of the Deaf and Dumb* 1 (October 1847).

16. Thomas H. Gallaudet, "The Natural Language of Signs I," *American Annals of the Deaf and Dumb* 1, no. 1 (October 1847); and Thomas H. Gallaudet, "The Natural Language of Signs II," *American Annals of the Deaf and Dumb* 1, no. 2 (January 1848).

17. Gallaudet, "Essay on Signs."

18. Stone, "Address upon the History of Deaf Mute Instruction."

19. Gallaudet, "The Natural Language of Signs II," p. 80.

20. Gallaudet, "Essay on Signs."

21. Gallaudet, "The Natural Language of Signs II," p. 93.

22. Gallaudet, "The Natural Language of Signs I," pp. 59–60.

23. Edwin John Mann, *The Deaf and Dumb: or, A Collection of Articles Relating to the Condition of Deaf Mutes; Their Education, and the Principal Asylums Devoted to Their Instruction* (Boston: D.K. Hitchcock, 1836).

24. Roch-Amboise Bébian, "Essay on the Deaf and Natural Language, or Introduction to a Natural Classification of Ideas with Their Proper Signs," in *The Deaf Experience*.

25. Berthier, Ferdinand. "The Deaf Before and Since the Abbé de l'Epée," in *The Deaf Experience*.

26. Ibid.

27. Laurent Clerc, in *A Tribute to Gallaudet,* p. 112.

28. Ibid.

29. For example, see (a) Isaac Lewis Peet, "Moral State of the Deaf and Dumb Previous to Education and the Means and Results of Religious Influence Among Them," *American Annals of the Deaf* 3 (July 1851); and (b) Harvey Peet, "Notions of the Deaf and Dumb before Instruction," *American Annals of the Deaf* 8 (October 1855).

30. Quotation taken from Harvey Peet, "Notions of the Deaf and Dumb before Instruction." p. 36.

31. Roch-Amboise Bébian, "Essay on the Deaf and Natural Language, or Introduction to a Natural Classification of Ideas with their Proper Signs," in *The Deaf Experience*.

32. Gallaudet, "The Natural Language of Signs II" p. 82.

33. Ibid., p. 86.

34. Ibid., p. 86.

35. Ibid., p. 81.

Chapter 3

1. All quotations from Audree Norton are from personal communication with the author (May 2004).

2. All quotations of Bernard Bragg are taken from personal communication with the author (April 2004).

3. From the files of Edna Levine, courtesy of Bernard Bragg.

4. Ibid.

5. Ibid.

6. Ibid.

7. George Fellendorf, personal communication with the author (April 13, 2004).

8. Alexander Graham Bell, *Memoir upon the Formation of a Deaf Variety of the Human Race* (Washington, DC: Alexander Graham Bell Association for the Deaf, National Academy of Sciences, 1883).

9. Edward Miner Gallaudet and Alexander Graham Bell, *Education of Deaf Children, Evidence of Edward Miner Gallaudet and Alexander Graham Bell* (presented to the Royal Commission of the United Kingdom on the Condition of the Blind, the Deaf and Dumb, etc.), ed. Joseph C. Gordon (Washington, DC: Volta Bureau, 1892), paragraph 21,868.

10. Ibid., paragraph 21,872.

11. Ibid., paragraph 21,984.

12. Ibid., paragraph 21,579.

13. Alexander Graham Bell, "Fallacies Concerning the Deaf," *American Annals of the Deaf* 29 (January 1884).

14. *Education of Deaf Children,* paragraph 21,635.

15. Ibid., paragraph 21,457.

16. Bell, "Fallacies Concerning the Deaf."

17. *Education of Deaf Children,* paragraph 21,407.

18. Ibid., paragraphs 21,540 and 21,541.

19. Ibid., paragraph 21,357.

20. Ibid., paragraph 21,518. See also Bell, "Memoir upon the Formation," chap. 6.

21. *Education of Deaf Children,* paragraph 21,522.

22. Ibid., paragraph 21,841.

23. Ibid., paragraph 21,721.

24. Ibid., paragraph 21,722.

25. Ibid., paragraph 21,643.

26. Reprinted in Gallaudet and Bell, *Education of Deaf Children,* pp. 82–86. The paper originally appeared in the Proceedings of the Fifth National Conference of Principals and Superintendents of Institutions for Deaf-Mutes, 1884, pp. 182–94.

27. *First Annual Report of the Clarke Institution for Deaf Mutes at Northampton, Massachusetts for the Year 1867* (Springfield, MA: Samuel Bowles and Company, Printers, 1868).

28. *Seventh Annual Report of the Clarke School for the Deaf for the Year 1874* (Springfield, MA: Samuel Bowles and Company, Printers, 1875).

29. Miriam Forster Fiedler, *Developmental Studies of Deaf Children* (Washington, DC: American Speech and Hearing Association, 1969).

Chapter 4

1. Address of President James H. Cloud, "Proceedings of the Fourteenth Triennial Convention of the National Association of the Deaf," *The Silent Worker* 37, no. 5 (February 1925).

2. Rae, "Introductory."

3. Alexander Graham Bell, "A Few Thoughts Concerning Eugenics," *National Geographic* 19 (1908): 188–23.

4. Benjamin Franklin, *The Complete Works of Benjamin Franklin,* ed. John Bigelow (New York: G.P. Putnam's Sons, 1887–1888), pp. 296–99.

5. Quoted in David R. Roediger, *Working Toward Whiteness, How America's Immigrants Became White.* (Cambridge, MA: Basic Books, 2005).

6. See, for example, *Americanization Studies, the Acculturation of Immigrant Groups into American Society,* vols. 1–10 published separately during the 1920s by Harper Brothers. Reprinted in 1971 by Patterson Smith Publishing Corporation, Montclair, NJ.

7. American School for the Deaf, Annual Report, 1851, pp. 23–44.

8. Jack R. Gannon, *Deaf Heritage, a Narrative History of Deaf America* (Silver Spring, MD: National Association of the Deaf, 1981), pp. 237–54, an admirable compilation of the names and some histories of Deaf publications.

9. Gannon, *Deaf Heritage,* p. 246.

10. T. V. Archer, "Conference on Lip Reading as a Means of Communication in Teaching," in Proceedings of the 19th Convention of American Instructors of the Deaf, 1911.

11. Alice T. Terry, "Our Pursuit of Happiness," Proceedings for the Eleventh (Special) Convention of the National Association of the Deaf 40 (1915): 76–80.

12. For other points of view, see Susan Burch, *Signs of Resistance, American Deaf Cultural History, 1900 to World War II* (New York: New York University Press, 2002), pp. 149–55; and Gannon, *Deaf Heritage,* pp. 255–59.

13. John E. Purdam, "Report of the Impostor Bureau," in Proceedings of the Fourteenth Triennial Convention of the National Association of the Deaf, *The Silent Worker* 37, no. 5 (February 1925): 227.

14. John E. Purdam, "Help Unmask the Deaf-Mute Impostor," *The Silent Worker* 36, no. 9 (June 1924).

15. "Not Dependents," *The Silent Worker* 27, no. 7 (April 1915): 130.

16. Burch, *Signs of Resistance,* pp. 155–67.

17. "Mutes Skillful Drivers," *The Silent Worker* 37, no. 9 (June 1925).

18. "The Deaf as Drivers," *The Silent Worker* 39, no. 6 (March 1927).

19. "Town's Men Direct Fight for Deaf to Get License," *The Silent Worker* 35, no. 7 (April 1923).

20. "Proceedings of the Fifteenth Triennial Convention of the National Association of the Deaf," *The Silent Worker* 39, no. 10 (July 1927).

21. Alice T. Terry, "Eugenics," *The Silent Worker* 30, no. 6 (March 1918).

22. Burch, *Signs of Resistance,* p. 143.

23. Terry, "Eugenics."

24. Terry, "Our Pursuit of Happiness."

25. "Proceedings of the Fourteenth Triennial Convention of the National Association of the Deaf," *The Silent Worker* 37, no. 5 (February 1925): 229.

26. Ibid.

27. See, for example, Amos Draper, "The Attitude of the Adult Deaf Towards Pure Oralism," *American Annals of the Deaf* 40 (1895). Draper was a Deaf professor at Gallaudet College.

28. Anonymous (A Semideaf Lady), "The Sign Language and the Human Right to Expression," *American Annals of the Deaf* 53 (1908).

29. Ibid.

30. See, for example, Draper, "The Attitude of the Deaf Towards Pure Oralism."

31. Douglas C. Baynton, *Forbidden Signs, American Culture and the Campaign Against Sign Language* (Chicago: The University of Chicago Press, 1996), pp. 78–80.

32. "Resolutions," in Proceedings of the Fifteenth Triennial Convention of the National Association of the Deaf, *The Silent Worker* 39, no. 10 (July 1927): 382.

33. Baynton, *Forbidden Signs,* pp. 60–61.

34. *Education of Deaf Children,* paragraph 13,166.

Chapter 5

1. Burch, *Signs of Resistance.*

2. "Proceedings of the Fifteenth Triennial Convention," p. 362.

3. Ibid., p. 384.

4. *Report of the Trustees and Superintendent of the Institute for the Deaf and Dumb and Blind Colored Youth of the State of Texas 1887–1888* (Austin, TX: State Printing Office, 1888).

5. All information about the Institute for the Deaf and Dumb and Blind Colored Youth from its founding until the post–World War II years was obtained from the yearly "Report of the Trustees and Superintendent" and the later Board of Control Reports, all of which were obtained through Texas School for the Deaf Museum. Specific facts are referenced to the years of individual reports in the main body of the text.

6. Information on the later years of the BDO was gleaned principally from conversations with Oliver Blaylock and Betty Henderson, two former BDO students.

7. For more information about National Black Deaf Advocates, see the Web site http:/www.nbda.org.

Chapter 6

1. See, for example, Noam Chomsky, *Syntactic Structures* (The Hague, The Netherlands: Mouton, 1968), p. 52, for a succinct summary of the ideas about generative grammar that would have been familiar to researchers at the time that Stokoe began his work.

2. Jack R. Gannon, *Deaf Heritage, A Narrative History of Deaf America* (Silver Spring, MD: National Association of the Deaf, 1981), p. 367.

3. Leonard Bloomfield, *Language* (New York: Holt, Rinehart and Winston, Inc., 1933).

4. William C. Stokoe, "Sign Language Structure: An Outline of the Visual Communication Systems of the American Deaf," in *Studies in Linguistics,* Occasional Papers #8 (Buffalo, NY: University of Buffalo, 1960).

5. William Stokoe, Dorothy Casterline, and Carl Croneburg, *A Dictionary of American Sign Language on Linguistic Principles* (Washington, DC. Gallaudet Press, 1965).

6. De l'Epée, *The Method of Educating the Deaf and Dumb.*

7. Years ago the author was introduced to a Deaf man, and we spent several hours in signed conversation. During much of this time I was vaguely aware that there was something unusual about his signs, but there were no difficulties in comprehension. It was not until after we had conversed for some time—not until there was a lull in the

conversation—that I noticed that he had six fingers on each hand. Apparently, extra fingers do not constitute significant linguistic variation.

8.   William C. Stokoe, Jr., *Semiotics and Human Sign Languages,* (The Hague, The Netherlands: Mouton & Co. N.V., Publishers, 1972).

9.   Ibid., p. 112.

10.   Ibid.

11.   Ibid., p. 35.

12.   Gallaudet, "On the Natural Language of Signs I."

Chapter 7

1.   Scott K. Liddell, *Grammar, Gesture, and Meaning in American Sign Language* (Cambridge: Cambridge University Press, 2003).

2.   See, for example, Edward S. Klima, and Ursula Bellugi, "Modulation of Meaning," in *The Signs of Language* (Cambridge, MA: Harvard University Press, 1979), p. 182, for a discussion of how details in sign production affect meaning.

3.   Klima and Bellugi, *The Signs of Language,* chap. 1.

4.   Gallaudet, "On the Natural Language of Signs II."

5.   Michael Gasser, "The Origins of Arbitrariness in Language," http:/www.cogsci.northwestern.edu/cogsci2004/papers/paper574.pdf.

6.   See, for example, Klima and Bellugi, *The Signs of Language,* chap. 5.

7.   Karen Emmorey, *Language, Cognition, and the Brain, Insights from Sign Language Research* (Mahwah, NJ: Lawrence Erlbaum Associates, Publishers. 2002), p. 52.

8.   Liddell, *Grammar, Gesture, and Meaning in American Sign Language,* chap. 5.

9.   For a more complete discussion of blending, see Liddell, *Grammar, Gesture, and Meaning in American Sign Language.*

10.   David P. Corina, Howard Poizner, Ursula Bellugi, Todd Feinberg, Dorothy Dowd, and Lucinda O'Grady-Batch, "Dissociation between Linguistic and Nonlinguistic Gestural Systems: A Case for Compositionality," *Brain and Language* 43 (1992): 141–47.

11.   K. Emmorey, D.P. Corina, and U. Bellugi, "Differential Processing of Topographic and Referential Functions of Space," *Language, Gesture, and Space,* ed. Karen Emmorey and Judy S. Reilly (Mahwah, NJ: Lawrence Erlbaum Associates, 1995), pp. 43–62.

12.   D.P. Corina and S.L. McBurney, "The Neural Representation of Language in Users of American Sign Language," *Journal of Communication Disorders* 34 (2001): 455–71.

13.   H.J. Neville, D. Bevelier, D. Corina, J. Rauschecker, A. Karni, A. Lalwani, A. Braun, V. Clark, P. Jezzard, and T. Runner. "Cerebral Organization for Language in Deaf and Hearing Subjects: Biological Constraints and Effects of Experience," *Proc. Natl. Acad. Sci. U.S.A.* 95 (February 1998): 922–29.

14.   See, for example, M. MacSweeney, B. Woll, R. Campbell, P.K. McGuire, A.S. David, S.C.R. Williams, J. Suckling, G.A. Calvert, and M.J. Brammer. "Neural Systems Underlying British Sign Langauge and Audio-Visual English Processing in Native Users," *Brain* 125 no. 7 (July 2002): 1583–93.

15. Kuniyoshi Sakai et al., "Sign and Speech: Amodal Commonality in Left Hemi-spheredDominance for Comprehension of Sentences," *Brain* 128 (2005): 1407–17.

Chapter 8

1. Samuel Gridley Howe, *Barnard's American Journal of Education* (December 1867). See also Mary Swift Lamson, *The Life and Education of Laura Dewey Bridgman, The Deaf, Dumb, and Blind Girl.* (Boston: New England Pub. Co., 1878), p. 1.

2. Samuel Gridley Howe, *Laura Dewey Bridgman,* ed. unknown (Watertown, MA: Perkins School for the Blind, 1889(?)), p. 55.

3. Ibid., p. 56.

4. Ibid., p. 174.

5. Ernest Freeberg, *The Education of Laura Bridgman* (Cambridge, MA: Harvard University Press, 2001), p. 1.

6. Charles Dickens, *American Notes* (London: Chapman Hill, 1874), chap. 3.

7. Helen Keller, *Teacher, Anne Sullivan Macy: A Tribute by the Foster Child of Her Mind* (Westport, CT: Greenwood Press, 1985).

8. Keller, *Teacher.*

9. The speech can be found in its entirety in Keller, *The Story of My Life,* pp. 392–93.

10. Regi Theodore Enerstvedt, *Lexicon of Impairments: With Emphasis on Hearing, Visual and Multi-Sensory Impairments,* vol. 5, *Sy-Z* (Oslo: Skådalen Kompetansesenter, 1999).

11. Robert J. Smithdas, *Life at My Fingertips* (Garden City, NY: Doubleday & Co., Inc., 1958), pp. 150–51.

12. Ibid., p. 58.

13. Nancy O'Donnell, personal communication (September 2005).

14. Steve Collins and Karen Petronio, "What Happens in Tactile ASL?" in *Pinky Extension and Eye Gaze, Language Use in Deaf Communities,* ed. Ceil Lucas (Washington, DC: Gallaudet University Press, 1998), pp. 31–34.

15. Harry C. Anderson, personal communication (July 2005).

Chapter 9

1. Thomas F. Fox, "Convention Prelude," in Fifteenth Triennial Convention of the National Association of the Deaf, *The Silent Worker* 39, no. 10 (July 1927).

2. It has not always been this way. Although Alexander Graham Bell wanted to eliminate sign language and the Deaf as a social class, he took the time to learn sign language and, by all accounts, enjoyed the company of Deaf people. See, for example, Albert Ballin, *A Deaf Mute Howls* (Washington, DC: Gallaudet University Press, 1998).

3. Claire L. Ramsey, *Deaf Children in Public Schools* (Washington, DC: Gallaudet University Press, 1997).

4. Gallaudet, "The Natural Language of Signs I," pp. 57–58.

5.   Richard T. Miyamoto, Derek M. Houston, and Tonya Bergeson, "Cochlear Implanation in Deaf Infants," *The Laryngoscope* 115 (August 2005): 1376–80.

6.   Duncan Grahame-Rowe, "Where No Implant Has Gone Before," *New Scientist* (January 10, 2004).

7.   Gunilla Preisler, Anna-Lena Tvingstedt, and Magareta Ahlström, "Interviews with Deaf Children about Their Experiences Using Cochlear Implants," *American Annals of the Deaf* 150, no. 3 (2005).

8.   John B. Christiansen and Irene W. Leigh, "Children with Cochlear Implants, Changing Parent and Deaf Community Perspectives," *Archives of Otolaryngology, Head and Neck Surgery* 130 (May 2004): 673–77.

9.   Leaving a historical record in the form of public statuary has a long history among American Deaf. In addition to these statues, there is another statue on a similar theme that was erected near the site of the old Hartford campus in 1953, and in 1998 a pair of granite memorials were placed at the graves of Laurent and Eliza Clerc. The inscription reads: "Dedication in memory of Laurent and Eliza Clerc, April 17, 1998, by friends of the National Association of the Deaf, Gallaudet University Alumni Association, and the American School for the Deaf."

10.   Dr. Corson's use of the term "total communication" is not quite standard. The term total communication is more commonly associated with a form of visual communication that was most popular during the 1970s. A simultaneous mixture of sign and speech, total communication was intended to reach all Deaf, regardless of whether they signed or read speech. He uses the term in a generic sense.

Index

Institute for the Deaf and Dumb and
Blind Colored Youth

of experimental proof, 130–31, 145;
after 1900, 135, 138, 148–55, before
1900, 10, 27–30, 33
Experiment in Television, 43–50

Fellendorf, George, 47, 49–52
Fiedler, Miriam Forster, 66–67
Fingerspelling. *See* Manual alphabet
fMRI (functional magnetic resonance
imaging), 153–54
Foster, Andrew, 113
Fox, Thomas F., 181
French Sign Language, 9, 18, 35–37, 119

Gallaudet, Edward Miner, 91–92
Gallaudet, Thomas Hopkins: early
failures, 22–23; early life, 21–22; early
understanding of signed language, 25;
experiments with signed language, 24–
25, 27–30, 33, 127, 136, 159–60;
final understanding of signed
language, 30–35, 87, 202–3;
observations on deafness as culture,
192; recognition of, 75, 197–98, 202;
relationship with Clerc, 23–24;
religious views, 22, 33, 39–41
Gallaudet College, 48, 90, 97, 117, 177,
197–98
*Gallaudet Guide and Deaf Mutes'
Companion,* 77
Galton, Sir Francis, 83
Garrett, Julius, 95, 101–2, 112
Gasser, Michael, 138
God and language, 11, 38–41, 77–78,
159–60, 163, 168

Haywood White, Mattie B., 108
Hearing aids, 194
Heinicke, Samuel, 13–15
Henderson, Betty, 109–10, 113
Holland, William: early life, 100; early
years at Institute, 100–101;

educational philosophy, 101–3, 111;
legacy, 112; second term at Institute,
105–6; view of deafness, 103
Hotchkiss, John Burton, 91–94
Howe, Samuel Gridley: attitude toward
signed language, 161–62; early years,
159; as an educator, 157, 161–62; as a
scientist, 160, 163
Hudgins, Ruth, 48

Imposter Bureau, 79–81
Integration, oral philosophy of, 52, 57,
59–62, 63, 64. *See also* Mainstreaming

Jenkins, Samuel J., 104–5, 112
Johnson, Amanda A., 101–2, 112

K (author and teacher at American
School), 25, 26
Keller, Helen, 158, 164–68, 170
Klima, Edward S., 135–36

Language and the organization of the
brain, 147–55
Language of conventional signs, 91
Language of thought, 55, 58, 161
Late-deafened as a privileged class, 84–85
Least restrictive environment, 187–92
Lesion studies: definition of, 148–49; of
D.N., 152–53, 155–56; of W.L.,
149–51
Levine, Edna, 46–47, 49
Liddell, Scott K., 131
Life without language, 37–39, 159–60
Linguistics: as branch of science, 129,
131, 145; characteristics
distinguishing signed and spoken
languages, 144, 155; characteristics
shared between signed and spoken
languages, 139–40, 147–48, 151, 155;
difficulties inherent in the study of,
132, 145, 148; existence of sublexical

structures, 139–40, 151; a three-dimensional signed language grammar, 141–47, 152–53. *See also* American Sign Language; Dual Channel Activity; Modality; Natural language of signs; Signed language

Lipreading. *See* Speech reading

Long, Major Stephen H., 34–35

Loring, George, 74–75, 161

Mainstreaming: definition of, 51–52; effects on signed language skills, 57–58, 200, 203; and the linguistic environment, 51, 57–58, 190–93. *See also* Integration; P.L. 94-142

Mann, Edwin John, 34

Manual alphabet: use by Deafblind, 161–62, 166–67, 169, 173–74; 176; use by the sighted signers, 25–26, 55, 117, 124

Martha's Vineyard, 60

Massey, Otis, 108

Massieu, Jean, 22–23

McKinney, J. W., 105

Memories of Old Hartford, 92–93

Methodological signs, 10–12, 14, 19, 25–26, 32, 36, 64

Modality and language: according to Bloomfield, 117; according to Gallaudet, 30–34; according to Stokoe, 117–28; 131; post-Stokoe ideas, 139–55; relative difficulty in learning spoken vs. signed languages, 134–35; in tactile signed language, 174–77. *See also* American Sign Language; Dual channel activity; Linguistics, Natural language of signs; Signed language

Morpheme, 118

NAD (National Association of the Deaf): comparison with ethnic organizations, 73, 79, 83; and Deaf children, 88–89, 198; Deaf support for, 97, 203; and driving rights of Deaf, 82–83, and eugenics, 83–85; and peddlers, 79–81; some presidents of, 76, 79, 84; and racial discrimination, 97, 113; and signed language, 85–88, 90–91; and tax relief for the Deaf, 81

The National Exponent, 77

National Theatre of the Deaf: creation of, 46–47; goals, 45–47, 49–50, 52; value of, 45–46, 49, 67, 89

Native American Sign Language, 30, 34–35, 110

Natural language of signs: dual channel activity, 29, 33–34; early conception of grammar in, 33, 45, 139; evolving understanding of, 24–35; experiments with, 27–30, 33; iconic nature of, 30–33; 132–33, 135–36; "language of the countenance," 26, 28–29; as a language of the Deaf, 24, 26, 34; as the language of instruction, 25–26; 40–41, 65–66, 74, 85–90, 101; as the "natural" language of the Deaf, 17, 26, 40–41; and religion, 11, 33, 39–40, 77–78, 86; as a universal language, 12, 14, 18, 26, 28–31, 34–35. *See also* American Sign Language; Signed language

NBDA (National Black Deaf Advocates), 109, 113–14

NFSD (National Fraternal Society of the Deaf), 73, 78, 80, 97, 203

NIDCD (National Institute on Deafness and Communication Disorders), 183

Norton, Audree, 45–46, 50

Oberlin College, 100

Oral Education: claims for, 55, 65–67, 78, 89; criticism of, 64–67, 78, 84, 86, 88, 90, 166; early efforts in, 9, 13–15;

About the Author

JOHN TABAK is the author or co-author of a number of books including the five-volume *History of Mathematics* published by Facts On File. He is currently writing a series of books about energy production and its environmental consequences. He is a freelance writer and a mathematician with a professional and personal interest in American Sign Language.